Performance Research is an independent, peer reviewed journal published by Routledge for ARC, a division of the Centre for Performance Research Ltd, an educational charity limited by guarantee, which works with the support of the Arts Council of Wales. Performance Research acknowledges support from the University of Wales, Aberystwyth, De Montfort University and Dartington College of Arts.

Performance Research welcomes responses to the ideas and issues it raises and is keen to consider proposals for articles and submissions. Please address all correspondence to:

Clancy Pegg
Journal Administrator
Performance Research
Market Road
Canton
Cardiff CF5 1QE
Wales, UK

Tel: +44 (0) 1 222 388848
Fax: +44 (0) 870 055 7873

Email: post@perfres.demon.co.uk

Performance Research is published three times a year by Routledge, 11 New Fetter Lane, London EC4P 4EE UK A full listing of Routledge journals is available by accessing http://journals.routledge.com

Enquiries concerning subscriptions should be addressed to Routledge Journals
Subscriptions
PO Box 362
Abingdon
Oxfordshire
OX14 3WB
UK
Tel: +44 (0) 1235 401060
Fax: +44 (0) 1235 401075
email: routledge@carfax.co.uk
For sample copy requests please contact the Subscriptions Department

ISSN 1352–8165

Annual subscription rates:

£ (Sterling):	Institution £110	Personal £30
US$:	Institution $175	Personal $45

Members of the Centre for Performance Research (CPR) will receive Performance Research as part of their membership. For further information please contact:

Adam Hayward
Centre for Performance Research
8 Science Park, Aberystwyth
Ceredigion SY23 3AH
Wales, UK

Tel.: + 44(0)1970 622133
Fax: + 44(0) 1970 622132
Email: cprwww@aber.ac.uk

Design: Secondary Modern
Typeset by Type Study, Scarborough, UK
Printed in the UK by Bell & Bain, Glasgow

EDITORIAL STATEMENT

Performance Research is a peer reviewed performing arts journal published three times a year. It is international in scope with an emphasis on contemporary European performance. The journal aims to promote a cross-disciplinary exchange of ideas and stimulate discourses surrounding established, experimental, speculative and prospective performance work. Each issue combines thematic and general content from the current field of performance research and practice.

SUBMISSIONS

The editors are interested in encouraging submissions and proposals for forthcoming issues. We welcome proposals using visual, graphic and photographic forms, including photo essays and original artwork for the page, as well as substantial articles and in-depth performance, archive and book reviews. There is no payment for articles except in the case of commissions for which funding might be sought. It is the responsibility of authors to seek permission for all visual and other copyright material.

Proposals may be submitted on one sheet of A4 containing an abstract, proposed word count and description. Unsolicited articles may be submitted for consideration by email attachment, on disk or double spaced in hard copy. Detailed guidelines for preparing text will be sent either on request or on acceptance for publication. Proposals are considered at least nine months before publication.
Proposals and articles, including reviews, should be sent to:

Clancy Pegg, Administrator, Performance Research, Market Road, Cardiff, CF5 1QE, Wales, UK.
Email: post@perfres.demon.co.uk

PLEASE NOTE that proposed submissions do not necessarily have to relate to issue themes. We actively welcome submissions on any area of performance research, practice and scholarship.

FORTHCOMING ISSUES

The next three issues of Performance Research will be entitled *On Cooking* (Spring 1999), *On Line* (Summer 1999) and *On Silence* (Winter 1999).

On Cooking. This issue will explore themes reflected in the overlap between Performance, Food and Cookery. It will look at food in performance and food as performance art; the performative in cookery and its staging in the kitchen and at the table. Articles and artists' pages will develop piquant analogies and correlations between the processes in cooking and performance making. They will give testament to the theatricality of food and speculate on food as a model for theatre: multi-sensory, processual and communal.

On Line. Emerging digital media, information and communications technologies are changing the ways in which we understand and experience time and space, place and body. These developments challenge us to redefine existing strategies and forms of performance, and to create fresh approaches and alternative environments for performance making and composition. *On Line* will explore these changing conditions as they relate to performance practice and discourse. The editors invite materials from individuals and groups involved in exploring territories where emerging technologies and performance overlap and intersect, as well as excavations of the histories of performance and technology.

On Silence. The greatest irony about silence is that there has been so much said about it. In fact, in this noisiest of centuries, silence has emerged as one of the richest areas of critical enquiry and most powerful elements of artistic expression. For the final issue of this millennium, Performance Research will look at its nature, uses and meaning across the fields of performance. We wish to explore silence as metaphor, as practice, as absence, emptiness and experience, political silence and silencing, musical and visual silence, and the place of silence in the history of the avant garde, as well as linguistic and philosophical approaches to silence.

Preface

This issue, *On Ritual*, completes volume three of *Performance Research*: a volume which has been entirely edited by 'guests': Nick Kaye for *On America*, David Williams and Mark Minchinton for *On Place* and now Günter Berghaus; with each of the core editorial team, Claire MacDonald, Ric Allsopp and myself, 'shadowing' each of the guest editors. Shadowing Günter has been both challenging and enlightening as I followed him down quite extraordinary paths. His breadth of vision, historical range and global reach has amazed me and the material gathered over a two year process at times bewildered me. At each meeting new material was presented that ranged from the arcane and the antiquarian to the new age and the pagan. What is presented here is a small selection from the material gathered and received; at one point Günter passionately pleaded for a double issue, a bumper edition, and I regret not being able to oblige as I am well aware of the many excellent submissions that we have not had space to include. As we reach the end of this millennium the interest in ritual practices is indeed burgeoning and the writing about them diverse and compelling.

I should like to thank all our guest editors of this volume for their conscientious and sustained work; we look forward to their continuing involvement with the journal . Next year the pendulum swings in the opposite direction; as I write I am finalising *On Cooking* which I have been editing, *On Line* will be edited by Ric Allsopp with Scott deLahunta and then this fourth volume, and the millennium, will close with *On Silence* edited by Claire MacDonald. We have already been thinking about the year 2000 and beyond and we wish to return to keeping the first issue in every volume un-themed, open, all-inclusive. And so the first issue of volume five will be 'off' theme to be followed by two 'ons': *On Animals* and *On Memory*. Whilst we have always welcomed and will continue to welcome submissions that do not directly relate to the announced theme we do hope this will firmly signal our desire to publish material on any area of performance research, practice and scholarship. We shall be pleased to receive proposals, submissions and responses and we also hope this open issue will allow dialogues and conversations raised within previous issues and between issues to continue.

We are also keen to create participatory events around the launch of each issue as a way of both marking the occasion and also expanding the debate in relation to the material published. We were able to launch

Performance Research 3(3), pp.v-vi © Routledge 1998

On Place at the Centre for Performance Research's international conference Points of Contact: Performance, Pasts and Place, in September this year; the journal travelling with delegates as complementary reading material throughout this itinerant event. We would like to build upon this modest start and gradually hold more public events which through talks, debates and panel discussions respond to the contents of an issue of PR; contest them, expand them and advance them. We also wish the event to be a performance; entertaining and challenging. For *On Cooking* we plan to stage a 'foodie' event as part of the 5th Performance Studies Conference: Here Be Dragons, to be held in Aberystwyth, Wales, UK between April 9th and 12th 1999. We will keep readers and subscribers informed of these developments.

Finally, I should like to mention a few other developments within the editorial team. We want to expand our review section, particularly with regard to books and performance events and so we have invited David Williams to co-ordinate our book reviews and Toni Cots, theatre researcher and producer, who splits his time between Copenhagen and Barcelona, to co-ordinate performance reviews and advise us on which emerging artists and companies to profile. We are committed to extended book and event reviews that engage with the issues raised by the material and place them in a broader context. Clusters of books and perhaps a venue's entire season or a festival's curatorial vision will become a subject for review. We are particularly pleased that this issue contains reviews of 'old' books. It was an idea in the original proposal for this journal that we should occasionally review an antiquarian book, or mark a book's anniversary, or revisit and review a book of particular significance. For *On Ritual* many books were eligible for such regard and we are pleased to begin the process with works from Richard Schechner and Mercia Eliade.

Richard Gough, Llanrhystud, Wales. October 1998

Editorial

The idea of editing a publication on ritual arose some five years ago, when I became aware that as we were approaching the end of the millennium, a substantial increase of ritual practices, both in the social world and in the theatre, could be observed. I formulated some preliminary thoughts on this phenomenon and presented these at various conferences, colloquia and symposia in Europe and the Americas. The response to my ideas was such that, in 1996, I suggested to the editorial board of *Performance Research* that an issue be dedicated to this topic. My initial call for papers found an extremely positive response from both theatre scholars and practitioners. This rather unexpected echo indicated to me and my colleagues that we were indeed dealing here with a theme close to the pulse of the *Zeitgeist*.

In the course of the following two years I corresponded with more than a hundred people in order to follow up the many interesting suggestions, proposals and abstracts received and to finalize the shape of this issue. Although one number of *Performance Research* cannot aspire to offer a comprehensive overview of the complex phenomenon of ritual, I felt that at least a significant range of approaches and examples from various cultures and historical periods should be represented. Therefore, when selecting contributors and commissioning papers, I tried to arrive at a balance between general essays and case studies, scholarly analyses and artists' statements, European and non-western traditions.

The study of ritual requires an inter-disciplinary approach, which at least in principle is also reflected in this publication. Ritualism needs to be analysed from a number of angles by anthropologists, biologists, archaeologists, sociologists, psychologists, theologians, theatre scholars, and so on.

It seems obvious that no *one* theory can explain the salient features of this multifaceted performative behaviour and that each must be complemented by others. As we have experienced with previous issues of *Performance Research*, it was in the end much easier to win collaborators from the academic field than to persuade artists to put pen to paper and to offer statements on their creative activities. By bringing together scholars from several disciplines I hope to have edited an issue that gives due attention to at least some of the key traits and features of ritual practices, so rich in symbolic references and emotional ramifications.

Günter Berghaus

Performance Research 3(3), p.vii © Routledge 1998

On Origins: Behind the Rituals

David George

Everyone knows the theatre originated out of ritual; the textbooks tell us so: 'The origins of theatre go back far into the past, to the religious rites of the earliest communities' (Hartnoll 1968: 7). They even know what these rituals were: 'Songs and dances in honour of a god, performed by priests and worshippers dressed in animal skins, and of a portrayal of his birth, death and resurrection' (ibid.). If one asks how they (can) know this, they tell us that 'even now similar ceremonies can be discovered among primitive peoples' (ibid.). Despite their conceding that the process 'must have been a slow one and it is not possible to pinpoint exactly the various stages' (ibid.: 8), the primary sequence is unquestioned – and universal: in a recent exposé of the inadequacies of most textbooks' coverage of Asian theatres, Carol Fisher Sorgenfrei castigated a number of authors for not – 'correctly' – identifying the origins of Noh (and Chinese and Indian theatre, etc.) in shamanism (and Shinto harvest rituals, ancestor worship, etc., etc.; Sorgenfrei 1997: 229, 237, 241).

Ritual has been a popular explanation for the otherwise puzzling fact that theatre clearly originated at different times and in different places that had no connection to each other; hence it seems to invite some transcultural theory of unitary origin. The obvious structural parallels between ritual and theatre have seemed to supply a suitable candidate; all that is needed is the proof. Since, however, no one was there 'in the beginning' to record the transition, evidence necessarily cedes to speculation, and fact to deduction: pollen is found on some Neanderthal bones and from it are deduced burial rites and, therefore, religious consciousness; a skeleton is found with one arm chopped off – 'evidence' of surgical procedures, medical care, compassion, goodness. A sketch on a cave wall of what could be a man wearing an animal mask and skins is enough to deduce a tribe with shamans – who, other scholars then argue, later became actors. There are, however, half a dozen possible reasons why a man might wear, say, reindeer antlers on his head other than his being a reindeer shaman, and a number of further reasons why someone else should draw one (e.g. to record a successful hunt; to demonstrate to young hunters how reindeers move; because it was a fashion, or a crown – some kind of insignia; or simply a fantasy doodle, a vision). There is no urgent reason to identify that figure as a dancing reindeer shaman rather than an actor except ideological prejudice which prefers a history of human development in which *homo religiosus* anticipated *homo ludens*. Even if he were a reindeer shaman, he must have derived from somewhere the value of dressing up, the efficacy of assuming another persona; he must have either learned or been born with that ability and to have noted it at work all around him. Acting (or, more strictly speaking, performing) is older than shamanism – which depends on it.

The consensual agreement on theatre's origins masks real uncertainties; we will never remove them all, but at least our methodology, our logic could be tight. Origins need, at least, some theory of *why* one thing *should* emerge out of another, what

• Krishna Worshipped. Photo: David George

Performance Research 3(3), pp.viii–14 © Routledge 1998

it took with it, what it left behind. That, however, only exposes the really tricky issue, namely that, although origins are ultimately the *result* of a series of deductive speculations, that result is then relabelled as a cause and placed first. Origins are typical of the logical inversion characteristic of all causal argument, the process whereby causes, which – by definition – come *before* effects, are causes only because they *have had* effects, and so come actually *after* them. A cause is 'that which produces an effect': cause and effect are correlative, but causes *are* causes only because and after they have effects. The solution is to recognize that cause-effect is, in the end, not an historical sequence so much as a logical pair – which can be reversed. As Nietzsche loved to point out: the sequence whereby the pin caused the prick which caused the pain is actually a reversal of the sequence whereby the pain caused me to locate the prick caused by the pin: causes and effects always demand testing by re-inversion (did theatre precede ritual?).

That, however, is still not the end of the methodological and philosophical problems. Cause and effect, origin and result, must *share* some element; something must pass from the one to the other. Causality requires both *continuity* between the cause and the effect and yet substantial *change* from cause to effect. As the great Buddhist philosopher Nagarjuna argued: if the cause contains the effect, it is not a cause (it is at best an effect-cause); but if it does not somehow contain the effect, then how can it work?* 'If the effect were identical with the cause, there is no production, as nothing new emerges; if they were different, there is no continuity between cause and effect' (Murti 1955: 121).

* cf. Kalupahana 1991.

The ritual origin of theatre may, in other words, seem logical, but one culture's logic is another's fallacy: the solution which the Buddhist philosophers and logicians came to was to abandon causes altogether and replace them by conditions. Conditions are always necessary in causal theories, being the prerequisites for some action to be performed: 'Something which must be present if something else is to take place'. Causes require apposite conditions but – as the father of modern western causal philosophy, John Stuart Mill, eventually had to conclude too – in the final analysis, the selection of one of those conditions as the cause is arbitrary. The result is that a linear, causal sequence in time is replaced by a spatial network within which 'causes' are exposed as arbitrarily selected from the sum of conditions – selected on ideological not logical grounds.

In other words – and summarizing this lengthy but necessary philosophical preamble: the early Buddhist philosophers decided, and contemporary western philosophy now accepts this too, that if you analyse any situation down into its cause and conditions, you will find that you do not need – or cannot pin down – a cause at all: all you need, all you find is a flux of conditions, mutually influencing each other. It is very likely (it is inevitable) that human beings, programmed to find causal chains, will go on constructing them – still today when Chaos and Complexity theory are beginning to discover a reality very much like that described in later Hua-Yen speculations as 'Indra's Net of Jewels', namely a universe in which all phenomena are 'interdependently originated' ('conditionally coproduced', 'co-dependently arising').†

† Thomas Cleary, *Entry into the Inconceivable: An Introduction to Hua-Yen Buddhism* (Honolulu, HI: University of Hawaii Press, 1982); Garma C. C. Chang, *The Buddhist Teaching of Totality. The Philosophy of Hwa Yen Buddhism* (Philadelphia, PA: Penn State University Press, 1971); Steve Odin, *Process Metaphysics and Hua-Yen Buddhism* (Albany, NY: State University of New York Press, 1982).

In sum: originist theories are like all causal arguments: post-hoc reconstructions of hypothetical sequences in which the logic of discovery is reversed and the identification of cause out of conditions arbitrary. A more useful model may be to replace the whole notion of linear, temporal sequence by recognizing a network of interlocking, mutually influencing conditions: one reason for indulging in this excursus on Buddhist logic is to illustrate the crucial point: origins are in the end not historical so much as ideological, the conclusions of cultural prejudice.

Ritual origin theory tells us that rituals are

(were) already theatrical. That may seem obvious, but one obvious possible implication – namely that ritual may, therefore, have itself evolved out of theatre rather than the other way round – is seldom even considered. Such an explanation (which could be supported on cultural evidence*) will, however, have to confront as its most trenchant opponent cultural prejudice. One reason why theories of origin (in general, as such) are so popular in the West is because it is a culture with an historical religion, both in the sense that Christianity sees the workings of God in history and in defining that God as the Originator. Not all gods share that function; not all cultures have that much respect for history; some religions have no theory of origins at all, but the most damning problem with the whole method is its built-in evaluation system. Far from a ritual origin in some way ennobling theatre, it does the opposite: declaring it a fall from grace, a suspect institution, constantly in need of rejustification by connection to some new service – moral, social, political. This serves and reflects well the prejudices of a culture that – since the beginning – has found theatre sufficiently suspicious to want to ban it, tame it, expose it: Jonas Barish's (1981) daunting catalogue of western denunciations of the theatre's innate hypocrisy and devilish deception reveals the real origin of theories of Ritual Origin.

*cf. George 1987; Harrison 1978: 19.

There are sufficient conceptual and theoretical problems with ritual origin theory to suggest the need for a re-examination – notably of the question not asked, namely: if not out of theatre then out of what did *ritual* originate?

The final problem with origin theories is that they have a nasty habit of infinitely receding, the identification of one cause leading to the investigation of *its* origin and so on until one ends up with God or some similar unquestionable premise.

Elsewhere (George 1987) I have argued both that the sequence can be reversed and that where it can be shown that drama could have evolved out of ritual, then the religious ontology of that ritual must have had some latently 'dramatic' element

already. That element can be identified – at least conceptually: all religions establish their own legitimacy by some story or myth of revelation in which a transcendental region of god(s) and an immanent region of humans came into contact. All religions therefore postulate a split universe – one with inverse proportions of transcendental and immanent areas and beings – and hence the need for some 'cross-over realm', some 'liminal space' where the Revelations can occur – as well as people to live in and work through them. The ability to create such liminal realms is a function and characteristic of rituals, but the capacity to do this can be traced much further back – deep not into history but into human cognition. Rituals are traditionally reserved for specialists, but they exploit only a talent and an ability that everyone has, no less than the ability to perform creatively with and in liminal realms.

The argument to be investigated is therefore this: if it is true that ritual and theatre are in some way related, then one needs to identify clearly the transitional stages, their logic and cultural implications, and/or trace *both* back to some common – cognitive – origin, either way revealing their 'mutual conditionality' and 'co-dependent arising' rather than some putative sequential order.

IN THE BEGINNING . . .

Various candidates have been proposed for the 'mother ritual' of 'Ur-drama': ancestor worship, burial and commemoration rites, fertility cults, initiation rites, bhakti cults and the most popular choice: shamanism. Margot Berthold writes: 'The theater of primitive peoples rests on the broad foundation of primary, vital impulses. From them it draws its mysterious powers of magic, conjuration, metamorphosis – from the hunting spell of the stone-age nomads, from the harvest and fertility dances of the first tillers of the fields, from initiation rites, totemism, and shamanism, and from various divine cults' (Berthold 1972: 2).

The differences are significant: rituals form a continuum between two distinct definitional types – 'mystical' rituals in which a believer seeks direct

Les Trois-Frères. Sorcerer. (Drawing by Breuil.)

experience of a transcendent accessible to all, and 'magical' practices in which specialists demonstrate their particular access to special powers (cf. George 1987). Shamanism belongs to the second category and is undoubtedly theatrical in its use of costumes, props, dance, although its chief attraction is the way it appeals to and reflects a culture which conceives of 'primitive religion' as incipient trickery, and the theatre which is supposed to have evolved out of it as a form of hypocrisy and deception. Because the typical history of a shaman is to progress from possession by a spirit to control over that spirit (Lewis 1971: 54–6; Blacker 1975: 24), theatre is presumed to occur when a shaman substitutes for ecstatic possession by a spirit an impersonation of that spirit – and of his own authentic trance (Kirby 1975: 9–10; Eliade 1964: 6). There is no doubt that such transitions do occur. Lévi-Strauss gives the fascinating and instructive example of the Eskimo Quesalid who, disbelieving the shamans, set out to expose them: he became a

pupil of a famous shaman and learned from him the tricks of the trade. So skilfully did he learn them that this man, who set out to expose them, became the most famous and successful shaman in the whole area – not because he contacted spirits better, but because he skipped actual possession completely and concentrated on acting it most convincingly (Schechner 1977: 174). His whole story can be complemented by the confessions of a famous Indian 'ritual actor', Panicker, who explains his success as a Teyyam performer by confessing: 'I see *teyyam* as an art not as a belief. As far as my technique is concerned, no one can surpass me. No one can tell from my performance that I am not a believer. I am not a believer. I am a good performer. But I never tell anyone that I don't believe' (Richmond *et al.* 1990: 137).

Because shamanistic ritual does not become theatre just when and because the shaman becomes an actor; it becomes theatre when the clientele too makes a cognitive shift, when they become an audience which now sees through the deception. Such a recognition of the shaman as trickster can have only two denouements: either his clientele leave him for a more credible seance or they begin to enjoy it now as theatre. That step is assumed: according to Ur-drama theory, theatre emerges when an original meeting of belief with ecstatic possession is replaced by a new encounter – between skilful pretence and happy scepticism, but it means that the whole institution has to pass first through a stage of disbelief and even contempt. That stage is indeed recorded in the one surviving classical play that dramatizes the purported ritual origin of western theatre, Euripides' *The Bacchae* – the only extant tragedy on the Dionysian theme in which we can examine the transition, because Pentheus is the Ur-spectator, a sceptic who does not believe all that mumbo–jumbo about altered states of consciousness and divine possession and ecstasy: the ritual participants pulled him down from his seat and tore him limb from limb.

In sum: shamanism theory achieves simultaneously two culturally desirable effects: a definition of theatre as originating in a confidence trick and sham; and exposure of trance, possession, contact with other spheres as a superstition which even the natives learn not to believe in. But:

> There are radical differences in the relationships between a person in trance and others who accept it as trance, a person in trance and others who do not believe in that trance, a person not in trance and others who believe he is in trance, and a person pretending to be in trance and known to be pretending. Each step is conditional on a cognitive leap which first defines this new form as a different kind of performance.
>
> (George 1987: 134 f.)

The multiple cognitive shifts involved in these transformations are so drastic that what we have here must be defined as a 'new origin'.

Any theory of origin (any causal theory) must be able to identify the two crucial components of continuity and change between two phenomena. In the case of shamanism and theatre, the continuities are superficial (appurtenances: costumes, props, dance,

plot) but the changes are radical, cognitive: shifts from real possession to simulation, from belief to deception. Except that theatre is, actually, not deception at all: an audience knows it is being deceived, welcomes it; an actor's pretence is overt. If one defines performances in terms not of their superficial appurtenances but of the relationships they establish between their participants, and the cognitive structures which inform those relationships, then theatre practises a much more complex epistemology than shamanism theory can embrace. Theatre may not enjoy a very elevated status in western culture, but even so, a phenomenological reduction of its cognitive presuppositions reveals

> the ability to conceive of other worlds, alternative realities, and to perform them; to 'see' one person as both character and actor and to adopt a split consciousness and a split affective system as well; to live in two planes of reality simultaneously, projecting oneself into other consciousnesses, other space–time matrices with different rules, which presuppose the ability to conceive of other consciousnesses and other 'realities' and to translate signs into things and back again. Actors and audiences perform very advanced cognitive operations, and it would not be at all difficult even on the basis of such a rudimentary listing of its presuppositions to derive a religious consciousness from a theatrical consciousness.
>
> (George 1987: 156)

Because ritual too is – ultimately and originally – not so much a set of practices as also a cognitive model, one that conceives of a split universe, at once transcendent and immanent, dividing and doubling space–time into parallel here/nows, and the community into believers/non-believers, initiates/outsiders. Ritual originates out of the need to create liminal realms, to inhabit cross-over areas, theatre out of the realization that one can be two things at the same time, can inhabit two time–spaces simultaneously: the cognitive structures of ritual and theatre are very close. That *could* mean not that one evolved out of the other but that they have a common origin, an origin to be found not in the constructed chronologies of history, but in the archaeology of cognition, deep not in time but in the most basic act, the one we all begin with as soon as we are born.

Studies of infant cognition reveal that, from the age of a few days, even a few hours, babies perform.* This aptitude and its practice are basic to human development; we learn both who others are and who we ourselves are by performing.

> * The following is based on the work of Andrew Meltzoff and M. Keith Moore: cf. 'Infants' understanding of people and things: from body imitation to folk psychology', in Bermúdez *et al.* 1995; Andrew Meltzoff, 'Foundations for developing a concept of self', in *The Self in Transition*, ed. Dante Cicchetti and Marjorie Beeghly (Chicago: University of Chicago Press, 1990).

It has long been recognized that infants learn through imitation; without this ability an infant could never learn the social codes. More recent studies have revealed that they would not even learn how to feel, because it appears that emotions are not somehow pre-natal, pre-existent, switched on at birth and then seeking appropriate avenues of expression, but are also learned by observation and reproduction. John Campbell summarizes Meltzoff's work: 'The hypothesis is that when the infant sees someone with a particular expression, he uses his innate capacity to imitate it, and this *in turn* leads to having the emotion in question, so the infant now knows what is going on in the other person' (Bermúdez *et al.* 1995: 38; emphasis added).

This is a classic example of a causal re-inversion: it is not, after all, emotions that precede and 'cause' their expression, but the other way round. This already has major implications for acting theory, suggesting as it does that tapping into the emotions in order to act them out may be a less reliable and useful tool for an actor to mobilize than practice in emotional imitation, since it seems to demonstrate that assuming an expression can itself trigger the associated emotion – the basis of David Best's pioneering revision of classical western theories of performance, Susanna Bloch's laboratory

• Shaman – dancer in trance. Photo: David George

experiments and the fundamental practices of much Asian theatre.*

* cf. Best 1974; Bloch *et al.* 1995.

But there is more to it than that: learning the communication and expression codes of one's culture by imitating another person's gestures is effected by looking first at others and then at one's own reproduction of their expressions. The most important of these are facial, and imitating someone else's face cannot be done so simply; infants have to learn to compare not two visual images but one visual image with an internalized, imagined version of their imitation of it. In other words, they learn not just to imitate, but to perform. The terms need definitional specificity: Bermúdez *et al.* define an *act* as different from an *event* because it involves 'essentially goal-directed movement' (1995: 7). Acts are intentional and provide a basic sense of self because they make us discover a physical world which resists them. A sense of self and a first cognition of an objective world are complementary. What differentiates a *performance* then from an *action* is that this new capacity not only involves goal-directed, intentional activity, but operates by comparison with some ideal model in that intention is now compared with achievement. Marvin Carlson argues that performance in all its senses requires first 'a certain distance between "self" and behavior', a certain incipient self-consciousness, and is, second, an activity measured against some standard of achievement (Carlson 1996: 4–5). Paraphrasing Richard Bauman, 'all performance involves a consciousness of doubleness, through which the actual execution of an action is placed in mental comparison with a potential, an ideal, or a remembered original model of that action' (ibid.: 5).

That, it appears, is what infants practise 'from the beginning'. Research in this field is ongoing and suggests a new model of primary human cognition, one of immense significance for anyone interested in revising the cultural status of performance. Within this model, an infant becomes almost immediately aware of a world of *events* occurring; it then *acts* in that world, beginning to construct continuities (reappearances of similar acts) and hence causalities. It learns to store representations and to copy and perfect its own production of them, correlating intentions with achievements. The whole syndrome is creative, voluntary, imaginative and active: we perceive, record, compare, adjust, improve – it is the most 'original' of all sequences, the origin of all performances, the primary performance.

This fundamental syndrome then becomes, of course, the basis for play – arguably a better origin for theatre than ritual, not least because it offers deep cognitive parallels. Western models of play as socialization, learning and catharsis are also cultural constructions and contrast sharply with Hindu conceptions, for example, in which play has a religious, metaphysical status: *Lila*. Hindu theatre – also *lila* – can claim a direct connection to this metaphysical dimension – and does so proudly, assuming a direct religious affiliation with no need for any intervening passage through ritual.

There are, it is true, arguments that Hindu theatre too evolved out of ritual, the origin of Sanksrit drama being located in Vedic rites – notably the so-called dialogic hymns of the *Rgveda*.†

† cf. Lidova 1994: 125, note 50; George 1986: 84, note 46.

However, Natalia Lidova in her study *Drama and Ritual in Early Hinduism* (1994) notes that 'no scholar has traced as yet direct links between the Sanskrit drama and particular rites' (1994: 53). The *Rgveda* itself records 'danseuses' (*nrtu*), and actors (*śailūṣa*) are mentioned in the equally old (circa 3000 BC) *Sukla Yajurveda*: which came first? The myth of origin in the *Natyasastra* resolves the issue by conceiving theatre as a fifth Veda, invented to combat people's addiction to sensual pleasures, desire and greed, jealousy and anger. It is true that theatre is presented as an invention of the gods and that Brahma is said to have taken recitation from the *Rgveda*, song, acting and aesthetics from the other three Vedas. However, the new institution did not therefore evolve out of the others or out of their associated rituals, but is something new, with its own function and purpose, designed, it is said, 'to give relief to unlucky persons who are afflicted with sorrow and grief or work and will be conducive to observance of duty as fame, long life, intellect and general good, and will educate people' (Richmond *et al.* 1990: 26).

Not only is theatre recognized here as a new institution with its own special – pedagogic – function: it can trace itself independently back to a religious origin, not to a ritual, but to a God, who himself dances, and another, who regularly appears in disguises – avatars. In a culture such as that you can even have 'ritual theatre', an institution which is ritual and theatre simultaneously,* a hybrid form which can thrive only in cultures which conceive of per-

* These genuine hybrid forms, it can be observed, are not performed by the Brahmin ritual specialists but are drawn from the very opposite end of the social and political – the caste – spectrum: Richmond *et al.* 1990: 125.

formance as primary – manifest in the conceptualization of Shiva as cosmic dancer, Vishnu as cosmic actor, and more generally in a theology which argues that gods, being perfect, *can* only play (George 1986: 23 f.). One of the most vital expressions of this 'theatrical theology' is Krishna – himself one of Vishnu's favourite roles. If one were to trace the origin of his ritual theatre – the Raslila – one would find not simply a theatre that somehow evolved out of a ritual, but also a ritual that itself exploited the paradigm of theatre as conceived in Hinduism. This 'co-dependent arising' had perhaps already occurred in the early days of Sanskrit drama; Natalia Lidova argues that it evolved not out of Vedic ritual, but out of puja worship dedicated to the Saiva Agamas (1994: 43 ff.). Facing the crucial issue that 'historical succession would be possible only if the rite, desacralized in its spontaneous evolution, gave rise to its successor, the drama, as it died away' (ibid.: 53), and noting that the *Natyasastra* suggests rather a 'mutual conditioning' of rite and drama, she concludes that the Sanskrit drama 'did not succeed to the rite, neither did it originate out of the rite, but evolved parallel to it' (ibid.: 52). Instead of a linear historical sequence, Lidova proposes a process of cross-fertilization, in which the increasing anthropomorphic tendency in Hindu worship fed on the theatre quite as much as vice versa:

'Paintings, and sculptures of gods, most probably received their attire, make-up and postures from actors who played gods. Instead of imitating iconographies from static images which appeared out of the blue no one knows when, the stage, with its sophisticated tradition of enacting Hindu myths, produced sets of divine features later fixed in paintings and statuary' (ibid.: 106).

Lidova focuses on Shiva, but if one were to transfer one's attention to Vishnu and specifically Krishna, then her thesis could be demonstrated in precise detail. For the historical evolution of the Raslila plays reveals that the iconic images which young boys originally imitated, were themselves derived from the theatre. The *Bhagavata Purana* draws on the theatre for its imagery and metaphors of Krishna quite as much as the Raslila draws on the *Purana* for its plots. In the *Purana*, Krishna as God plays the role of Krishna the cowherd, just as the actor of Krishna today plays the god playing the cowherd. The Krishna of the *Purana* is no longer the Krishna of the *Bhagavad Gita*: the lawgiver of the *Gita* has become the playful, irresponsible, beautiful child of the *Purana*, who now appears in mystical visions to a new generation of saints and prophets – as a player, as an actor. The *Bhagavata Purana* is thick with explicit metaphors and similes from drama and theatre. Krishna is described as playing a 'role', concealed in his maya; the gods are shown applauding him, in the guise of cowherds, 'as actors do to cheer up another actor'; Krishna has 'a charming personality, like an accomplished actor'; he and his brother are described as 'exceedingly beautiful like actors on the stage'; 'dressed like an actor decorated with a wreath of sylvan flowers, peacock feathers and tender shoots, beautiful with mineral paints'.[†] It is not only

[†] cf. George 1986: 24.

the god himself; the whole universe is theatrical – a world of *lila* generated by *maya* – and when Krishna departs it, he tells his devotees that it is by acting plays that he can still be contacted and persuaded to return. This is what the original gopis did, and one can trace a sequence whereby later devotees then took on the personalities of the

• Krishna Painting. Courtesy Museum of Fine Arts, Boston

original gopis, enacting them in real life, adopting their names, identities and costumes. At first, they worshipped an icon (called already a *svarupa* – the entity itself – not a *murti* – image or representation), which was then substituted by young boys in static poses (such as they still assume at the opening *arati* worship in Raslila performances today) and finally by actors, re-presenting Krishna's sports in the very places and on the very anniversaries of their original enactments.

What each stage in this progression did is no less than bring out the latent theatricality of the theology itself, a process which can be followed in the career and writings of Vallabhacarya, whose whole theology of reincarnation is based on a redefinition of time as multistratified, layers of time coexisting just as theatrical time always coexists with 'real time'. The connection is not merely an allusion: Vallabhacarya theology conceives of time–space as infinitely multilayered, Krishna endlessly and eternally performing all his sports simultaneously, so that when a devotee

exists on the equivalent *lila*-plane of consciousness, he or she enjoys direct testimonies, first-hand experiences of divine presence. This state of consciousness is called '*alaukika*', a term derived from the *Natyasastra*, where it originally designated the realm of dramatic illusion.*

* ibid.: 18 f., 36 f.

In sum: Hinduism exhibits a pattern whereby ritual and theatre alternate in inspiring each other – from which it may be further deduced that the origins of both are to be found not just in each other but in some common origin: in primordial performance. That is why they have made a god out of it, because Shiva as Nataraja does what all gods must do: represents a primordial power, in this case the primordial power of performing. To worship a dancing God is, however, not to claim a ritual origin: it is to claim the equal status of dance and religion just as Vishnu – representing the primordial power of appearing only through others – enrols the gods in a theatrical ontology just as much as deriving theatre from their mode of being.

This paradigm can be repeated for other cultures and other religions too. Japan has a legendary origin of dance in a heavenly dancer – Uzume; danced rituals – Kagura (Shinto ceremonial dances, performed by *miko* – usually the daughters of priests); and evidence of cross-fertilization. Although the shamanistic origins of Noh have been exaggerated, there is a good case for arguing that a ritual (a 'Zen seance') grew out of commercial professional theatre: I have set both arguments out in detail elsewhere.* They reveal how even a religion such as

* ibid.: 28 f., 35–7; George 1987: 129.

Buddhism, which shares western disquiet about the sensual temptations inherent in theatre, can have at the same time a deep respect for performance – as a medium to enlightenment. Dogen once wrote about 'playing joyfully' in *samadhi*, and referred to enlightenment itself as 'joyous play'. Hee-Jin Kim comments: 'It [Enlightenment] is the activity of *homo ludens* par excellence' (Kim 1987: 52, 60).

Tibetan Buddhists have deified dance too but here it is not just a question of dancing Bodhisattvas, dancing oracles, dancing meditations. If it can be argued that performance is a primary cognitive, epistemological capacity and a theological state-of-being, then Buddhist philosophy completes the process by proposing performance as a primary ontology too.†

† George 1987; a new publication, *Buddhism as/in Performance*, to be published in Delhi by D. K. Print in 1998 has a lengthy chapter on this topic.

'Im Anfang war die Tat' (In the beginning was the Deed): Faust's blasphemous challenge is Buddhist orthodoxy, although, strictly speaking, Buddhism has no theory of origins, partly because in Buddhism time is simply adjectival, a property of all living things, and partly because Buddha himself refused to answer questions of origin due to their implicit metaphysical assumptions: 'Behind all these mistaken views and "unfit questions" lies the assumption that there is an entity which is denoted by the grammatical subject of verbs, while the Buddha's reply asserts the existence of an event described by the verbal notion, but denies that it is legitimate to infer the existence of a real subject from the verbal form' (Collins 1982: 105). When the early Buddhist philosophers began to transform the Buddha's own sayings, teachings and insights into a systematic philosophy, they found themselves deconstructing things (nouns) down into their qualities (adjectives). They discovered, however, that those properties and qualities exist only in time, with the result that nouns crumbled into adjectives which danced away as verbs. Conze writes: 'The own-being of the thing is dissolved into the conditions of its happening' (Conze 1973: 240), or as Guenther puts it: 'Things . . . are hypotheses symbolizing possible ways in which events may be connected' (Guenther 1971: 141).

The essential ephemerality of performance – which has caused so much concern in western thinking – is confronted as the basic fact of existence, with the result that the criterion of a thing's existence in Buddhism is not some moment of pure being but the performance of generative actions: 'The criterion of existence is the performance of certain specific actions' (Vyas 1991: 12); 'There are no "things" in Buddhism, only processes' (Johannson 1979: 217); 'Things do not exist; only events exist' (Chang 1971: 81).

What applies to things applies also to people: western theories of acting have always had fundamental problems because of a categorical dualism of self and role, in which the former is the locus of authenticity, the latter of pretence. Western directors interested in somehow restoring to theatre some sense of holiness or authenticity have sought methods of exposing that self behind the roles; Buddhism had from the beginning a simpler solution: dissolve the self completely. Malalasekera writes: 'In the Buddha's teaching, the individual's being is, in fact a *becoming*, a coming-to-be, something that happens, i.e., an event, a process' (Malalasekera 1968: 66).

This was already the Buddha's insight and teaching: 'Train yourself in such a way that there is only seeing in what is seen, there is only hearing in what is heard, there is only sensing in what is sensed, there is only cognising in what is cognised.

• Dancing Buddah. Photo: David George

ritual drama, but all respect meditation as the path to enlightenment, and in Buddhism meditation is itself a performance: 'Contemplation is the stage of fruition of the theater of mind. When the practitioner has reached this stage, the multiple realities coded in cosmology and enacted in mythopoeic drama may "come alive" in direct experience' (Laughlin *et al.* 1967: 163). Buddhist meditation sets up a basic binary, splintering the 'Self' into 'I-spectator' of 'me-parts' performing in a world of transient, ephemeral events. As K. K. Inada writes: Buddha asks one to be 'both spectator and participant of the activities'.[†]

† In *Buddhist and Western Philosophy*, ed. Nathan Katz (New Delhi: 1981), 275.

This is true of all Buddhist meditation, but especially so of Tibetan, Tantric 'visualization' methods: the Tantric Buddhist in meditation is a kind of psychic dramatist and director, fabricating an hallucinatorily vivid theatre-in-the-mind, and then becoming also an actor in that world; so by meditating one exchanges one's own personality for that of one's favourite character – the deity one visualizes. These visualizations are minutely detailed, involving rehearsals, costumes, props, sets: 'The mind becomes a stage which can be lit up at will for enacting the brilliantly coloured, vivid transformation scenes which cut through the sense barriers and permit mystical union with the sacred Source' (Blofeld 1970: 49). But visualization meditation aims not just at the pursuit of wisdom; the fully visualized deity must then be reabsorbed by a sort of Stanislavskian mystical empathy, the point of the whole technique being to see oneself *as* the deity in order to *become* the qualities which that deity represents and then to act them out – for the benefit of all. 'He vividly visualizes himself as the deity and grasps the divine pride or ego; he directs the power of the deity into himself and becomes, in effect, the transformer through which the divine power can pass out of the realm of knowledge and into the world of events' (Beyer 1973: 66).

Perhaps the most startling example of this is a danced meditation called Chöd, an advanced practice of the Nyingmapa sect: 'A rite to achieve

Then you will not be recognised in terms of what is seen, heard, etc. (i.e. as the seer of something, as the hearer of something, etc). . . .That will be the end of suffering.'[*]

Mookerjee comments: 'How completely the Buddha had rid himself of the notion of a fixed being is well-established by all the passages where he replaces the actor by the act itself' (1975: 168). In the words of Shwe Zan Aung: 'In Buddhism there is no actor apart from action' (1929: 7), or as Buddhadasa Bhikku puts it: 'The doing is done but no doer is there; the path has been walked but no walker is there' (1935: 23).

* Translation by Lily de Silva of the passage in the *Bodhi-vagga* of the Udana, from 'Sense experience of the liberated being as reflected in early Buddhism', in *Buddhist Philosophy and Culture*, ed. D. J. Kalupahana and W. G. Weeraratne (Colombo: 1987), 17.

This performative ontology and psychology flow over into fully developed Buddhist ritual dramas – the Chams. Not all Buddhists practise dance or

Enlightenment in this lifetime by a risk-taking venture. If he succeeds,' writes Evans-Wentz, 'he may go straight to Nirvana, having penetrated beyond Maya' (1958: 282). Chöd is an extreme example of visualization meditation in which the yogin creates imaginary figures of such hallucinatory vividness than he cannot distinguish them from material, physical beings. This, in all visualization meditations, leads to realization that the material, physical world too is no more than a mind-emanation, no more real than imaginative constructs, the difference being that in Chöd this is taken to an extreme in that the yogin 'may even make them physically as "real" as his own body' (Evans-Wentz 1958: 281) and be so convinced of their reality that they can kill him. It is practised in solitary and sacred places, usually a Himalayan snowfield or a place where corpses are chopped to bits and given to the wolves and vultures, and Evans-Wentz – who has published the Chöd text in translation in his invaluable collection *Tibetan Yoga and Secret Doctrines* – has no hesitation in calling it a 'mystic drama, performed by a single human actor, assisted by numerous spiritual beings, visualized, or imagined, as being present in response to his magic invocation' (ibid.: 282). Because the great gift of theatre to this religion is that it facilitates the cognition of reality as an illusion, 'an imaginative creation given illusive existence by its creator' (ibid.: 281). Chöd goes further: both creating a theatrical illusion and then seeking to penetrate beyond, to the Void, for *chöd* means, literally, 'to cut off' – egoism, passion, karmic inheritance, the Self. Simultaneously director, choreographer, performer and spectator, the lama must have put in years of preparation and rehearsal before attempting this rite: he must memorize the whole ritual including the dance steps, the mantras, the rhythmic beating of the damaru drum and the sounding of the thigh-bone trumpet. 'Alone in the wilderness with no other aid at hand than his own *yogic* power, he must face the strange elemental beings which the ritual evokes and dominate them; or, failing, risk an unbalancing of mind and psychic constitution, possibly leading to madness or even death' (ibid.: 280).

CONCLUSION

The relationship between ritual and theatre has traditionally been approached historically – the former identified as preceding and (it is argued, 'therefore') being the source/origin of the latter. Much in this approach may be objected to on methodological grounds – its 'fallacy of emergence', its cultural universalism, porous causalities, and – not least – the evidence that the sequence depends in the end on ideological assumptions. In a culture whose dominant religion conceives of God as the Great Originator, religious studies tend to be obsessed with notions of origins, but religion is not just – or even necessarily – about origins, but just as arguably about perfection. Religious rituals seek and offer encounters with perfection – imploringly, apologetically, enticingly and sometimes mimetically. That is where performance already comes into the picture, because 'all performance involves a consciousness of doubleness, through which the actual execution of an action is placed in mental comparison with a potential, an ideal, or a remembered original model of that action' (Carlson 1996: 5).

The urge to emulate, to perform, precedes the concept of the sacred and even though it can be shown that there has been a shift from ritual to theatre in some cultures,* those rituals themselves already depended on the ability to perform.

*Notably where colonialists and missionaries have destroyed local belief systems and preserved their 'masquerades' as entertainment: cf. Nwabueze 1982.

These performances heal – temporarily – the split universes of religions: every religion requires regular acts of re-revelation to re-establish the connections between transcendent and immanent strata of time, space and consciousness. These acts are too obviously theatrical for some cultures not to have adopted the theatre for their religious purposes, because the theatre is a highly suitable medium to create parallel, alternative time–spaces poised somewhere between material representation and imaginative construct, between perception and conception.

Rather, however, than continuing to search for

more 'proof' that theatre informed ritual or that ritual preceded theatre, what has been proposed above is abandonment of the whole historical method along with its in-built causalities, inversions and hypotheses and adoption instead of the model which Buddhist philosophy practises on the basis of its performance ontology: the conception of phenomena as 'mutually arising', 'co-dependently originating'. Instead of endlessly constructing putative, heuristic histories, it may be more useful to recognize that when we find a variety of similar phenomena we take this as evidence not that one derived from another but that they have some common, deeper origin, one that is cognitive rather than cultural. 'Co-dependent arising' makes good sense of much Hindu material; it would make better sense of the relationships between Zen and Noh than any linear, causal model; it would do justice to other phenomena in other cultures too – such as, for example, the subtle interactions between the ritual Sanghyang Dedari and its secular equivalent, the Legong.* * cf. George 1991: 36.

Such a basic revision of classical methodology and its cultural assumptions will, however, meet with some resistance: proposing performance as a foundational psychological capacity, the primary epistemological base and ontological model is a radical challenge to classical western logocentrism: 'Im Anfang war das Wort.' Buddhist philosophy replaces the precedence of the Word with the priority of the Event, but cultures which do not or cannot accept the primacy of performance over substance must have problems with theatre, which can only be a betrayal of something else.

Performance is a strange reality; its space, time and persons are all radically different from those we experience in other realities; and until recently, those other realities have been ascribed some greater degree of truth. The theatre has suffered from that, especially in the West, whose cultural arbiters have regularly had problems with it, disturbed by its ephemerality, its illusory quality, and, above all, by the fear that it represents some alternative and therefore blasphemous act of alternative creativity. Theatre in the West has always been haunted by the drama, by the word, by the idea and thus by the metaphysical assumption that any representation must be a distortion of some original, transcendent truth. Only the wholesale jettisoning of that metaphysics can possibly emancipate the theatre from entrapment in its own metaphor.

Disguised as theatre, performance has had to wait a long time for its contemporary emancipation, but one can conjecture that theatre-people must have already found their marginalization puzzling. People kept accusing them of practising deception, not understanding how one can live with the creation of artefacts that have no continuous material base. Theatre-people shrug: we live in a world of elusive temporality; isn't that what the world is really like? They always knew that their worlds were 'unreal', the product of their wills, consciousness, perceptions, desires, that they had no substance, existed only in time. Paradoxically, it was theatre-people who never made the cognitive and emotional mistakes which Buddhists spend their lives refuting. No one needed to tell them about impermanence, temporality, insubstantiality, dependent arising. But then Buddhism has never had problems with other realities, positing a virtually infinite number of parallel universes – necessary if every possible expression and manifestation of the basic forces in the universe is to be realized. None of these universes has any priority over the others: all of them are fictions, maya-like, a creation, a construct of the mind: they are all 'theatres'. Originally . . .

BIBLIOGRAPHY

Aung, Shwe Zan (1929) 'An introductory essay to the compendium of Buddhist philosophy', in *Compendium of Philosophy*, London: Pali Text Society and Oxford University Press.

Barish, Jonas A. (1981) *The Antitheatrical Prejudice*, Berkeley, CA: University of California Press.

Bermúdez, José Luis, Marcel, Anthony and Eilan, Naomi (eds) (1995) *The Body and the Self*, Cambridge, MA: MIT Press.

Berthold, Margot (1972) *The History of World Theater. From the Beginnings to the Baroque*, New York.

Best, David (1974) *Expression in Movement in the Arts*, London.

Beyer, Stephan (1973) *The Cult of Tara: Magic and Ritual in Tibet*, Berkeley, CA: University of California Press.

Blacker, Carmen (1975) *The Catalpa Bow: a Study of Shamanistic Practices in Japan*, London.

Bloch, Susana, Orthous, Pedro and Santibanez-H, Guy (1995) 'Effector patterns of basic emotions', in Phillip B. Zarrilli (ed.) *Acting (re)considered*, London: Routledge, 186–218.

Blofeld, John (1970) *The Tantric Mysticism of Tibet*, New York: Arkana.

Buddhadasa Bhikku (1935) *Heart-Wood from the Bo Tree*, place to come: Suan Mok.

Carlson, Marvin (1996) *Performance: a Critical Introduction*, London and New York: Routledge.

Chang, Garma C. C. (1971) *The Buddhist Teaching of Totality: The Philosophy of Hwa Yen Buddhism*, Philadelphia, PA: Penn State University Press.

Collins, Steven (1982) *Selfless Persons*, Cambridge: Cambridge University Press.

Conze, Edward (1973) *Buddhist Thought in India*, Ann Arbor, MI: University of Michigan Press.

Eliade, Mircea (1964) *Shamanism*, London and New York: Princeton University Press.

Evans-Wentz, W. Y. (1958) *Tibetan Yoga and Secret Doctrines*, Oxford University Press.

Gaster, T. H. (1975) *Thespis: Ritual, Myth and Drama in the Ancient Near East*, New York: Gordian.

George, David E. R. (1986) *India: Three Ritual Dance-Dramas*, Cambridge: Chadwick-Healy.

George, David E. R. (1987) 'Ritual drama: between mysticism and magic', *Asian Theatre Journal* 4(2) (Fall): 154–60.

George, David E. R. (1991) *Balinese Ritual Theatre*, Cambridge: Cambridge University Press.

Guenther, Herbert V. (1971) *Buddhist Philosophy in Theory and Practice*, Harmondsworth, Mx: Penguin.

Harrison, Jane Ellen (1978) *Ancient Art and Ritual*, Bradford on Avon.

Hartnoll, Phyllis (1968) *A Concise History of the Theatre*, London: Thames & Hudson.

Johansson, Rune E. A. (1979) *The Dynamic Psychology of Early Buddhism*, Oxford: Curzon Press.

Kalupahana, David J. (1991) *The Mulamadhyamakakarika of Nagarjuna*, New Delhi: Motilal Banarsidas.

Kim, Hee-Jin (1987) *Dogen Kigen Mystical Realist*, Tucson AZ.: University of Arizona Press.

Kirby, E. T. (1975) *Ur-drama: The Origin of Theatre*, New York.

Laughlin, Charles D., Jr, McManus, John and d'Aquili, Eugene G. (1967) 'Mature contemplation', *Zygon: Journal of Religion and Science* 28(2).

Lewis, I. M. (1971) *Ecstatic Religion*, Harmondsworth, Mx: Penguin.

Lidova, Natalia (1994) *Drama and Ritual in Early Hinduism*, Delhi.

Malalasekera, G. P. (1968) 'The status of the individual in Theravada Buddhist philosophy', in *The Status of the Individual in East and West*, ed. C. A. Moore, Honolulu, HI: University of Hawaii Press.

Mookerjee, Satkari (1975) *The Buddhist Philosophy of Universal Flux*, New Delhi: Motilal Banarsidas.

Murti, T. R. V. (1955) *The Central Philosophy of Buddhism*, London.

Nwabueze, Patrick P. (1982) 'From ritual to entertainment', PhD thesis, Bowling Green State University, Ohio.

Richmond, Farley P., Swann, Darius L. and Zarrilli, Phillip B. (1990) *Indian Theatre: Traditions of Performance*, Honolulu, HI: University of Hawaii Press.

Schechner, Richard (1977) *Essays on Performance Theory*, New York: Routledge.

Sorgenfrei, Carol Fisher (1997) 'Desperately seeking Asia: a survey of theatre history textbooks', *Asian Theatre Journal* 14(2): 223–58.

Vyas, C. S. (1991) *Buddhist Theory of Perception*, New Delhi: Navrang.

Shamanism in Britain Today

Graham Harvey

There is no etymological link between Shaman and Sham, but some responses to the activities of Shamans (or those who call themselves Shamans) suggest there should be. This chapter explores the various activities commonly labelled Shamanism in contemporary Britain. It is divided, somewhat artificially, into seven sections. A brief introduction to Shamans of indigenous, small-scale societies is intended not as a yard-stick against which all other forms can be measured, but as a indication of what it is about Shamanism that seems so attractive and enticing. It also notes that there is nothing distinctive about the ambiguity of responses to Shamanism, and indeed that 'sham' might be an intentional part of Shamans' performances. Following sections are devoted to the Shamans of today's Britain: core Shamans, Jungian-style therapists, 'white Indians', techno-Shamans and Pagan eco-activists. In drawing conclusions from this discussion, the final section asks what these movements have in common and questions criticism of them as inauthentic or illegitimate. Is it possible to condemn (neo-)Shamans without undermining the entire anthropological (or indeed academic) enterprise? Even if the contextualization of shamanic practice in the West is unlike other 'traditional' forms, might this be acknowledged as appropriate either as a celebration of modernity or as a postmodern critique?

FROM SIBERIA WITH POWER

Academics have introduced the activities of Shamans to a wider audience. Indeed, it is academic systematizing, universalizing and publicizing that turned a host of discrete, local, disparate and even unique phenomena into a new -ism, Shamanism.

Recognizing that Shamanism is a construct is necessary as a preface to this discussion of the Shamans of Britain precisely as a counter to that condemnation of the new Shamanisms which ignores the academic invention of the -ism in the first place. Whether appropriate or not in other contexts the construct is powerful for many people.

Siberian Shamans (the 'classic' type if only because that is where the name comes from) have been known to academics for over three hundred years (Hutton 1993). Shamanism, however, has become more popular since Mircea Eliade (1964) championed its (re)presentation as 'the archaic techniques of ecstasy'. This focus on states of consciousness and the techniques by which they are altered has been persuasive and certainly facilitates the attempt to say what Shamanism is (or might be) in a few short sentences. Thus, Shamans deliberately do what everyone else does regularly and easily, i.e. change states of consciousness (from concentration on reading, to careful listening in case that sound was an intruder, to wistful dreaming about a holiday or a tea-break). Everyone occasionally has to cheer themselves up or to relax. However, Shamans alter moods or states more dramatically, both in terms of the means employed and in terms of the purpose. Shamans (as presented by Eliade at least) effect the more dramatic state of ecstasy, a controlled trance in which the practitioner journeys to the worlds of spirits. And the heart of the matter, for Eliade, is that Shamans use a repertoire of similar techniques to achieve this state. They might, for example, drum, dance, chant, fast, or suffer pain, hunger or sleep-deprivation. All these and other methods effect dramatic changes in the practitioner's state of consciousness. That these are the

Performance Research 3(3), pp.15-23 © Routledge 1998

effect of alterations in brain chemistry is of interest to some interpreters, and sometimes becomes simply reductionist (Vitebsky 1995: 148).

Eliade's use of 'archaic' alerts us to the fact that his exposition of Shamanism is part of his broader programme of elucidating the history of religions as the history of religion (singular) with an original tripartite cosmos (upper, middle and lower worlds) and rituals in which people return to 'sacred time'.* But if 'archaic' is a loaded word within Eliade's own cosmology, the word 'traditional' is similarly polemical (although rarely as deliberately as Eliade's 'archaic') in other discussions of the practices of Shamans. It asserts that there are pure, authentic and legitimate forms existing in some non-western, pre-modern, small-scale societies against which western modernity can be opposed. Rejection of the insistence that 'tradition' is unchanging and timeless enables a much richer exploration of the practices of Shamans and other real people. The following paragraph suggests aspects of shamanic practice not yet noted sufficiently above.

* For further criticisms of Eliade's 'Shamanism' see Smith 1987 and Noel 1997.

What Shamans do is rooted in their cultural worlds, which vary considerably. The academic and popular use of the name Shaman for those who control (and sometimes those who are controlled by) spirits, regardless of their own language, is now nearly universal, but it should not suggest that all those called Shamans are the same. When used carefully the name refers to those who work, in symbiotic relationships with spirits, as healers and/or as finders of information (detectives or researchers) for their community. In only a few cultures is Shamanism a profession of choice. More often, Shamans describe their initiation as a matter of being abducted and attacked by spirits – i.e. as an unwelcome experience. Sometimes initiation arises out of severe illness, and Shamans feel *compelled* to serve their communities (human and spirit). A focus on the techniques employed and the states of consciousness achieved should be subordinate to exploration of the powerful and empowering encounter with spirits that is at the heart of

what Shamans do (Lewis 1989). This too requires elucidating within a discussion of the relationships between Shamans and their human communities.†

† For an excellent example of this see Humphrey and Onon 1996. Vitebsky (1995: 88–90) also illustrates the traditional and ubiquitous 'shamming' of Shamans.

CORE SHAMANS

If Eliade highlights 'the techniques of ecstasy' as the centre of Shamanism, Michael Harner has popularized the idea that there is a 'core' to Shamanism which can be useful to anyone, anywhere.‡ Following his anthropological research (1972) among the Jívaro and Conibo, Harner wrote a pioneering resource book for new Shamans, *The Way of the Shaman* (1980). The first, more ethnographic chapter summarizes his anthropological work and indicates just how far Harner had 'gone native'. In the rest of the book, and in his workshops and teaching, he is more interested in the 'core' of Shamanism extractable from within diverse cultures. It is this that he makes available for people throughout the world to 'integrate into their own lives'. It is this that his followers have promulgated.

‡ Aldous Huxley, Carlos Castaneda, Joan Halifax and others predate or parallel Harner in re-contextualizing Shamanism in the West, but Harner's version has proved more popular, especially as it does not require the use of psychotropics.

Typically, core Shamanism is taught in weekend workshops and evening events which are advertised in centres and magazines dedicated to Shamanism, and in New Age bookshops and magazines. Longer courses (residential for a couple of weeks, or a series of weekends) are also available. Some of these are labelled 'Basic', others 'Advanced', but practitioners do not limit themselves to a single attendance at a 'basic' workshop. A reluctance to name oneself 'Shaman' is typical, although it seems acceptable to claim to have a shamanic world-view. However, there is a looser sense in which participation in shamanic workshops is seen as entitling people to describe their experiences as shamanic and therefore themselves as (at least potential) Shamans. Some workshops might even encourage the idea that it is possible to become a Shaman by making the accoutrements of Shamanism (drums and fans, for example).

First encounters with workshops will entail a brief orientation to shamanic world-views and techniques. Participants become familiar with the names and locations of traditional 'shamanic' societies – the Evenk, from whose Tungus language 'Shaman' comes, are particularly noted, however little of their actual culture or life-style concerns workshoppers. The idea (and sometimes the real existence) of Otherworlds above, below or beside the ordinary, everyday world, is introduced. But essentially workshops are about experience. It is not enough to talk about Shamanism, the course entails action, performance and participation. Adverts offer choices of 'finding your power animal', 'dancing with the spirits', 'contacting your spiritual power', 'divinatory journeys', 'drum making', 'journeying to non-ordinary reality', 'questing for knowledge and power for oneself and others'. More advanced workshops teach participants to 'work with the dead', 'find a shift of perception', 'strengthen your own relationship to Spirit', 'utilize the places of power in the landscape' and 'tap the cyclical power of the moon, menstruation and the seasons'.*

* Examples drawn from a variety of UK and US magazines and fliers.

In practice and performance these tend to mean very similar things. To the accompaniment of rhythmic music (typically drums but maybe rattles or chanting), people are guided in imaginatively visualizing a journey. Usually they lie on the floor in a dimly lit room and may blindfold their eyes or be covered by a blanket to enable shamanic vision to work.† The expectation, rhythms and ambience effect an alteration in mood or state of consciousness which enables participants to become receptive. The facilitator then narrates a journey for participants to follow 'spiritually' or in their Imagination.‡ Initial journeys are usually in quest of a 'power animal' or 'totem creature', understood to

† Although this appears silly in Jones's 1994 critique of John Matthews (1991), it might actually seem 'traditional' in the light of Vitebsky (1995: 146).

‡ Capitalized to suggest something more powerful and 'real' than 'mere illusion'.

be close to one's true-self and expected to be a guide on further journeys. Such animals might be found in the roots of trees or in caves visualized while a drum heartbeat encourages a sense of safe and easy movement. Later journeys may be to find knowledge about death, the reason for an illness, the importance of an ancestral site, patterns to paint on one's own drum and so on. Workshops might encourage forays into the (outer) 'natural' world to find parts of 'power animals' with which to adorn drums, costumes and surroundings.

The (other)world in which the core Shaman journeys is most often understood to be an inner world akin to the Jungian 'unconscious'. 'Spirits' encountered in these journeys are most often thought of as parts of one's self. They are rarely hostile, and never any more dangerous than other parts of oneself. The traveller can turn away from any uncomfortable situation and return on another occasion when he or she feels better equipped to integrate disturbing parts of the persona into a more holistic sense of self. Finally here it is worth noting that core Shamans typically reject the use of stimulants to help achieve altered states of consciousness – sometimes workshoppers are instructed to avoid even tea and coffee for a day or two before a workshop. The core shamanic journey is achieved by the individual aided only by the deeper, truer self, his or her companions and someone playing rhythmic sounds. Tape-recordings of suitable rhythms are available.

JUNGIAN THERAPEUTIC MYSTERIES

Many of those who engage in Harner-style core Shamanism, and especially the facilitators of the workshops promulgating it, also practise as healers or therapists. Their interests, activities, techniques and discourses are continuous with those of core Shamanism. That is, both forms engage in rhythm-assisted inner-journeys in search of knowledge about themselves, which can be summarized as 'power and healing'. Therapists are treated separately here simply to highlight the fact that they also 'work' for others: clients, patients, or seekers.

Therapies that work on or with the mind, soul, state of consciousness, sense of well-being or disease, psyche, or whatever our deep 'inner' life is to be called, have been enlivened by 'shamanic' understandings. Jung and his devotees entice us to explore our inner worlds, which are presented as more than individual, though always deeply personal. Rather than the cold distance of allegedly scientific medicine such therapists engage the Imagination, the Imaginal, fantasy, desire, hopes and fears – their own as much as those of their clients or patients. Shamanism provides a language with which to describe what these therapists want to do, and techniques with which to do it. They may reject the real existence of Otherworlds and Spirits, but they do 'believe' in the power of seemingly cognate Innerworlds. Shamanic journeys, supported by drum heartbeats and the softly spoken words of the therapist, take the client/patient towards the goal of wholeness.

Some of these therapists present what they do as a means of dealing with 'soul loss' by 'soul retrieval'. They assert that there is some part of a human being (and perhaps other living beings in the shamanic world) which can be separated from the whole person. In dreams and imaginings this 'soul' travels, experiences and learns. But just as an accident can separate a person's hand from the body, so too trauma can sever the soul or some part of it. Some Shamans see it as their role to journey after that soul, to recover it and return it to its rightful place. In the West the majority of shamanic therapists see themselves as guiding their client/patient on this journey – that is, the client shamanizes. Again using rhythms and visualization, the therapist guides the traveller deep within him- or herself to encounter not only memories but the coded reimaginings of traumatic events. Archetypal forces are encountered and either recruited as helpers or confronted as hindrances to the development of well-being. Some therapists ritualize their work with crystals, incense and tubes through which intruding 'spirits' are (symbolically?) sucked out of their clients/patients. The most accessible introduction to this style of

Shamanism is Caitlín Matthews's *Singing the Soul Back Home* (1995).

WHITE INDIANS

A scan of neo-shamanic literature and workshop advertisements reinforces the suspicion that many neo-Shamans are playing at being 'Indians'. They adopt feathers, drums, hyphenated pseudonyms referring to natural phenomena, and other indicators of Hollywood clichés. Their participation in sweat lodges, even leadership of such a lodge, often fails to affect their individualistic, self-obsessed quest for yet another immediate spiritual experience.

Western culture holds a pervasive understanding that indigenous peoples are wiser, nobler, purer and more spiritual than whites. It has held this idea since shortly before the nearly successful beating of such peoples into near total extinction – up until then it was busy attempting genocide. Such neo-Shamans' solution to 'our' lack of spirituality is not to challenge western culture or its roots but to appropriate from 'native' peoples. They might put it rather more positively, of course: this is learning from people with an unbroken way of living a sacred life, and is done with respect so it redresses the balance and does challenge modernity to learn to live differently. Is it merely ironic that the archetypal film 'Indians', the Sioux/Lakota, are now the archetypal spiritual resource (or fashion style-guide) of British neo-Shamans? The end-result of this process is that 'disciples' of alleged 'medicine men' lead workshops in which people are enabled to address 'all our relations' while walking 'the red road'. The 'plastic medicine men' (Churchill 1992) share with their 'white Indian' followers the understanding that integral parts of a nation's culture are in fact elements of a universal human spirituality in the making.

CYBERIAN TECHNO-SHAMANISM

Meanwhile away from suburbia (or its rural retreat centres for the elite), in country barns or inner city clubs, Shamanism has found new techniques in

• Heating the Grandfather Rocks. Photo: Graham Harvey

new technology. The pervasive idea that Shamanism is centrally concerned with ecstasy animates the techno-shamanic experimentation with trance and an insistence on the immediacy and authority of experience. Rhythmic music and dance are the predominant techniques employed to induce trance, although psychotropic (and sometimes hallucinogenic) substances are sometimes employed. Labelling this form of Shamanism 'techno' implies that technology marks it out from other ('traditional') forms, and is its defining characteristic. Drums, sweat lodges, incense and mirrors are no less technological than drum machines, synthesizers, lights and fractal patterns. All these human artefacts can be envisaged similarly, as being of cosmic importance (although some techno-Shamans treat their technology as mere equipment).

'Cyberia' (rather than 'techno') is probably more evocative of what is important here (Rushkoff 1994). This is a form of Shamanism that challenges modern understandings of personal and social identity, while building on scientific *and* 'pre-modern' understandings of the world. Blending 'traditional' shamanic world-views and techniques with Chaos science, the Cyberian Shaman enters Other-worlds in ecstatic trance-dance. Some rehabilitate hallucination not as 'false vision' but as 'enlightening vision' or 'hallucignosis' (Ebersole 1995: 256–63). In his *Food of the Gods* Terence McKenna asserts:

> Not all shamans use intoxication with plants to obtain ecstasy. . . . Yet none of these methods [drumming, manipulation of breath, ordeals, fasting, theatrical illusions, sexual abstinence] is as effective, as ancient, and as overwhelming as the use of plants containing chemical compounds that produce visions.
>
> (McKenna 1992: 6)

So, in epic dance events, consciousness-altering drugs, rhythmic music and colourful fractal patterns combine with the World-Wide-Web's information highway to provide an experience of 'at-one-ness' with all things and access to (apparent?) omniscience. Mysticism and technology combine, as they always have. Perhaps wisdom cannot be gained in this way, but information and knowledge can.

Media coverage of raves might suggest that they are solely concerned with drug-induced hedonism. They might be more accurately considered as egalitarian and communal arenas for achieving significant, co-operative ecstatic experiences. For participants it is important that this is a communal experience. There are

> no performers, no audience, no leaders, no egos. For the fractal rule of self-similarity to hold, this also means that every house club must share in the cooperative spirit of all clubs.
>
> (Rushkoff 1994: 159–60)

The whole experience takes everyone to the awareness of 'oneness'. For at least some of the participants and many of the organizers of such events this is considered shamanic, and is expressed in terms of an animated, interconnected cosmos. Just as everyone lives *in* Gaia, in the Earth – whether knowing it, or liking it, or not – so everyone lives in Cyberia, but some do so consciously, deliberately, willingly and creatively.

It remains to note examples of recent journeys in Cyberia's raves. The Secular Order of Druids has always been intimately involved with youth and counter-culture, especially its various popular musical manifestations. In a large indoor rave in the English Midlands they recently proclaimed the rave's organizer to be 'the first bard of the dance of this age' and presented him with robes and an oak sapling, to be planted later. The Megatripolis club in London opened with a Druid ceremony. The white robes of the Druids might have been created especially for the lights, colours and patterns of these events. Dragon Environmental Group have facilitated ceremonies at a number of clubs and

other venues. Return to the Source, at the Brixton Academy, includes a regular and central chakra journey and trance dance among its dance events – partially replicated in a double CD (Return to the Source 1995). One Chaos Magickian, who seems typical, told me that, apart from enjoying raves, he goes when the energy is high and lets the momentum swing him higher in order to do his 'work'. When people's consciousness is already altered and connected to everything, it provides a context for making the changes 'according to Will' that are understood to be the essence of magic (Harvey 1997: 88).

PAGAN ECO-SHAMANS

Alongside the idea that Shamanism has something to do with altered states of consciousness and the techniques for achieving them, it is popularly thought that Shamanism is rooted in direct experience of living nature. This perception is radicalized among the final group of British Shamans to be considered here, Pagan eco-Shamans. Gordon MacLellan argues that

> Modern shamans may be: personal healers: shamans who help people listen to themselves; community healers: shamans who help people listen to each other; patterners: shamans who help the community listen to/relate to the world around them.
>
> (MacLellan 1996: 142)

The first two categories seem to describe most of the western Shamans introduced so far. This section is concerned with the 'patterners' among contemporary Pagans. They are encountered in their guises as environmental educators and/or front-line eco-activists.

The environmental educators use contemporary environmental tools and locations. They are involved in computer-based environmental networks and educational programmes, tree-planting and city farms. Museum- and school-based educational programmes in which ecological principles and practices are encouraged can be natural contexts for such patterner Shamans. Even when the connections made in these events are principally with the 'natural' world rather than the Otherworld, this is shamanic in a culture in which 'wildlife' is as alien as 'spirits'. Indeed, in modernity a re-connection with one's embodiment is shamanic (Harris 1996).

Pagan eco-activists confront destructive road-, quarry- and house-building because they share the shamanic experience of a world full of life in which humans are members of a community of life. Everything has 'soul(s)', everything is 'spirit(s)', everything is alive and 'all that lives is holy'. Inspired musicians (bards?) and colourful drama remind others – including passive TV watchers – that they too are participants in these matters of life and death. Eco-actions are dramatic ceremonies far more than they are political protests. In between actions, drum sessions, dance and other techniques for altering states consciousness are employed as means of celebration and of maintaining neighbourly communication with the defended place. Everything about life in the camps is envisaged not only as protecting but also as evoking the land and its life.

Popular romantic notions of nature (and of the 'green and pleasant land') are radically vitalized in environmental education and eco-actions.* The central job of Pagan, patterner Shamans in our culture is to reintroduce people to the land and to help them find for themselves ways of relating to the living world.

*See Taylor 1995 for global perspectives on similar movements.

CONCLUSION

This chapter has introduced a number of different contexts in which the label 'Shaman' is claimed or applied. It is now necessary to ask what it is that 'Shaman' and 'Shamanism' refer to that other words do not. The fact that we need to borrow a foreign word and coin a neologism suggests that something new is evident. The Shaman cannot be exactly the same as a priest, magician, doctor, juggler, or visionary. However, perhaps more interesting than these simple questions of historical semantics, is the question of whether all the forms of Shaman discussed here share any common ground at all.

Perhaps a brief rehearsal of the facts will clarify the significant details here. The word 'Shaman' is of Siberian (specifically Tungus-speaking Evenk origin). It applied to religious specialists who lived in symbiotic relationship with 'spirits'. Shamans can be considered to control spirits, in that they call

• Sweatlodge Framework. Photo: Graham Harvey

them to work on behalf of clients or patients, but at the same time they can be considered to be controlled or even possessed by the spirits. These Shamans became interesting to the West because of their altered states of consciousness and their methods of affecting such alterations. Similar people and practices were then 'discovered' in many other parts of the world. Anthropology, the emerging academic discipline most interested in Shamans, had two abiding interests: a quest for the earliest forms of human culture, and an understanding of the diverse ways of being human. The quest for origins inspired considerable academic, and eventually popular, enthusiasm. Coincidentally with postwar quests for alternative and instant experiences, the historian of religions, Mircea Eliade, offered an attractive systematization of the allegedly original cosmology underlying what proper Shamans should do: namely Shamanism. The diverse phenomena that now bore a single label were neatly packaged as 'the archaic techniques for achieving ecstasy'. It was not long before the package was opened and the techniques utilized in a variety of popular forms (neo-, techno- and eco-Shamanisms, for example). Some academic observers continue to deride this popularization and distinguish between 'real', 'traditional' Shamans and their deluded imitators. Essentially, the former live in small-scale, pre-literate societies, the latter in western suburbia.

Here we return to the link between 'Shaman' and 'sham'. Most, if not all, the types of Shaman discussed fit uneasily, at best, into their cultural context. They can seem both centrally important and completely marginal. They can reveal something essential about a culture while at the same time appearing quite eccentric. Their serious engagement with the business of life and death is often enmeshed with trickery and shamming. They might be chosen by spirits, but they also chose to perform, playfully at times.*

* This is admirably clear with reference to 'traditional' Shamans in Humphrey and Onon (1996), and with reference to neo-Shamans in Lindquist (1997).

What any Shaman means by 'spirits' is at best ambiguous – are they as real as trees, or are they simply to be treated as if they were real? Shamanizing is almost always rooted in dramatic performance, which should not be explained too quickly as aiding observers to suspend disbelief. Playful, unsystematic role-playing is as important to many Shamans as achieving ecstasy. All Shamans display these paradoxes and refuse to be neatly categorized. This much at least is common ground.

What then is the value of the rejection of western Shamans by academic observers? If 'traditional Shamanism' is itself a systematized figment of academia, imposed on the diverse ways in which distinct cultures engage with the world (and their Otherworlds), it can hardly be appropriate to criticize those who have further reinvented Shamanism. Late-modernity's shamanic workshoppers are taking seriously the ideology on which anthropology, and perhaps the entire academic exercise, is built. As Howard Eilberg-Schwartz argues:

> Twentieth-century anthropology has insisted that we have a great deal to learn about ourselves from the study of the other. . . . This is the myth that justifies the anthropological enterprise, a myth that says that the study of the other leads to enlightenment.
>
> (Eilberg-Schwartz 1989: 87)

Without such a purpose, academia becomes simply a source for arcane information for trivia games and pub quizzes.

As for the practice of Shamanism in Britain, in the contexts and ways noted above, it has developed beyond the pursuit of ecstasy for its own sake and its practitioners are beginning to say so. Though immediacy of experience and instant gratification are central to late-modernity, the experience of encountering non-ordinary states of consciousness is already a transformation of humanity that might be liberating. In at least some forms of Shamanism, trances and the real or symbolic existence of spirits may be involved. Such connections with living beings or life-sources might be implicated in the 'healing' that is generally understood to be essential to shamanic practice – traditional and new. While shamanic *techniques* have been made prominent by academics and practitioners, it is the power of an unusual, intense experience that has captivated the western imagination in search of soul. Some realize this is traditionally found in relationships with others. Some utilize the techniques precisely in order to encounter the ensouled others with whom we share this living planet.

Finally, it does seem legitimate to request an honest recognition by Shamans that at least some of what they do is imaginative, creative, playful performance. Of course, this should not be declared during the performance, or the real business of healing souls and putting soul back into life would be impossible. This is to agree with Dan Noel's valuing of a

> soulful spirituality, in artful touch with dreams and imaginings, including especially those which connect us to our wounding, [which] can be a shamanic spirituality of imaginal healing.
>
> (1997: 211)

It does not, however, forget that the Shaman is 'the one caught in the middle; the spider in the web, perhaps. Or maybe the fly' (MacLellan 1996: 141).

REFERENCES

Castaneda, Carlos (1968) *The Teachings of Don Juan: a Yacqui Way of Knowledge*, Berkeley: University of California Press.

Churchill, Ward (1992) 'Spiritual hucksterism: the rise of the plastic medicine men', in Ward Churchill, *Fantasies of the Master Race*, Monroe, ME: Common Courage, 215–28.

Ebersole, Gary (1995) *Captured by Texts: Puritan to Post-Modern Images of Indian Captivity*, Charlottesville: University Press of Virginia.

Eilberg-Schwartz, Howard (1989) 'Witches of the West: neopaganism and goddess worship as enlightenment religions', *Journal of Feminist Studies in Religion* 5(1): 77–95.

Eliade, Mircea (1964) *Shamanism: Archaic Techniques of Ecstasy*, New York: Pantheon.

Halifax, Joan (1979) *Shamanic Voices: a Survey of Visionary Narratives*, New York: Dutton.

Harner, Michael (1972) *The Jívaro: People of the Sacred Waterfalls*, Berkeley: University of California Press.

Harner, Michael (1980) *The Way of the Shaman*, New York: Bantam; reissued (1990) San Francisco: Harper & Row.

Harris, Adrian (1996) 'Sacred ecology', in Graham Harvey and Charlotte Hardman (eds) *Paganism Today*, London: Thorsons, 149–56.

Harvey, Graham (1997) *Listening People, Speaking Earth: Contemporary Paganism*, London: C. Hurst.

Humphrey, Caroline and Onon, Urgunge (1996) *Shamans and Elders: Experience, Knowledge and Power among the Daur Mongols*, Oxford: Oxford University Press.

Hutton, Ronald (1993) *The Shamans of Siberia*, Glastonbury: Isle of Avalon Press.

Huxley, Aldous (1954) *Doors of Perception*, New York: Harper.

Jones, Leslie (1994) 'The emergence of the Druid as Celtic Shaman', *Folklore in Use* 2(1): 131–42.

Lewis, Ioan M. (1989) *Ecstatic Religion: a Study of Shamanism and Spirit Possession*, London: Routledge.

Lindquist, Galina (1997) *Shamanic Performance on the Urban Scene: Neo-Shamanism in Contemporary Sweden*, Stockholm: Stockholm University.

McKenna, Terence (1992) *Food of the Gods*, London: Rider.

MacLellan, Gordon (1996) 'Dancing on the edge: Shamanism in modern Britain', in Graham Harvey and Charlotte Hardman (eds) *Paganism Today*, London: Thorsons, 138–48.

Matthews, Caitlín (1995) *Singing the Soul Back Home: Shamanism in Daily Life*, Shaftesbury: Element.

Matthews, John (1991) *The Celtic Shaman*, Shaftesbury: Element.

Noel, Daniel (1997) *The Soul of Shamanism: Western Fantasies, Imaginal Realities*, New York: Continuum.

Return to the Source (1995) *The Chakra Journey*, London: Return to the Source, RTTS CD2.

Rushkoff, Douglas (1994) *Cyberia: Life in the Trenches of Hyperspace*, London: HarperCollins.

Smith, Jonathan Z. (1987) *To Take Place: Toward Theory in Ritual*, Chicago: University of Chicago Press.

Taylor, Bron (ed.) (1995) *Ecological Resistance Movements*, New York: SUNY Press.

Vitebsky, Piers (1995) *The Shaman*, London: Macmillan.

The Aztec Ritual Sacrifices

Mutsumi Izeki

INTRODUCTION

The Aztecs or the Mexicas* were the people who established the last empire of the entire Mesoamerican history, which lasted for more than three thousand years until the Spanish Conquest in AD 1521. At the time of the Spanish Conquest, the Mexica empire extended from the Gulf of Mexico to the Pacific Ocean and from what is now north-central Mexico to Guatemala. From the capital of Tenochtitlan, the Mexicas ruled over those areas by means of alliance, tribute and trade. In the gaining of their territories, war and sacrifice were considered to be essential.

* The term 'Mexica' means exclusively those who originated from outside the Central Valley of Mexico, and founded and inhabited the imperial capital of Tenochtitlan in the late post-classic period, from the mid-twelfth century to 1521. And the term 'Aztec' is generally used as a generic name for the Nahuatl-speaking people, who lived in the valley under the control of the Mexica empire.

The practice of human sacrifice was not the innovation of the Aztecs themselves but part of the Mesoamerican tradition. According to González Torres (1992: 56–62), human sacrifice might have been practised from quite an early period in the Mesoamerican history. In her work she mentioned some archaeological facts from which she infers the existence of human sacrifice in the pre-classic and classic periods.† In Tlatilco, the pre-classic site in the Central Valley, several tombs with intentionally decapitated skulls and dismembered bodies have been found, which suggests a certain form of ritual slaying. Also some stone sculptures and reliefs found in the Olmec regions

† In Mesoamerican chronology the pre-classic corresponds roughly to the period from 1,500 BC to AD 0 and the classic to the period from AD 0 to 900.

make us assume the existence of ritual human sacrifice there in the pre-classic period. In Teotihuacan, the most influential city in the classic Mesoamerica, many remains of human sacrifice dedicated to the newly built pyramids as guardians or offerings have been discovered (Cabrera Castro and Cowgill 1993; González Torres 1992: 60). Archaeological excavations have revealed some other evidence of human sacrifice in Monte Albán and the Maya region (González Torres 1992: 60–2).

Human sacrifice was considered by the Aztecs not only as a means to show their political power, but also as an important ritual to maintain the order of the universe. They performed human sacrifice and auto-sacrifice in almost every festival, and offered human hearts and blood to their gods. Several forms of cruel sacrifice were practised by them: extracting a victim's heart and flaying the dead body; killing a victim with arrows; pushing a victim from the top of a pyramid; throwing a victim into fire or water; etc. Those forms of human sacrifice had particular meanings in the feasts and were dedicated to certain deities. However, the main purpose was to nourish the earth with a large quantity of blood and to energize the sun and other gods by dedicating to them the human hearts of the victims. In the same manner, auto-sacrifice, or bloodletting through piercing ears, elbows, and shins with sharp maguey (agave) spines or filed bones, were rituals that were designed to offer one's blood to the deities.

In almost all the Aztec ceremonies, offerings of food, flowers, papers, clothing and incense to the gods played a crucial role. Some types of death sacrifice, such as the dispatching of animals, were normally employed in all important rituals.

• Flaying a man in honour of the God 'Xipetolec. Sahagún (1953–8): Bk 2, plate 1)

Performance Research 3(3), pp.24–31 © Routledge 1998

However, as Nicholson (1971: 432) mentioned, ritual human sacrifices were practised among the Aztecs 'on a scale not even approached by any other ritual system in the history of the world'.

This article examines the notion of human sacrifice among the Aztecs through mythology, ethnohistorical documents and archaeological remains, and aims to rethink their concept of death.

THE ORIGIN OF SACRIFICE IN THE AZTEC MYTHS

The mythological events played out by the gods in the primordial time always define the values of life and thought of present human beings. Aztec mythology tells that the creator deities sacrificed themselves to produce new worlds and new life, including human beings. For this reason, the people believed that they had to offer humans in return in order to nourish the solar and earth deities who were the sustainers of the whole creation. The myths were recorded by the Spanish conquerors and some educated natives after the Conquest, as well as by the Aztec people on sculptures and in painted manuscripts before the arrival of the Spaniards. Various accounts, such as *Leyenda de los soles,** *Historia de los Mexicanos por sus pinturas,*† *Historia de México*‡ and *Florentine Codex*§ narrate different stories of the origin and purposes of sacrifice performed by the gods in mythological time.

* In *Códice Chimalpopoca* (1992: 119–28).

† In Garibay (1985: 23–57).

‡ ibid.: 91–116.

§ Sahagún (1953–81: Bk VII, 3–9).

The Aztec believed that four previous eras, or Suns, existed before the present world, which is the Fifth Sun. Both *Leyenda de los soles* and *Historia de México* tell the same version of the creation of human beings. In order to create the present race of humans from the human bones of the last creation, Quetzalcoatl, the god of life and wind, went to Mictlan, the underworld ruled by Mictlantecuhtli, the god of death. Having overcome the difficulties set up by Mictlantecuhtli, finally he retrieved the bones and took them to Tamoanchan, the place of origin. Then the goddess called Quilaztli or Cihuacoatl ground the bones into powder, and Quetzalcoatl and all the other gods shed drops of their blood on it. Thus, the present humans were created by mixing the bones of the extinct race, who had been changed into fish at the end of the fourth world, with the self-sacrificial blood of the gods.

According to *Historia de México*, after the destruction of the Fourth Sun, the gods Quetzalcoatl and Tezcatlipoca took charge of new creation. They descended from the sky and saw the goddess Tlaltecuhtli, who looked like a beast crawling on the sea. Then, in order to create the earth, the two gods transformed into great serpents and tore her body into two pieces. They made the earth from the upper half of her body and took the other half to the heaven, but this incident angered other deities. To compensate for the damage they had done to Tlaltecuhtli, all the deities descended to console her and ordered that all plants needed for human life would sprout from her. However, at times she cried and required human hearts and blood in return for giving sustenance to human beings. This story tells the reason why people had to offer human sacrifice to the earth.

Leyenda de los soles and *Florentine Codex* narrate the creation of the Fifth Sun in Teotihuacan, the place of the gods. After the creation of the earth, people, and their food and drink, all the gods got together in darkness at Teotihuacan to decide who was to become the new sun. The god Nanahuatl was chosen: after four nights of penance he jumped bravely into the divine flames, but though the newly born sun appeared on the eastern horizon, it did not move at all. Finding that the sun needed to be revived in order to follow its path, all the other gods had to kill themselves and offer their lives to it. The self-sacrifice of the gods finally set the sun in motion. Therefore, the Aztec people kept offering human hearts to the sun for the purpose of preventing the cessation of its motion due to lacking energy.

Historia de los Mexicanos por sus pinturas contains a different version of the creation of the sun and human beings. It says that Quetzalcoatl threw his son into the great fire and from there the sun came

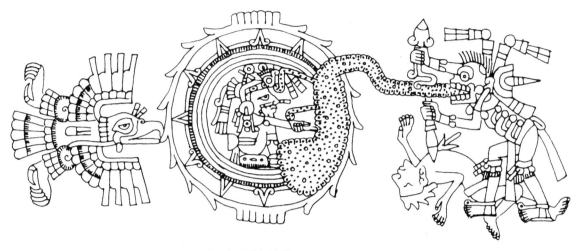

• 'Mictlantechtli' offering a human heart to the sun in the underworld. Códice Laud (1994: plate 24)

out to light the world, but the sun needed human hearts and blood. Then Tezcatlipoca created 400 men and 5 women to feed the sun, and the gods invented war to obtain hearts and blood for the sun. It also tells that the first god who started auto-sacrifice or blood-letting was the god Camaxtle or Mixcoatl, other nomina of Tezcatlipoca. He imposed auto-sacrifice on humans as a rite to perform when they were in need of begging the gods for something.

The Aztec mythology indicates that the present world was created and ordered through the self-sacrificial acts of the deities. As Matos Moctezuma (1995: 42) says, the principle of sacrifice would be crucial in producing life. And human beings were created for the purpose of giving their lives to the gods to maintain the whole creation. This whole idea represents the notion that life and death are continuous and complementary.

RITUAL SACRIFICES DURING FESTIVALS

In the Aztec culture, the solar year was divided into eighteen months of twenty days each, the system which was based on their religion and corresponded to their agricultural cycle. Each month was dedicated to a certain deity, and specific feasts were celebrated with human sacrifice as an indispensable ritual. Many historical sources relate to those feasts, but the ethnohistorical documents recorded by Sahagún (1953–81), Durán (1977) and Torquemada (1976) are considered to contain the most informative details of the rituals.

Ritual death of a human being was called *tla-camictiliztli* in the Nahuatl language and was regarded as a culmination of any ceremony. There were various forms of rituals before slaying, but most of the *tlacamictiliztli* were performed by the extraction of the victim's heart. The extracted hearts and the blood were believed to nourish the gods. The blood of victims was also considered to be filled with the vital power to communicate with the supernatural world (González Torres 1992: 116). The priests in charge of ritual sacrifice daubed the statues of the gods with the collected blood and sprinkled it on a sacrificial stone and the stairs of the temple pyramid, for the purpose of consecration. The purpose of throwing the bodies of victims from the top of the temple pyramid is thought to have been to sanctify the stairs with their blood (ibid.).

Rituals before and after the heart extraction could be as follows: flaying of a victim in the month Tlacaxipehualiztli; shooting a victim with arrows in Huey Tecuilhuitl; and sacrifice by fire in Xocotl-huetzi.

'Flaying of men' in Tlacaxipehualiztli, the second month of the year, dedicated to the god

Xipe Totec (Our Lord the Flayed One), began with the captives of war at dawn on the first day of the feast. Then followed gladiatorial combat. Afterwards, victorious warriors who were regarded as impersonators of Xipe donned the flayed skins of their captives. They wore the skins for twenty days, engaging in mock skirmishes throughout the capital, begging alms and blessing those who gave them food and offerings. After twenty days, the dried and smelly skins were thrown into a cave.* According to Couch (1985: 100), this month coincides with the end of April in our calendar, the beginning of the rainy season, which corresponds to the time of germination just after planting in the agricultural cycle of the central valley. As Miller and Taube (1993: 188) suggest, wearing the flayed skins symbolizes agricultural renewal. A Xipe impersonator wears the old skin until it gets dried, and the young man emerges again from the cracked skin. This event represents germination of a seed from the dried soil.

* In the Aztec culture, a cave was thought to be a place where this world and the supernatural world meet.

The eighth month, Huey Tecuilhuitl or 'Great Feast of the Lords', was dedicated to the goddess of young maize. In this month, a young woman was decapitated and flayed, and the blood was offered to the statue of the goddess. After dancing and enjoying the feast, people went to a spacious chamber, in which the sacrifice by shooting arrows would take place. Durán (1977: 227) describes the ritual as follows:

> Then they (the shooters or archers) gathered their bows and arrows. Prisoners and captives of war then appeared who were crucified upon a high scaffolding which stood there for that purpose. Their arms and legs extended, they were all bound to one board or another. Then the archers dressed in the divine garb shot them with great fury. This was the sacrifice of the goddess; it was performed in her honor. . . .
>
> Once the wretches had been slain by the arrows, they were cast down. Their chests were opened, their hearts were extracted, and their bodies were delivered to their owners, together with [the body of] the young woman who

had been skinned – all for feasts and banquets of human flesh.

The context of this ritual is interpreted as follows: by shooting victims with arrows and decapitating the impersonators of the goddess, the Aztecs intended to obtain greater quantities of blood, which they offered to the goddess in return for her divine protection of fertility.[†] Since the impersonators were thought to become the divine beings after sacrifice, the eating of their dead bodies meant the extracting of divine power from them.[‡]

[†] This interpretation was mentioned by Dr Elizabeth Baquedano in a lecture at the Universidad Nacional Autónoma de México (1995).

[‡] Cf. Miller and Taube (1993: 55).

The tenth month, Xocotlhuetzi or 'Great Fall of the Xocotl Fruit', corresponded to the period just before the harvest of the year (Couch 1985) and was dedicated to the god of fire. It was often called Huey Miccailhuitl, 'Great Feast of the Dead', as many slaves were sacrificed by fire. Fire sacrifice was a major rite in this month and it was carried out in the following manner (Durán 1977: 205):

> After dawn all those who were to be sacrificed were dressed in the garb and habit of the main gods, and according to seniority they were placed in a row next to the great fire. . . . Then came five other ministers and one called Tlehua. [This Possessor of the Fire] swept carefully around the glowing coals. When he had finished sweeping, they took the 'gods' one by one, alive as they were, and cast them into the fire. Half-roasted, before they were dead, [these victims] were pulled out and sacrificed, their chests opened.

Fire sacrifice was a fairly common form of offering humans to the gods of fire. This ritual sacrifice is thought to be the reproduction of the myth of the creation of the Fifth Sun, in which the god Nanahuatl killed himself in divine fire to transform himself into the sun. Fire, like water, was believed to have power to purify and consecrate the human offerings and to change them into divine beings or divine power. As the ceremony of Xocotlhuetzi coincided with the beginning of the dry season, I assume that fire sacrifice was required to revitalize

• A fire sacrifice dedicated to the goddess 'Cihuacoatl'. Durán (1984: vol 1, plate 21)

the sun, which was often identified with the god of fire.

The ultimate purpose of the Aztec ritual sacrifices would be defined as communication with the divine world. Since 'death' brings new life in their religion, as we saw in the previous section, the people might have regarded human sacrifice as a way to give vital energy to the deities; in other words, a way to transform human beings into the gods themselves.

ARCHAEOLOGY OF RITUAL SACRIFICE

Archaeological remains found around the Aztec capital support the idea that sacrifice and regeneration were closely related. Among the most important artefacts employed in ritual sacrifice are the Chacmool, a three-dimensional reclining figure found atop the temple, the Cuauhxicalli, or 'eagle vessel', and Tzompantli, or 'skull racks'. Both Chacmools and Cuauhxicallis were used as

receptacles for hearts and blood of human sacrifice. Chacmools sometimes contain the carved figures of the water-earth deities, who bring fertility and require a lot of human sacrifice in the Aztec religion. A variety of Cuauhxicallis exist, but most of them are commonly depicted with the representations of human hearts, the solar disk, and the earth deities, all of which are related mythologically to the concept of sacrifice and new life. Tzompantli, a wooden scaffold containing sacrificed human skulls pierced horizontally by crossbeams, was considered as 'a tree laden with fruit' (Miller and Taube 1993: 176). Some stone sculptures of Tzompantlis with the motifs of skulls and crossed bones have also been found. It is often pointed out that Mesoamerican thought identified skulls and bones with plant seeds as 'a source for regeneration and life' (Baquedano 1988: 193).

Baquedano (1989a, 1989b, 1993) studied the death motifs depicted on the earth deities on the sculptures. Many representations of Tlaltecuhtli, the lord of earth, are shown in a crouching position, or the posture of giving birth, with arms upraised, an open jaw, and the motifs of crossed-bones, skulls and other skeletal figures. Those symbols denote the idea that new life requires death or sacrifice. What is stressed here is that the death motifs in Aztec art contain the symbolism of regeneration, new life and afterlife within themselves.

THE CONCEPT OF DEATH

The Aztec conceived time as cyclical, which is embedded clearly in their calendar system based on the solar cycle. The cycle of risings and settings of the sun provided the perfect metaphor for life and death. Therefore, the movement of the sun assured that 'there was an order beneath the chaotic surface of life, an order that ensured that death was not an end but the prelude to rebirth' (Markman and Markman 1992: 85). Besides the evidence of ritual sacrifice seen above, the Aztec concepts of afterlife and of soul will assure this concept of continuous death and rebirth.

In Aztec religion there were four worlds to which the dead might go: (1) Mictlan, the underworld, for those who die of old age or by normal causes; (2) Tlalocan, the eternal spring paradise, for those who die in water-related accidents, or having been struck by thunderbolts, or of particular kinds of sickness; (3) Tonatiuh Ilhuicac, the place of the sun, for those who die in war or are sacrificed, or for women who die in childbirth; (4) Chichihualcuauhco, for the dead children. The dead were believed to go on living in those worlds or there to be transformed into other beings.

The Aztec had a very unique concept of soul. The soul was thought to consist of three elements: *tonalli* is the life-force and fate represented by the calendric sign of one's birth, and when one dies, this is the only part that descends to the underworld; *ihiyotl* is the air, which spreads throughout the entire body during lifetime and which leaves the body as gaseous matter when one dies; *teyolia* is the heart, which goes to the heaven. As for the composition of the soul, Furst (1995: 182) states that 'the body was a collection of multiple rather than unitary souls' and that death meant just the separation of the compound soul and the returning of each component to each provenance.

Many scholars have described the Aztec concept of life and death as continuous, like the Indian concept of cyclic and repetitive time. Others have explained that life and death are the complemental forces which cannot be conceived separately, like yin and yang of Taoism, as death always implies rebirth. However, there would be another aspect which describes death as a time to metamorphose into another being in order to continue one's endless life. The Aztecs believed that sacrificial victims became divine beings after being slain, that the dead lived an afterlife, and that each part of a soul went back to its provenance. These ideas clearly show that death is just one of the major stages of endless life, the stage in which one transforms into another being and starts living life as a different being.

REFERENCES

Baquedano, Elizabeth (1988) 'Iconographic symbols in Aztec elite sculptures', in Nicholas J. Saunders and Olivier de Montmollin (eds) *Recent Studies in Pre-Columbian Archaeology*, British Archaeological Reports International Series 421(i), Oxford: British Archaeological Reports, 191–203.

Baquedano, Elizabeth (1989a) 'Aztec earth deities', in Glenys Davies (ed.) *Polytheistic Systems*, Edinburgh: Edinburgh University Press, 184–98.

Baquedano, Elizabeth (1989b) 'Aztec death sculpture', PhD dissertation, University of London.

Baquedano, Elizabeth (1993) 'Aspects of death symbolism in Aztec Tlaltecuhtli', in Jacqueline de Durand-Forest and Marc Eisinger (eds) *The Symbolism in the Plastic and Pictorial Representations of Ancient Mexico*, Bonner Amerikanistische Studien 21, Bonn: Holos Verlag, 157–62.

Broda, Johanna (1983) 'Ciclos agrícolas en el culto: un problema de la correlación del calendario mexica', in Anthony F. Aveni and Gordon Brotherston (eds) *Calendars in Mesoamerica and Peru: Native American Computations of Time*, British Archaeological Reports International Series 174, Oxford: British Archaeological Reports, 145–65.

Cabrera Castro, Rubén and Cowgill, George (1993) 'El Templo de Quetzalcóatl', *Arqueología Mexicana* I(1): 21–6.

Códice Chimalpopoca (1992) Mexico: Universidad Nacional Autónoma de México.

Códice Laud (1994) *La pintura de la muerte y de los destinos: libro explicativo del llamado Códice Laud*, intro. and expl. Ferdinand Anders and Maarten Jansen, Graz: Akademische Druck- und Verlagsanstalt, and Mexico City: Fondo de Cultura Económica.

Couch, N. C. Christopher (1985) *The Festival Cycle of the Aztec Codex Borbonicus*, British Archaeological Reports International Series 270, Oxford: British Archaeological Reports.

Durán, Fray Diego (1977) *Book of the Gods and Rites and The Ancient Calendar*, ed. and trans. Fernando Horcasitas and Doris Heyden, Norman, OK: University of Oklahoma Press.

Durán, Fray Diego (1984) *Historia de las Indias de Nueva España e Islas de la Tierra Firme*, Vols I and II, Mexico: Editorial Porrúa.

Furst, Jill Leslie M. (1995) *The Natural History of the*

Soul in Ancient Mexico, New Haven, CT and London: Yale University Press.

Garibay, Angel A. (ed.) (1985) *Teogonía e historia de los Mexicanos*, Mexico: Editorial Porrúa.

González Torres, Yolotl (1992) *El sacrificio humano entre los Mexicas*, Mexico: Instituto Nacional de Antropologia e Historia.

López Austin, Alfredo (1989) *Cuerpo humano e ideología*, Vol. 1, Mexico: Universidad Nacional Autónoma de México.

López Luján, Leonardo (1994) *The Offerings of the Templo Mayor of Tenochtitlan*, trans. Bernard R. and Thelma Ortiz de Montellano, Niwot, CO: University Press of Colorado.

Markman, Roberta and Markman, Peter (1992) *The Flayed God*, New York and San Francisco: Harper.

Matos Moctezuma, Eduardo (1995) *Life and Death in the Templo Mayor*, trans. Bernard R. and Thelma Oltiz de Montellano, Niwot, CO: University Press of Colorado.

Miller, Mary Ellen and Taube, Karl (1993) *The Gods and Symbols of Ancient Mexico and the Maya*, London: Thames & Hudson.

Nicholson, Henry B. (1971) 'Religion in pre-Hispanic central Mexico', in Robert Wauchope (ed.) *Handbook of Middle American Indians*, Vol. 10, Austin, TX: University of Texas Press, 395–46.

Sahagún, Bernardino de (1953–81) *Florentine Codex*, trans. A. J. O. Anderson and C. E. Dibble, Santa Fe: monographs of the School of American Research.

Sahagún, Bernardino de (1992) *Historia general de las cosas de Nueva España*, Mexico: Editorial Porrúa.

Taube, Karl (1993) *Aztec and Maya Myths*, London: British Museum Press.

Torquemada, Fray Juan de (1976) *Monarquía Indiana*, Vol. 3, Mexico: Universidad Nacional Autónoma de México.

Townsend, Richard F. (1992) *The Aztecs*, London: Thames & Hudson.

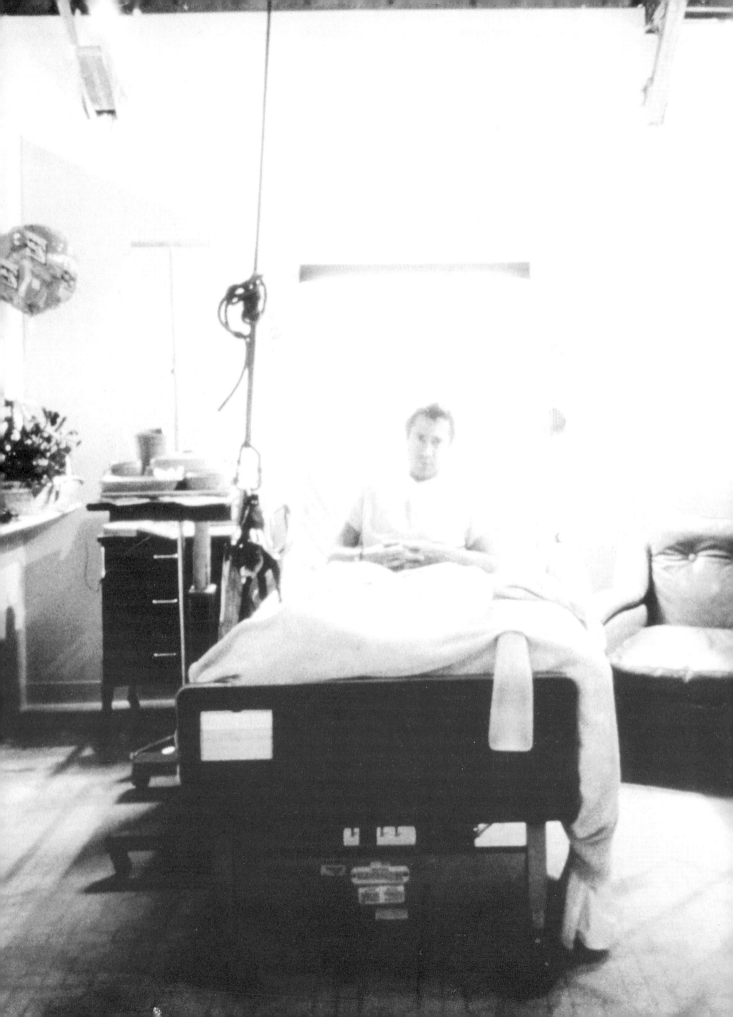

Sadomedicine: Bob Flanagan's 'Visiting Hours' and Last Rites

Linda S. Kauffman

1 ELEGY IN LIEU OF A PROLOGUE

From my home in Washington, DC, I went to California in 1991 to begin research on performance artists, film-makers and novelists who were seizing radical innovations in science, medicine and technology, ranging from MRI and PET scans to pharmaceutical, genetic and reproductive break-throughs.* Since our views of these developments derive wholly from what specialists – doctors, researchers, psychiatrists – report, artists are beginning to intervene, to serve as translators of this brave new world.

Bob Flanagan is one such translator, a shaman for the twenty-first century. Bob died of cystic fibrosis at the age of 43 on 4 January 1996. Cystic fibrosis (CF) is a hereditary disease that affects breathing and digestion; few victims live beyond their thirties. Bob attributed his longevity to his lifelong masochistic proclivities. His motto was: 'Fight Sickness with Sickness'. He traced his masochism back to childhood, when he spent long hours bound in bed. From childhood forward, he was prodded and probed, X-rayed, transformed into a medical specimen. No part of his body was immune, in any sense of the word.

Bob turned his twin 'maladies' – CF and SM –

* Segments of this essay appear in different form in Linda S. Kauffman, Bad Girls and Sick Boys: Fantasies in Contemporary Art and Culture (Berkeley and London: University of California Press, 1998); © Linda S. Kauffman and the Regents of the University of California.

into multiple forms of art: he was a poet, photographer, stand-up comic, actor in film and video, creator of beautiful objects, and radical body artist. In 'Visiting hours', he transformed the art museum into a hospital ward, defamiliarizing the rituals attendant on illness, death and dying. Bob actually moved into the art museum with his hospital bed, oxygen tank and other medical equipment. By installing himself and 'going inside' his own body, Bob exhibited what is past, passing and to come for the human body. Using his own body as a sexual and medical 'specimen', Bob redefined the meaning of ritual. He deconstructed the idea of the *museum* and of the *human* in the process.

3 January 1996, Long Beach Memorial Hospital

I've come to say goodbye to Bob. How does one bid farewell to a shaman – especially a satirical one who would mock the very title? His upper body is bloated, his hair is long, and he has a stubbly grey beard, like the muzzle of an old dog. If he had lived to be an old man, this is what he would look like. I feel I should leave quickly so he can sleep, but he clutches my hand and arm. Speech is difficult, but he's surprisingly alert and solicitous. Raised a Catholic, he tells me he's converted to Judaism for Sheree (Sheree Rose, his long-time companion, dominatrix and collaborator). 'You're probably relieved she just wanted to turn you into a Jew, instead of maybe a transsexual!' We laugh. I thank

• Bob Flanagan in bed. Courtesy Bob Flanagan and Sheree Rose

Performance Research 3(3), pp.32–40 © Routledge 1998

Bob for teaching me so much about gratitude and generosity, about living and creating. I kiss him farewell.

Friday 5 January 1996

Bob lies in a plain pine box in the chapel of Forest Lawn Cemetery, which is overflowing with mourners: artists, actors, writers, poets. Some in suits, some in leather, with shaved heads and tattoos. Some are children from Cystic Fibrosis summer camp, where Bob worked as a counselor for many years.

Tim Flanagan, Bob's brother, speaks: one of their sisters died in infancy from CF; another died at the age of 21 in 1979. 'Now this disease has finally left the Flanagan family,' he says.

A friend from Costa Mesa High School (which Bob and I both attended), reads W. H. Auden's eulogy for Yeats.

Memories overwhelm me:

• After visiting Yeats's grave in 1994, I interviewed J. G. Ballard, who told me that in retrieving Yeats's body from France, the Irish mixed up the bodies: a *French* soldier is buried under Ben Bulben! Bob *loved* this story.

• On 22 September 1994, WBAI in New York City hosts a radio call-in show before the New Museum opening of 'Visiting hours' to help people understand Bob's work. They urged all the people who work in the museum, including the janitors and guards, to participate in this 'teach-in'. The atmosphere is festive: Bob is cheerfully propped up in bed, installed as master of revels in the museum and at the party later that night, surrounded by Lynne Tillman, Andres Serrano, David Leslie, Laura Trippi, Kirby Dick, Gary Indiana, Jane DeLynn, Ira Silverberg, and of course, his ministering angel, Sheree.

• On 27 June 1995 Bob's urgent telephone call comes back to me: would I infiltrate the Christian Action Coalition's meeting in the Rayburn Building in Washington, DC to see if they violated his copyright? (They did.) The meeting was a last-ditch effort to kill the National Endowment of the Arts by staging a 'degenerate art' show, in which

Bob's work was featured prominently. (Ironically, Bob never received NEA funds.). I think again of Auden's words about intellectual disgrace staring from every human face, and about the seas of pity lying locked and frozen in each eye.

As J. G. Ballard once said, *Deep assignments run through all our lives: there are no coincidences.* Alice Wexler's *Mapping Fate* is about her family's struggle with Huntington's disease and their search for a cure; she once arranged for the doctor who discovered the CF gene to meet Bob. Now a bitter wind and moon are rising over the hill in the cemetery; Alice and I are hugging each other at his grave.

Do we map fate or does fate map us? That is one question ritual poses.

2 RITUALS OF SADOMASOCHISM

The rituals of sadomasochism are by now familiar to any one who has read de Sade or *The Story of O*: the 'bottom' relinquishes all power and puts herself in the hands of a 'top', who slowly strives to heighten the sensation of pleasure through pain. The function of ritual is the pursuit of the absolute in pleasure. This entails rigorous discipline, a curriculum of tests. In Sade, the women keep journals and receive chastisements. The implicit attraction of the regimen is that it permits women to cast off the traditional roles of daughter, wife, mother. Bob turns the Sadean regime on its head, for by putting himself in the role of the woman, he tests not just the thresholds of pain and pleasure, but the taboos against violating prescribed masculine roles.

Robert Mapplethorpe's photographs of the forbidden world of gay male sadomasochism took s/m out of the closet and into the art museum. But Flanagan, in collaboration with Sheree Rose, makes us realize how little theorizing has been devoted to *heterosexuality*, which for so long has been presumed to be 'natural'. Male heterosexual submissives, moreover, constitute a substantial subculture, one that until recently was wholly unacknowledged because their existence defies too many taboos. Only recently have books like

Different Loving by Gloria G. Brame, William D. Brame and Jon Jacobs (1993), which is devoted to heterosexual sadomasochism, begun to receive serious, widespread attention. Flanagan exposes one of commercial s/m's best-kept secrets: the majority of customers are not sadistic men seeking submissive women. Instead, a growing number of men are willing to pay substantial sums to be clothed in diapers, put in playpens, suckled with bottles. Bob and Sheree understand this world from both ends, so to speak, for in addition to staging their sexuality for art audiences, Sheree once worked professionally as a dominatrix, earning, in Bob's unabashedly gleeful words, 'Buckets of money'.*

On the one hand, such playacting permits men to return unashamedly

* All quotations are from personal conversations and interviews with Bob Flanagan and Sheree Rose between 19 February 1993 and 4 January 1996.

to the pre-oedipal bliss of harmony with the mother. On the other hand, they enjoy being punished, spanked, made to clean house, do dishes. Since these men are often highly successful in public life, their sexual proclivities suggest a strong compulsion to repudiate masculine authority and privilege privately.†

† Anne McClintock, 'Maid to Order', *Social Text* 37 (1993): 87–116.

One function of sadomasochistic ritual, then, is to create an environment for regression. Flanagan places particular emphasis on the pre-oedipal stage, before the infant is socialized, before the unconscious is censored. His rituals revel in narcissism and exhibitionism. He is a psychic omnivore: everything revolves around his needs, his demands, his libidinal dynamism. He is aggressive in his passivity. All his life, he confesses, he has been

Nothing but a big baby; and I want to stay that way, and I want a mommy forever, especially a mean one; because of all the fairy tale witches, and the wicked stepmother.‡

‡ *Bob Flanagan: Supermasochist*, ed. V. Vale and Andrea Juno (San Francisco: Re/Search Publications, 1993), 64.

The 'mean mother' is the phallic mother who punishes, spanks, disciplines. Far from being terrified of her, Flanagan wanted to be her slave.

When he met Sheree, he got his wish. Instead of ostracizing him, she relished her role. Before meeting Bob, Sheree was in a very traditional, constraining marriage, so part of her pleasure with Bob had a 'certain revenge aspect of ordering a man about', with a little smirk on her face. Who wouldn't let a man who lusts to vacuum have his way? He scrubbed the floors with a toothbrush (inspired, perhaps, by the film, *Mommy Dearest*).

The secret every masochist knows is how difficult it is to find a 'top' who will indulge his fantasies. As Bob notes wryly, every masochist hates to confess that he is really the one in control. He cheerfully recounts how he enlisted Sheree's participation in his fantasies. She ordered him to write daily about their sex acts: the result was *Fuck Journal* (Hanuman Books, 1987), composed in the course of one entire year of their relationship. Together, they created art in alternative performance spaces like LACE (Los Angeles Contemporary Exhibitions) that highlighted the ritualistic aspects of s/m: the carefully choreographed interaction between dominator and dominated; the fetishistic use of leather, high heels, whips, and other props; the theatrical display of the body in scenarios borrowed from *The Story of O*. What made their acts unique was that Flanagan did not identify with Sir Stephen but with O herself: 'How desperately I wanted to be her.' S/m is a night-school for the senses; from de Sade forward, it has always had a pedagogic as well as a pornographic element. Eventually, Bob and Sheree were frequently invited to address the Society for the Scientific Study of Sex. They also collaborated with sexologist Robert Stoller, who substantially revised his views on perversion as a result of his discussions with them.

3 'VISITING HOURS'

'Visiting hours' is an installation that Bob and Sheree exhibited at the Santa Monica Museum of Art in 1992–3, the New Museum in New York City in 1994, and the School of the Museum of Fine Arts in Boston in 1995. This installation transforms the museum into a pediatric hospital ward, complete with a waiting-room filled with toys, s/m paraphernalia, medical X-rays and video monitors of his naked, bound body. In one section of the room, one comes upon Flanagan himself, propped up in a hospital bed, his home-away-from-home.

Flanagan's ritualistic art performances serve two functions: first, they stage psychic processes which are both conscious and unconscious; second, they juxtapose the social with the psychic. One of the many fascinating things about Flanagan is that he seems to have almost total recall about the images in popular culture that sexually excited him in early childhood: he remembers cartoons of Porky Pig in bondage, force-fed, with his bare bottom and open mouth, always being punished for his insatiable orality; Cinderella, sexily disciplined by her wicked stepmother and stepsisters. As a child, Flanagan instinctively recognized the latent obscenity and violence in fairy-tales and cartoons. They turned him on and he turned his 'play' into art.

The exhibit evokes the image of naughty, nasty children 'playing doctor'. Children concoct their own theories to explain birth, sexuality and sexual difference, as Flanagan illustrates in vivid detail. 'Visiting hours' is a ritual staging of infantile regression that explores childhood wishes head on. Those wishes turned out to be considerably more sexual than most people are willing to admit, saturated with a sense of childlike curiosity and sexual precocity. Signs of infantile existence litter the museum: a porta-potty, pacifiers, blankets, a crib that seems more like a cage, toys like a Superman doll and Visible Man, which is designed to teach children anatomy, although this one excretes shit, mucus and sperm. 'Visiting hours' evokes a scene the spectator has visited long before, but – as with the psychoanalytic session – its buried content comes to the surface only when restaged. Everything about the exhibit is uncanny, at once strange and disturbing, hysterical and

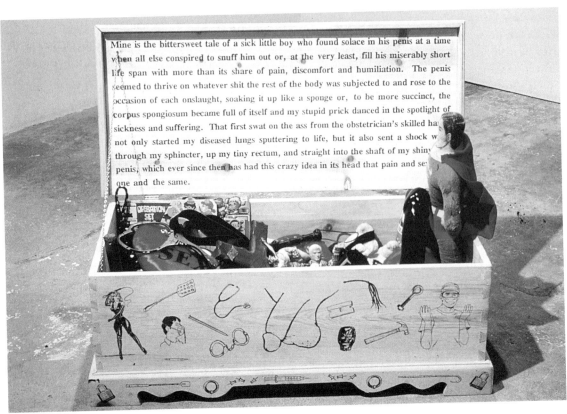

Mine is the bittersweet tale of a sick little boy who found solace in his penis at a time when all else conspired to snuff him out or, at the very least, fill his miserably short life span with more than its share of pain, discomfort and humiliation. The penis seemed to thrive on whatever shit the rest of the body was subjected to and rose to the occasion of each onslaught, soaking it up like a sponge or, to be more succinct, the corpus spongiosum became full of itself and my stupid prick danced in the spotlight of sickness and suffering. That first swat on the ass from the obstetrician's skilled ha[nd] not only started my diseased lungs sputtering to life, but it also sent a shock w[ave] through my sphincter, up my tiny rectum, and straight into the shaft of my shin[y] penis, which ever since then has had this crazy idea in its head that pain and se[x are] one and the same.

• Toy chest. Photo: Linda Kauffman

hilarious. A toy chest contains s/m paraphernalia, and stuffed animals sit in one corner. The writing on the toy chest confirms the exhibition's fairy-tale quality:

> Mine is the bittersweet tale of a sick little boy who found solace in his penis at a time when all else conspired to snuff him out or . . . fill his miserably short life span with more than its share of pain, discomfort and humiliation. The penis seemed to thrive on whatever shit the rest of the body was subjected to and rose to the occasion of each onslaught. . . . That first swat on the ass from the obstetrician's skilled hand not only started my diseased lungs sputtering to life, but it also sent a shock . . . straight into the shaft of my shiny penis, which ever since then has had this crazy idea in its head that pain and sex are one and the same.

Flanagan satirizes the quest for rational explanations of his twin 'maladies', CF and SM, by using medical language, comic colloquialisms ('snuff him out', 'whatever shit', etc.), and puns (the penis's crazy idea in its 'head'). Flanagan's narrative evokes the Hobbesian notion of life as 'nasty, short, and brutish', as well as Tristram Shandy's account of a prolonged and difficult quest for and through birth. Linguistically, the chest (of toys) parallels the chest (of the body). Another object in the exhibit is a wall of 1,400 alphabet blocks juxtaposing the letters CF and SM, as if to evoke the DNA codes, alphabets, letters that have become crucial in the gene research, which one day will provide a cure for cystic fibrosis.

Some of Flanagan's rituals are indebted to 'ordeal artists', like Chris Burden and Vito Acconci. In *Seedbed* (1971) Acconci masturbated under a ramp, while amplifiers projected the sound of his breathing throughout the museum. In 1990, his 'Adjustable wall bra' consisting of two mammoth cups, permitted visitors to curl up in the fetal position and watch cartoons. The cups pulse with music or with the sound of a woman breathing. Acconci, like Flanagan, brings babyism into the art museum.

We all know by now that femininity and masculinity are cultural constructs, neither innate nor natural. But Flanagan's art audaciously exposes the *process* of gender construction, particularly its weird ridiculousness. Rather than disavowing castration anxiety, Flanagan acts it out – he *performs* it. Rather than fetishizing the female body, he pokes and pierces his own. He was inspired in part by Rudolf Schwarzkogler, who 'had himself photographed (supposedly) slicing off pieces of his penis as if it were so much salami'.[*] Schwarzkogler's acts, however, are fake, whereas Flanagan's actions are real. He pierces the penis, attaches weights and clothespins, nails it to a board while singing 'If I had a hammer'. His acts are at once too literal for art, too visceral for porn, too satirical for either art or porn.

> [*] Barbara Rose, 'Is it art? Orlan and the transgressive act', *Art in America* 81:2 (February 1993): 82–7, 125.

Flanagan's rituals satirize the penis's prestige and the phallus's authority. Flanagan places our assumed ideology before our eyes. The foundation of the anti-pornography campaign, for instance, assumes that man is the oppressor, woman is victim. Pornography is the theory, rape the practice. Flanagan turns such clichés on their head. While Camille Paglia worships the penis and Andrea Dworkin damns it, Flanagan deflates it and them both.[†] Yet his art poses an equal threat to constructs of masculinity, for if Sylvester Stallone and Arnold Schwarzenegger can be viewed as 'living phalluses', displaying the pumped body in/as excess, Flanagan's display of his puny body satirizes macho bravado. Yet he is proud of the endurance his ritualistic acts require: he appears as a perverted version of Superman on the cover of *Bob Flanagan: Supermasochist*. Flanagan's rituals juxtapose two opposed fields of contest: confinement and escape, descent and ascent, reflected in his obsessions with such confining apparatuses as cages, ropes, or coffins, and his invented persona as a sexualized Superman and Houdini.

> [†] At the Clark Gallery in Washington DC, December 1993, Camille Paglia and her lover, Alison Maddex, curated 'True phallacy', which glorified penises in bronze, photography and painting; Paglia was videotaped at the opening reception for a Rapido TV Production for *World Without Walls*, Channel 4, London, produced by Peter Stuart, directed by Peter Murphy, broadcast 1 March 1994.

Flanagan's rituals fuse medicine with s/m to problematize the relationships between the social and the psychic, between disease and desire. Flanagan's mordant wit thwarts every cliché about death: he undermines pity with satire, fear with fervor. He confronts visitors with their own voyeurism by turning the tables. He, after all, is propped up in bed, watching *you* watch him. Visitors are forced to confront their own psychic investments and their own conflicting reactions: voyeurism and prurience, arousal and dread.

Is the function of ritual to answer questions, or to assuage the pain of insoluble enigmas? In this as in so many aspects of his art and his performances, Flanagan raises more questions than he answers. As if addressing an invisible interrogator, Bob has written the question 'Why?' on the wall of the museum, as though in answer to the visitor's implicit question, 'Why these practices?' Every wall in the museum is encircled with a string of answers to that single question:

> Because it feels good; because it gives me an erection; because it makes me come; because I'm sick; because there was so much sickness; because I say FUCK THE SICKNESS; because I like the attention; because I was alone a lot; because I was different; because kids beat me up on the way to school; because I was humiliated by nuns; because of Christ and the crucifixion; because of Porky Pig in bondage, force-fed by some sinister creep in a black cape; because of the stories of children hung by their wrists, burned on the stove, scalded in tubs; because of 'Mutiny on the Bounty'; because of cowboys and indians; because of Houdini . . . Because of what's inside me; because of my genes . . . Because they tied me to the crib so I wouldn't hurt myself . . . Because I'm a Catholic; because I still love Lent . . . Because it's in my nature; because it's against nature; because it's nasty; because it's fun; because it flies in the face of all that's normal . . . Because NO PAIN, NO GAIN; because SPARE THE ROD AND SPOIL THE CHILD; BECAUSE YOU ALWAYS HURT THE ONE YOU LOVE.

The answers reveal how consciously Flanagan appreciated, exploited and satirized rituals ranging from Lenten abnegation to a Sadean defiance of nature. Ritual, after all, is the language of paradox. No one knew this better than Sade: 'You shall know nothing if you have not known everything, and if you are timid enough to stop with what is natural, Nature will elude your grasp forever.'[*]

* Cited in Maurice Blanchot, 'Sade', in *The Marquis de Sade*, trans. Richard Seaver and Austryn Wainhouse (New York: Grove Press, 1965), 50.

The same is true of Flanagan's ritualistic confrontation with the question 'What is death?' He once told me that what surprised him most about 'Visiting hours' was how museum visitors turned him into a father-confessor. They sat by his bedside, sharing stories about their own experiences with cancer, leukemia and other diseases. Yet he is mercilessly satiric on the subject of the nobility of suffering, the romanticism of death. He won the hearts of the children in CF summer camp by refusing to sentimentalize death or condescend to them. Instead, he composed songs to the tune of Mary Poppins' '*Supercalifragilisticexpialidocious*':

> Supermasochist Bob has cystic fibrosis
> He should have died when he was young
>   but he was too precocious . . .
> Now 40 years have come and gone
>   and Bob is still around . . .
> With a lifetime of infections and his lungs all filled with
>   phlegm
> The CF would have killed him if it weren't for S&M.

He designed his own open casket: peering inside, I was startled first to see his face on a videoscreen, then my own! As medicine becomes increasingly technological, death becomes more and more abstract. We know we must die, but the knowledge remains theoretical until 'the end'. Flanagan maps this uncharted country with considerable courage, since the terminal disease is his own. Death, not sex, is the last mystique in contemporary culture, and doctors seldom pull back the curtain to give us a peek. Bob's rituals pull back the curtain.

The most moving ritual of all in 'Visiting hours' involved Bob's ascension: a pulley hoisted him from his bed to the ceiling, where he hung suspended upside down and naked. On opening night at the New Museum, an awed hush fell over the crowd of

• Alphabet Blocks. Photo: Linda Kauffman

jaded New Yorkers as Bob slowly ascended to the ceiling. Was he a combination of a *tableau vivant* and a nature morte, or a cross between Mantegna's St Sebastian and Chaim Soutine's butchered carcass? Will the prolonged and painful journey toward inevitable death be marked by an ascension and transcendence? Or does his ascension merely provide comfort for the living, not the dead? Tragedy is the imitation of an action of a certain magnitude, inciting pity for the sufferer and terror at the cause. One thing is sure: witnesses at this ascension felt pity and terror.

4 POST-HUMAN

'Post-human' signifies the impact technology has had on the human body. Any candidate for a pacemaker, prosthetics, plastic surgery, or Prozac – not to mention sex re-assignment surgery, *in vitro* fertilization or gene therapy – qualifies as

'post-human'. Artificial hearts, breasts, hair and organ transplants have already transported us into the cyborg world of tomorrow. By actually *moving into* the museum, Flanagan deconstructs the very concept of the *museum*, irrevocably transforming the pristine, inviolate art space with the messy debris of everyday life, sex and illness: intravenous tubes, bedpans, food and the ubiquitous oxygen tank nearby. He also deconstructs the cherished concept of the *human* by staging the elemental, alimental body, emphasizing its plasticity as an aesthetic – and technological – medium.

Bob Flanagan is a live model of the post-human, for he illustrates step by step how the human senses – taste, touch, smell, hearing, and sight – have been utterly reorganized by technology. Just as microscope, oscilloscope, speculum, X-ray not only altered *what* we saw but *how* we perceived the human body in the past, so today sophisticated imaging techniques (CAT scans, PET scans, MRI, etc.) raise scores of questions: 'What is pathology?', 'What is "sick"?' (One of Bob's performances was called 'Bob Flanagan's sick', which is also the title of Kirby Dick's award-winning 1997 documentary film, *Sick: The Life and Death of Bob Flanagan, Supermasochist*.) In one witty scene in the film, Bob nods to all the artists working in the wake of Artaud: the Viennese Actionists, Yves Klein, Fluxus, Nam June Paik, etc. But none can hold a candle to him, for he is the '*original* Mr. Derivative'! Flanagan used ritual to fulfil the prophecies of Artaud regarding the painful reorganization of the theatre, and the urgent demand for a new type of corporeal speech: 'We need above all a theater that wakes us up: nerves and heart.'* His rituals create a spontaneous corporeal force between his own 'shocked' neuro-muscular responses and those of the spectators, enlivened and updated by the new technologies that heighten interactivity.

* Antonin Artaud, *The Theatre and Its Double* (New York: Grove Press, 1958), 110.

While his work heralds the world of the post-human, that world is thus paradoxically peopled with ghosts: primitive rituals of sacrifice and purification; medieval rituals of fleshy mortification; mystical rites of body modification. Bob's performance rituals remind us of the link between sacrifice and eroticism, death and sensuality, following Bataille's theories on transgression and taboo. In the chapter on 'Christianity', Bataille laments that Christianity reduces religion to its benign aspect. He argues that 'Bacchic violence is the measure of incipient eroticism whose domain is orig-inally that of religion'.† Flanagan forces us to dissolve the dichotomy between divinity and obscenity. Toward this end, 'Visiting hours' juxtaposes images of Christ, the Crucifixion and the martyrdom of saints with sophisticated technological interventions: computer graphics; multiple video monitors displaying his splayed naked body contorted by pain and pleasure; MTV videos and musical sound-tracks from Nine Inch Nails and other heavy metal groups; Saturday morning

† Georges Bataille, *L'Erotisme* (Paris: Editions de Minuit, 1957); English-language edition as *Erotism: Death and Sensuality*, trans. Mary Dalwood (San Francisco: City Lights, 1986), 117.

cartoons; and the whole repertoire of medical imaging that permit us to see the human body opened up in ways never before imaginable.

Like the myth of the inviolate text, the myth of the inviolate body has been a long time dying. Through ritual, Bob Flanagan put the final nails in the coffin, using his own body as a masochistic and medical test case – a terminal case. By staging his own masochism, Flanagan violated a deeply ingrained taboo. Through ritual, he also dismantled our most cherished myths about sickness and health, death and dying, and challenged society's most cherished assumptions about the body's integrity and rectitude. Bob Flanagan was the real translator of the brave new world that already envelops us, for medical specialists cannot go *beyond* technology to analyze the underlying motivations and contradictory impulses inherent in it. Only art and ritual can do that. Bob's work was a sustained investigation into the function of ritual in sex, medicine and death. By confronting mourning and mutability, he forced us to ask what exactly we know about love and sex, life and death. Through ritual, he fused the virtual and the visceral, his personal and aesthetic identity. He was a shaman who lived without shame. He made his life a work of art.

Mental Illness as Ritual Theatre

Roland Littlewood

How do healing practices 'heal'?* It has recently been suggested that it is through their aesthetic and dramaturgical idiom (Kapferer 1979; Laderman 1991; Desjarlais 1992). This paper examines certain relatively discrete patterns which appear, historically and geographically, to be specific to industrialized cultures, especially to the United States and Britain, and which are generally referred to as mental illnesses. Can they be seen in a dramaturgical idiom? The psychiatric term 'culture-bound syndrome' has usually been taken to refer to: (1) local patterns of time-limited actions, specific to a particular culture, which, while regarded as undesirable, are recognized as discrete by informants and observers alike; (2) few instances of which have a biological cause; and (3) in which the individual is not held to be aware or responsible in the everyday sense; (4) the behaviour usually has a 'dramatic' quality, in the popular sense.

* This paper draws on material from 'The Butterfly and the Serpent', published in 1987 in *Culture, Medicine and Psychiatry*, 11: 289–335.

SYMBOLS AND SYMPTOMS

Such reactions frequently articulate a personal predicament, but they also represent public concerns, usually core structural oppositions between age-groups or the sexes. They have a shared meaning as public and dramatic representations in an individual, whose personal situation demonstrates these oppositions, and they thus occur in certain well-defined situations. At the same time they have a personal expressive meaning for the particular individual and have been regarded as functional, or 'instrumental': 'In situations of deprivation or frustration where recourse to personal jural power is not available, the principal is able to adjust his or her situation by recourse to "mystical pressure"' (Lewis 1971), that is, by appeals to values and beliefs that cannot be questioned, because they are tied up with the most fundamental concerns and political organization of the community. How 'conscious' the principal is of pragmatically employing the mechanism as a personal strategy is debatable , but it may be noted that observers frequently describe the reactions as 'dissociative'; Turner (1969) aptly calls this sideways recourse to mystical action 'the power of the weak'; the popular medical or psychiatric term is perhaps 'manipulation'.

'Wild Man behaviour'

Let us start by considering in more detail some non-western examples. 'Wild man behaviour' (*negi-negi, nenek*) is the term given to certain episodes of aggressive behaviour in the New Guinea Highlands. The affected man rushes about erratically, threatening people with weapons, destroying their property, blundering through the village gardens tearing up crops. Episodes last for a few hours or, at most, a few days; during them the wild man fails to recognize people and, on recovering, claims amnesia for the episode. This behaviour is locally attributed to possession by spirits, and treatment may include pouring on of water or exorcism, although observers have felt these measures were applied 'half-heartedly' (Newman

Performance Research 3(3), pp.41–52 © Routledge 1998

1964). The incipient wild man's announcement that he no longer wishes to eat and his rejection of his share of the prepared food advertise that his performance is about to begin. This is always public. 'It would be possible for a man to run wild in seclusion but no-one does' (Newman 1964: 3). The audience participate by feigning terror or attempting to mollify the principal, or alternatively pouring water over him and ostentatiously hiding weapons. To observers he retains a high degree of control. He is like a shaman in trance: 'though he flings himself in all directions with his eyes shut [he] nevertheless finds all the objects he wants' (Eliade 1964). In *negi-negi* and similar reactions there is 'a disproportion between the injury threatened and actually inflicted. It is generally more alarming to the white onlooker than the native' (Seligman 1928). Similar episodes of spear-throwing by Western Desert Aborigines remain constrained and relatively safe; only participants with organic brain syndromes are 'out of control'. If we examine the social context of the pattern, it typically occurs among young men, politically powerless, in situations such as working to pay back an enormous bride-price debt raised through a complicated network of kin. *Negi-negi* exaggerates this social dislocation to the point where the young man dramatically declines membership of his social community altogether. Resolution may include latitude in repayment. The net result is to restore and legitimate the status quo, not to question it.

Tikopian Suicide Swims

Audience participation is essential to *negi-negi* and to certain parasuicidal behaviours. In the Western Pacific island of Tikopia, aggrieved or offended women swim out to sea. As an islander comments: 'A woman who is reproved or scolded desires to die, yet desires to live. Her thought is that she will go to swim, but be taken up in a canoe by men who will seek her out to find her. A woman desiring death swims to seawards; she acts to go and die. But a woman who desires life swims inside the reef' (Firth 1961: 12). While completed suicide is regarded as a revenge on the community, the

pay-off for the survivor of a suicide swim includes enhanced status together with a renegotiation of the original problem. Thus an adolescent girl who is rebuffed or censured by parents reacts by exaggerating this extrusion, detaching herself further from the community, and the resolution restores the equilibrium. For the community, the tension between parental authority and filial independence is presented as dramatically as the account of a lovers' suicide pact in the American popular press.

Saka

Sympathy for the Tikopian suicide swimmer wanes with repetition; like *saka* among the Kenyan Waitata, the reaction can occur 'once too often'. Approximately half of married Waitata women were subject to *saka* ('possession') after a wish is refused by their husband, typically for an object that is a prerogative of men (Harris 1957). It is locally recognized that *saka* is clearly something to do with male/female relations. While women provide food for the family, they are also expected to supply domestic objects that can be purchased only through access to the profits of the sale of land or livestock. Such access is denied to women:

> Women are said to have no head for land or cattle transactions. They do not have the right sort of minds for important community affairs because they have little control over emotions and desires. Indeed femininity is made synonymous with an uncontrolled desire to acquire and consume. . . . In saka attacks, women are caricatured as uncontrollable consumers. . . . They are shown as contrasting in every way with men and the contrast is symbolised as a personal malady.
>
> (Harris 1957: 1054, 1060)

Harris argues that 'women can acquire male prerogatives or the signs thereof through illness', and compares the reaction to a European woman's 'sick headache' or 'pregnancy cravings'. While observers feel the reaction can be either 'real' or 'simulated', some local men say the whole reaction is a pretence. *Saka* is regarded by the Waitata simultaneously as an illness, as a possession by spirits, and as the consequence of a woman's personal wishes and her social role. Possession ceases when the woman's wish is granted by her husband or when he sponsors a large public ceremony, in which she wears male items of dress or new clothes.

Sar

Pastoral Somali women may become possessed by *sar* spirits who demand gifts and attention: 'Therapy really consists in spoiling the patient while ostensibly meeting the demands of the spirit as revealed to the expert therapist' (Lewis 1971). In patriarchal Islamic society, where women are excluded from the public realm, the outrageous behaviour of possession coerces husbands into gestures of reconciliation and consideration, while at the same time the formal public ideology of male dominance remains unchallenged. The cost of *sar* ceremonies may be such as to preclude the purchase by the husband of additional wives. The typical situation is a

> hard-pressed wife, struggling to survive and feed her children in the harsh nomadic environment, and liable to some degree of neglect, real or imagined, on the part of her husband. Subject to frequent, sudden and often prolonged absences by her husband as he follows his manly pastoral pursuits, to the jealousies and tensions of polygamy which are not ventilated in accusations of sorcery and witchcraft, and always menaced by the precariousness of marriage in a society where divorce is frequent and easily obtained by men, the Somali women's lot offers little stability or security. . . . Not surprisingly the *sar* spirits are said to hate men.
>
> (Lewis 1971: 75, 76)

Diagnosis of the performance as *sar* possession is in the hands of women and the treatment groups provide an organization for women in opposition to the public ritual of Islam dominated by men. The participation of women in such healing groups may be said to 'allow the voice of women to be heard in a male-dominated society, and occasionally enable participants to enjoy benefits to which their status would not normally entitle them' (Corin and Bibeau 1980). Such self-help groups may partially maintain the stigmatized ('sick') identity in opposition to

complete reversion to normative values; thus Janzen (1982) likens them to western groups such as Alcoholics Anonymous. In other societies they may even take on important roles including taxation, redistribution and welfare (Janzen 1978). Their organization may then provide, in contrast to a hypothesized 'homeostatic' function, whether individual or communal, a dynamic mechanism for social mobility and even institutional change.

FUNCTION AND OPPOSITION

To summarize: this pattern of reaction appears to occur where major points of political and cultural opposition are represented in a particular situation and thus, not surprisingly, where the everyday articulation of power relationships is not appropriate as solution to a perceived problem. Employing our western psychological categories, these ambiguous points may be represented as 'tensions'. Turner (1969) says such tensions do not imply that society is about to break up; they 'constitute strong unities . . . whose nature as a unit is constituted and bounded by the very forces that contend within it. [The tension becomes] a play of forces instead of a bitter battle. The effect of such a "play" soon wears off, but the sting is removed from certain troubled relationships.' As Harris (1957: 1064) comments about the *saka* attack, it 'allows a round-about acknowledgement of conflict, but in the *saka* dance there is again peace, dignity and festivity'. Indeed individual components of this key institution are included as parts of other rituals of the community. The performances appear characteristically to have three stages. In their course, the individual is *extruded* out of normal social relationships in an extension of the usual devalued or marginal social status. This is followed by a prescribed role, deviant but legitimate, which represents further *exaggeration* of this dislocation (frequently suggesting a direct contravention or 'symbolic inversion' of common social values) to unbalance the social equilibrium to such an extent that it is succeeded by *restitution* back into conventional and now unambiguous social relationships. 'The *saka* dance turns the *saka* attack on its head' (Harris 1957: 1060). The suicide voyager's 'attempt at detachment has failed, but he has succeeded in resolving his problem. He is once again absorbed and an effective catharsis has been obtained' (Firth 1961: 15).

A similar three-stage model of separation, transition and reintegration has been postulated for those psychosocial transitions usually glossed as 'rites of passage' (Van Gennep 1960), such as shamanic trance possession and women's cults in Africa (Turner 1969). While medical convention divides such patterns into 'symptoms' and 'treatment' I should prefer to consider them a single ritual complex. 'Attack and dance are two manifestations of a single situation . . . [they] can be translated into one another' (Harris 1957: 1061). Leach (1961: 135–6) suggests that ritual is 'normal social life . . . played in reverse' and offers the terms 'formality', 'role reversal' and 'masquerade' to represent the equivalent of our three stages. The prescribed deviant role amplifies the rejection by the community, frequently taking the form of behaviour which contravenes the core values of the society, female modesty or decorum. During this period, the principal is regarded as the victim of external mystical forces (which must be placated) and is not accountable. In *negi-negi* 'a man does not have a name'; he is an animal escaped from everyday social control (Newman 1964). Whilst I am emphasizing here the instrumental, rather than the expressive, aspect of this behaviour, I may gloss the personal experience for the principal (and audience) by the western term 'catharsis', similar to the collective experience of social inversions found in carnivals, licensed rituals of rebellion and contravention of norms in certain specific and tightly controlled situations. In large-scale societies (with a linear rather than a cyclical notion of time; Leach 1961), individual culture-bound reactions of 'hysterical conversion' may succeed the periodic and collective rites of role-reversal practised in smaller and more homogeneous groups.

Sociological explanations of symbolic inversion stress both group catharsis and the social marking of a norm by its licensed and restricted contravention.

The audience is placed between distress and safety, the position of 'optimal distancing' and balanced attention reserved for group catharsis (Scheff 1979). To describe the behaviour as a 'performance' is not to say that the 'actors' do not fully identify with their parts. Even in the more stylized display of the Balinese theatre, the actor portraying the witch Rangda may disrupt the performance by running amok and the audience follow suit (Geertz 1966); but some observers remain unentranced and direct the activities of the 'spectators'. For the community as a whole, social contradictions are demonstrated but shown to be susceptible to a solution, albeit a temporary and restricted one (for these contradictions are not ultimately resolved). The performance articulates these social oppositions for all members of the audience, but also permits individual identification with the protagonist. That sex-specific performances are appreciated equally by both sexes suggests that individual identification is perhaps less important than psychodynamic writers have suggested: ritual derives its efficacy and power from its performance.

THE 'MYSTICAL PRESSURE' OF MEDICINE

My model of culture-bound reactions thus involves non-dominant individuals, who display in their personal situations the basic structural social contradictions, expressed through the available intellectual tools, with recourse to 'mystical pressure' permitting personal adjustment of their situation by a limited contravention of society's core values. Each reaction involves dislocation, exaggeration/inversion and restitution. An attempt to look for equivalent 'western' reactions would appear quite straightforward apart from the notion of 'mystical pressure'. What unquestionable 'other-worldly authority', standing outside everyday personal relations, might serve to explain and legitimate them?

For small-scale traditional communities, social organization and normative principles and the categorization of the natural world and human relations to it are articulated through an intellectually tight system of cosmology, which we usually refer to as 'religion'. Religion is an ideology; it both describes and prescribes, binding the individual into society and into the natural order. Through its other-worldly authority it legitimates personal experience and the social order. By contrast, in the secularized West, Christianity has lost its power of social regulation and competes both with other religions and, more significantly, with a variety of alternative ideologies, moral and political. Where then can we find an equivalent 'mystical' sanction that integrates personal distress into a shared conceptualization of the world?

I would suggest that the legitimation of our present world-view lies ultimately in contemporary science, which offers core notions of individual identity, responsibility and action. In its everyday context as it relates to our personal experience, science is most salient in the form of medicine. In all societies illness is experienced through an expressive system encoding indigenous notions of social order. Whilst serious illness 'is an event that challenges meaning in this world. . . . medical beliefs and practices organise the event into an episode which gives form and meaning' (Young 1976). This obligation to order abnormality is no less when it is manifest primarily through unusual behaviour.

Professional intervention in sickness involves incorporating the patient into an overarching system of explanation, a common structural pattern which manifests itself in the bodily economy of every human being. Social accountability is transferred on to an agency beyond the patient's control. Becoming sick is part of a social process leading to communal recognition of an abnormal state and a consequent readjustment of patterns of behaviour and expectations, and then to changed roles and altered responsibility. Expectations of the sick person include exemption from discharging some social obligations, exemption from responsibility for the condition itself, together with a shared recognition that it is undesirable and involves an obligation to seek help and co-operate with treatment. Withdrawal from everyday social responsibilities is made socially acceptable through

some means of exculpation, usually through mechanisms of bio-physical determinism. 'When faced with a diagnosis for which he has equally convincing reasons to believe that either his client is sick or he is not sick, the physician finds that the professional and legal risks are less if he accepts the hypothesis of sickness' (Young 1976). To question the medical scheme itself involves questioning some of our most fundamental assumptions about human nature and agency. Because of its linking of personal experience with the social order, its standardized expectations of removing personal responsibility and initiating an institutionalized response, and its rooting in ultimate social values through science, biomedicine offers a powerful and unquestionable legitimate inversion of everyday behaviour. It will thus not be surprising to find many of our 'culture-bound syndromes' already included in psychiatric nosologies. Others we may suspect lie hidden in the fringes of general medicine. Lee (1981) shows how the symbolic inversions of Malay *amok*, *latah* and possession states continue, although the attribution of responsibility has been transferred from supernatural agencies on to a notion of illness.

BUTTERFLIES AND SERPENTS: THE MEDICALIZATION OF WOMAN

In all societies, women are 'excluded from participation in or contact with some realm in which the highest powers of the society are felt to reside' (Ortner 1974). They are excluded by a dominant ideology which reflects men's experiences and interests: 'The facts of female physiology are transformed in almost all societies into a cultural rationale which assigns women to nature and the domestic sphere, and thus ensures their general inferiority to men' (La Fontaine 1981: 347).

The core aspect of the female role in western society is reflected in the ideals still held out to women: concentration on marriage, home and children as the primary focus of concern, with reliance on a male provider for sustenance and status. There is an expectation that women will emphasize nurturance and that they live through and for others rather than for themselves. Women are expected to give up their occupation and place of residence when they marry and are banned from the direct assertion and expression of aggression. Their lack of power is attributed to their greater emotionality and their inability to cope with wider social responsibilities, for dependency and passivity are expected of a woman; her psychological image is of a person with a childish incapacity to govern herself and a need for male protection and direction. Contemporary western women are permitted greater freedom than men to 'express feelings' and to recognize emotional difficulties, enabling the woman to define her difficulties within a medical framework and bring them to the attention of her doctor.

Through childbearing, every woman in the West becomes a potential patient: Jordanova (1980) suggests that medicine and science are characterized by the action of men on women; women are regarded as more 'natural', passive, awaiting male ('cultural') organization. In the heraldry of the British Royal College of Psychiatrists, as sported on the neckties of its members, they continue this tradition as the Butterflies of Psyche, awaiting the Serpents of Aesculapius. Serpent and Butterfly are in an opposed but complementary relationship; action by one engenders the opposed complement in the other (Bateson 1958). There is a close historical relationship between the psychiatric notions of 'woman' and 'patient', and there is a similarity between neurotic symptom patterns and normative expectations of female behaviour.

OVERDOSES

A contemporary reaction which offers close parallels is parasuicide with medically prescribed drugs. As in hysteria, in this type of ritual theatre the normative situation of active male (husband, doctor) and passive female (wife, patient) is reflected in the drama of the hospital casualty department. The unease and anger which it evokes in the medical profession reflect its 'perverse' transformation of the clinical paradigm.

Women are closely identified with psychotropic medication. Whilst more women than men go to physicians and receive prescriptions, there is an even greater disproportion in the number of women receiving psychotropic drugs. During the year preceding a national sampling of American adults, 13 per cent of the men and 29 per cent of the women had used prescribed drugs, especially minor tranquillizers and daytime sedatives. These American rates are consistent with other western industrialized nations. Physicians expect female patients to require a higher proportion of mood-altering drugs than do less expressive male patients. These are perhaps the 'attractive healthy women who thoroughly enjoy being ill' (*Daily Express* 1984). That we are not dealing simply with a 'real' gender disparity in psychological distress is suggested by the symbolism of medical advertising. Women outnumber men by 15:1 in advertisements for tranquillizers and anti-depressants. One advertisement depicted a woman with a bowed head holding a dish-cloth and standing beside a pile of dirty dishes represented larger than life-size; the medical consumer is told that the drug 'restores perspective' for her by 'correcting the disturbed brain chemistry'. Psychotropic drug advertisements emphasize women as the patients; they are represented as discontented with their role in life, dissatisfied with marriage, with washing dishes or attending parent–teacher association meetings. Advertisements for psychotropic drugs tend to picture women as patients, while those for medications show men; within the psychotropic drug category alone, women are shown with diffuse emotional symptoms, while men are pictured with discrete episodes of anxiety because of specific pressures from work or from accompanying organic illness.

'Overdoses' of medical drugs are up to five times more common among women than men, especially in the age group 15–19. Among girls of this age in Edinburgh, more than one in every hundred take an overdose each year. Half of the episodes involve interpersonal conflicts as the major precipitating factor. Only a minority had made definite plans to

prepare for death and avoid discovery or subsequently regretted not having killed themselves.
Suicidal intent and risk to life appear to be low,
especially as overdoses are usually taken with
somebody close by: 59 per cent of attempters
commit the act in the presence of or near other
people.

While the reasons given by the individual for
taking overdoses may be expressive (explaining the
overdose as a result of a personal predicament and
associated feelings at the time of the act), they are
frequently pragmatic – that is, they are consciously
conceived in terms of the desired consequences of
the act, usually increased support or understanding. Overdoses can be interpreted as a transaction
between the woman and her intimate group. A
study of adolescent overdosers suggested they
viewed their act as a means of gaining relief from a
stressful situation or as a way of showing other
people how desperate they felt. Medical staff who
assessed their motives both regarded them as
expressive but also noted that adolescents took
overdoses in order to punish other people or change
their behaviour. Typically, a teenage girl took
tablets after a disappointment, frustration, or
difference of opinion with an older person (usually
a parent); many patients afterwards reported that
the induction of guilt in those whom they blamed
for their distress was a predominant motive for the
act. Thus, while overdoses can be seen as strategies
designed to avoid or adjust certain specific situations, the self-perception of the principal is of
social dislocation or extrusion: the reaction exaggerates this extrusion, offering a threat of refusing
membership in the human community altogether –
an inversion of normal life-seeking norms. As in
Tikopia (Firth 1961), attempted suicide is, among
other things, a dangerous adventure.

The conventional resolution of the inversion
involves its complement: medical intervention
returns the patient into everyday relationships. Not
surprisingly, the overdose meets with little professional sympathy, particularly when it is interpreted as an instrumental social mechanism rather
than the sign of underlying individual hopelessness

or psychiatric illness. 'Expressive' explanations
(communicating despair and aiming at withdrawal,
escape or death) are more acceptable and evoke
more sympathy or readiness to help in both doctors
and nurses than pragmatic motives. Doctors tend to
distinguish acts as either suicidal or 'manipulative',
and are more accepting of the 'wish to die' motive.

Women who take overdoses still gain access to
hospital, despite the physician's antipathy, since the
popular conception of suicidal behaviour is as a
discrete event, 'something that happens to one',
rather than something one intentionally brings
about. Relatives accept that the patient's problems
are outside her direct personal control, and
responsibility is thereby attributed to some agency
beyond the patient's volition. The official translation of the performance into *symptoms* takes place
under socially prescribed conditions by the
physician who alone has the power to legitimate
exculpating circumstances (Young 1976). As with
nineteenth-century hysteria, the resolution of the
reaction involves a 'mystical pressure', which repli-
cates the social structure in which the reaction
occurs. The drama of the scene in the casualty
department replays the male doctor/female patient
theme without questioning it, but it does afford a
degree of negotiation for the principal, who
induces a mixture of responses, mainly sympathy
and guilt, in close relatives and friends.

MENTAL ILLNESS AS THEATRE: PSYCHOPOLITICS, OPPOSITION AND INVERSION

Reactions like overdose, agoraphobia, shoplifting
and hysteria cannot necessarily be taken as
phenomenologically discrete. Many similar
patterns occur in non-western societies and
occured in the past in the West. Anorexia nervosa is
arguably an 'internalization' of the nineteenth-
century corset, similarly controlling female
sexuality by giving it an increased but restricted
salience. The spread of industrialization and its
associated tendency to individualize, psychologize

and assign pragmatic motives (and hence perceive socially standardized behaviours as 'only' ritual or theatre) might suggest that 'Western' variants will become more universal. Whatever the origins of *pibloktoq* ('arctic hysteria') in European/Inuit relations (Murphy 1982), the reaction is being 'replaced' by parasuicide (Harvey *et al.* 1976).

I have emphasized the specific social and symbolic meaning of certain performances in Britain and America which show similarities with my model of Third World culture-bound syndromes. While social meanings and behaviour may be superimposed on a variety of existing bio-logical patterns – as in premenstrual syndrome, adolescence, biological psychoses, drug intoxica-tions – I have restricted my discussion to reactions not primarily associated with human pathophysiol-ogy. These are public and dramatic presentations of core social issues; in a word, theatre or, to be more precise, *ritual* theatre, which offers a specific pragmatic tool for the principal actor and one which may at times end in her death.

The application of 'inversion' is not to imply that each gender simply adopts a role more directly opposed to the other. In the case of the male equivalents, domestic sieges and flashing, the pattern is an exaggerated ritual reassertion or parody of dominant (male) norms rather than their obvious inversion. Although they are clearly extra-ordinary behaviour relative to everyday articulation of the same symbolism, it would perhaps extend the notion of 'inversion' too far to include them.

In obesity, running amok, or parasuicide, it is the ritual threat that provides bargaining power. Sieges (separated or divorced men kidnapping their children) certainly take place in situations where the principal is excluded from full participation in dominant values. But the consequent performance is an assertion of such values. I have seen a number of husbands who became agoraphobic after a period of compulsory redundancy, during which the wife continued as the wage-earner. The female reactions also appear to be an exaggeration or *reductio ad absurdum* of normal sex roles, but in certain cases (agoraphobia, overdosing) women are, as we have

seen, already in an inverted and socially extruded position and the reaction is an extension of this accessible to the principal and her audience. Exag-geration of behaviour provokes a reciprocal response in men. The parody of gender-specific behaviour in women may be perceived as inversion of those values *which, at another level, men and women hold in common.* Anorexia, like obesity (its apparent reverse), has a close subjective relation-ship to male/female relations; for many partici-pants, both are phases in the same reaction. The ambiguity and 'overdetermination' of anorexia reflect a current ambiguity over female sexuality and child-rearing, which is not characteristic of the role of the woman as housekeeper (agoraphobic) or patient (overdoser). Coherence of the matured syndrome is shaped by interaction between the pro-fessional and the principal.

Particular elements of the 'Serpent/Butterfly' relationship thus appear to be employed distinc-tively in different reactions: doctor/patient in overdoses; public/private in agoraphobia; produc-tion/consumption in shoplifting. They are not dis-cretely related, however, and each reaction partly articulates the total complex, out of which other ritual situation-specific patterns can be generated. Thus, a bank manager's widow, faced with insoluble debts, attempted to rob a bank, where she was a well-known customer, undisguised and using her perfume spray as a gun. After a suspended court sentence facilitated the adjustment of her finances, she commented: 'I must have had a brain storm.' The popular notion of a brain storm affords exculpation as an overriding and irrational but excusable impulse, clearly aligned with the medico-legal concepts of 'diminished responsibility' and 'disturbed balance of mind'. This coexists with the professional and lay idea that at some unconscious level the reaction is 'understandable'.

The mystical power of biomedicine as 'external' justification for individual action, and the negotiat-ing 'space' it affords, seem relevant to those other performances in which patient enacts a *pas de deux* with doctor: Ganser Syndrome, compensation neurosis, irritable bowel, Munchausen's Syndrome,

Munchausen's Syndrome by Proxy, and chronic pain or loss of energy syndromes, apart from the many situations (such as non-compliance) where different explanatory models employed by doctor and patient afford the latter some control over the social drama. The mystical sanction of medicine seems less relevant to the two specifically male reactions, sieges and flashing (or other similar patterns such as the ritual stealing of cars by male adolescents), presumably because of the Serpent/Butterfly relationship (Culture:Nature :: Male:Female :: Active:Passive :: Doctor:Patient). Those 'medical' reactions that are more common among men, such as alcoholism, are more easily viewed as a 'response to stress' in themselves than as a dramatic and functional method of personal negotiation. For medical professionals themselves, whether male or female, the biomedical 'mystical pressure' is difficult to employ personally. While student nurses frequently take overdoses, the reaction is rare among qualified nursing staff: the recourse to biomedical sanction has to be more complex and more 'dissociated' than overdosing. A patient of mine is a married nursing sister of strict evangelical background, who has achieved a certain negotiating 'space' between the demands of specialized professional responsibilities and her role as an 'ideal mother' by hospital admissions for recurrent episodes of loin pain haematuria. During a psychotherapeutic session she recollected a 'dream-like' state, where she would temporarily leave her professional role to venesect herself, injecting the blood into her bladder. It is difficult to determine the extent to which the reactions are 'conscious' pragmatic attempts at adjustment; while to the theorist there is an element of parody in all of them, the irony is only rarely perceived by principal and audience. Participants certainly experience despair and self-hatred.

All the patterns I have described are likely to be found as part of an endogenous depressive illness; I suggest the mediating factor is the sense of extrusion and isolation, which is so characteristic of depression. My emphasis on semiotic rather than psychological or physiological antecedents should thus not be taken to mean that individual personality or biology are irrelevant in the choice of reaction. It is not surprising that agoraphobic patients are anxious people or have 'phobic personalities' or that anorexics were overweight as children. The final path is polysemous and over-determined: 'The efficacy of ritual as a social mechanism depends on this very phenomenon of central and peripheral meanings and on their allusive and evocative powers. . . . All symbolic objects make it possible to combine fixity of form with multiple meanings of which some are standardised and some highly individualised' (Richards 1981: 164–5). My nurse patient's venesection commenced after she had an extramarital affair (with an anaesthetist!) and an attempt to lose the subsequent pregnancy by severe dieting coincided with the death of her father. Nevertheless, the individual reaction is socially embedded: the male who takes an overdose or who develops anorexia is inevitably 'feminized'. Another patient of mine shoplifted from a London store, where her domineering mother was well known, ostensibly to purchase her own birthday present for her mother to give her later in the week. In this setting the mother stood in a relationship to her analogous to that of husband to wife; we would be surprised to find a man engaging in shoplifting in a similar relationship with his wife or even a son with his mother.

Reversal theory suggests inversions occur in a universal non-rational 'ludic' mode (Apter 1982), while many in the women's movement have emphasized that it is women who are 'conditioned to lose in order to win'. Devereux (1970) characterises this passive 'appeal of helplessness' as *chantage masochiste* (masochistic blackmail) and illustrates it with an agoraphobic case-history and the 'psychology of cargo cults'. Rather than characterize such life-threatening or constricting performances as simply 'self-punitive' or 'manipulative', with all the psychodynamic baggage that implies, we would prefer to see the powerless individual as enmeshed in a situation that she cannot control, one that reflects neither her interests nor her perspective, but which does afford room for manoeuvre by employing the dominant symbolism itself. If it were not a dangerous game, it would not work: physiological integrity is temporarily sacrificed to semiology. 'The stakes are high: they involve a real gamble with death' (Firth 1961: 15).

The dominant structures are only represented, possibly adjusted, but not challenged; whether self-help groups or women's therapy groups can, like women's groups in the Third World, actually develop into alternative political structures ('counter-cultures') (Turner 1969) is unlikely. It is interesting that these reactions are often 'resolved' through psychiatry: the psychiatrist, relative to other doctors, is more passive, more empathic, more 'feminine'. The inversion can, however, be institutionalized, either as an undesirable identity in relation to dominant norms (Open Door phobic groups) or as valued identities in their own right (the American Big Beautiful Woman [BBW] network). The irony of affirming a stigmatized identity is that this identity remains determined by the dominant culture.

STRUCTURE, FUNCTION AND ACTION

If, as Gregory Bateson claims, 'data from a New Guinea tribe and the superficially very different data of psychiatry can be approached in terms of a single epistemology' (Bateson 1958: vii), a variety of explanatory problems still remain. Thus, we have argued that many of these reactions can be interpreted as instrumental (function for) as opposed to the medical and semiological perception of them as reflections of 'stress' (functions of). Where is such instrumentality (which retains its symbolic dimension) located? In many instances of overdoses there is a clear pragmatic intention to alter personal relations; in anorexia nervosa functionality lies in the therapist's explanations in family therapy; in other instances it can be located in our own, more distanced, method of analysis. It is difficult to assign a uniform 'meaning' to any behaviour, particularly one which, once established, is available for fresh situations. 'What is instrumental for some

may be expressive for others; and moreover, the "etic" categories of instrumentality and pragmatism may be quite different from the categories of the people concerned' (Cohen 1985: 307–8). In general, such reactions can only continue, when they involve a common assumption that participants are 'not aware' of any immediate goal, thus allowing society to invoke the 'mystical sanctions' of biomedicine or the spirit world. It is of course difficult to distinguish pragmatic from 'unconscious' participation, even in such clearly iatrogenic reactions as the recent vogue for multiple possession. In the case of work disability symptoms ('compensation neurosis') the symptoms are now believed to continue longer after financial settlement than was formerly believed. In most instances it is more appropriate to talk of identification or 'fit' with models than 'intent'; but a complete description of the transformations of participant experience and reflexive self-perception by cultural typification lies outside the scope of this essay. Whilst the precipitating event would appear on our model to be some type of excessive 'stretch' between the oppositions, this may be no more representative of the central symbolic relations than a relative loss of self-determination.

A related issue is that of 'functioning' to preserve social homeostasis, emphasized by many scholars: rituals are taken as adjustment reactions for a society, allowing repressed impulses and potential rebellions to express themselves in harmless 'rituals'. As Kapferer (1979: 121) points out, 'rituals [may] function to paper over and to resolve conflicts and tensions'. This is often the case, but it is not necessarily so. To arbitrarily isolate individual institutions as 'functional' is often little more than seeing how the total field of data under the observation of the fieldworker must somehow make sense. Indeed, it is only a disguised form of description. Certainly, if our reactions may be glossed by the observer as 'rituals of rebellion' or even parodies, this is not the participants' exegesis: nineteenth-century hysterics do not seem to have been conscious of their part in what De Swaan (1981) calls a 'revolt enacted as mental disease'.

Standardized rituals can always lead to the development of new tensions. Thus, a common experience of family therapists working with neurotic patients is that therapy leads to marital separation. We cannot assume that the illness simply 'masked' an inevitable separation, for therapeutic assumptions and techniques carry their own models and implicit goals. To what extent can the reactions themselves be regarded as the direct representation of communal tensions rather than some relatively discrete and less central adjustment reaction? Functionalist and structuralist models have the advantage of a hierarchy of causality, allowing us to differentiate 'core' from 'adjustment' patterns. Functionalist explanations assume that rituals are occasioned by social tensions and that they are merely occasions when their tensions find expression, with the assumption that the precipitating cause of the discrete episode is identical with the social themes demonstrated in it.

While I argue that the reactions described articulate the opposition I have called Butterfly/Serpent (B/S), the initial precipitating event may be relatively unconnected with these themes (although articulating the Butterfly's inaccessibility to jural power). However, it is professionally shaped in the cause of medical diagnosis, exegesis and treatment along B/S lines. As the B/S relationship is present both between Butterfly and significant others before the reaction and in the biomedical construction of it, Butterfly's response becomes more truly Butterfly-like. Even after 'resolution' of the individual episode this sensitization continues as a potential vulnerability. 'Aspects of the everyday social experience and world of the actors are made to become explanations, or causes, of the illness event with which they have been brought into contact. Whether these explanations are antecedents to the illness event in the strictly logical sense often assumed in the functionalist argument is open to question' (Kapferer 1979: 121). Nevertheless, if the reactions reflect social oppositions and show that they are soluble without being challenged, they can be said to reinforce them.

The same phenomena are susceptible to a variety of theoretical explanations: reflection of social status or of stress; social catharsis; social homeostasis; cultural loophole; individual catharsis; role reversal; ritual theatre; entertainment; ritual reaffirmation of gender relationships; genesis of sorority or sodality; rite of passage; revolutionary prototype; resolution or expression of symbolic ambiguity; manifestation of lay or professional explanatory model of sickness; not to mention the expression of such basic impulses as distress, parody, play, adventure or revenge. Western neuroses may be represented simultaneously as all these. Claims to the primacy of a particular theory are ultimately arbitrary and are grounded in the particular perspective of the observer.

REFERENCES

Apter, M. J. (1982) *The Experience of Motivation: The Theory of Psychological Reversals*, London: Academic Press.

Bateson, G. (1958) *Naven*, 2nd edn, Stanford, CA: Stanford University Press.

British Medical Journal (1971) 'Suicidal attempts', 11: 483.

Cohen, (1985) Symbolism and Social Change. *Man* 20: 307–24.

Corin, E. and Bibeau, G. (1980) 'Psychiatric perspectives in Africa', *Transcultural Psychiatric Research Review* 16: 147–78.

Daily Express (1984) 'Wives hooked on illness are giving GPs a headache', 27 March, London.

Desjarlais, R. (1992) *Body and Emotion: The Aesthetics of Illness and Healing in the Nepal Himalayas*, Philadelphia: University of Pennsylvania Press.

De Swann, A. (1981) 'The politics of agoraphobia', *Theory and Society* 10: 359–85.

Devereux, G. (1970) *Essais d'Ethnopsychiatrie Générale*, Paris: Gallimard.

Eliade, M. (1964) *Shamanism: Archaic Techniques of Ecstasy*, Princeton, NJ: Princeton University Press.

Firth, R. (1961) 'Suicide and risk taking in Tikopia society', *Psychiatry* 2: 1–17.

Geertz, C. (1966) 'Religion as a cultural system', in M. Banton (ed.) *Anthropological Approaches to Religion*, London: Tavistock.

Harris, G. (1957) 'Possession "hysteria" in a Kenyan tribe', *American Anthropologist* 59: 1046–66.

Harvey, E. B. (1976) 'Utilisation of a psychiatric social work team in an Alaskan boarding school', *Am. Acad. Clin. Psychiatry* 15: 558–74.

Janzen, J. M. (1982) 'Drums anonymous: towards an understanding of structures of therapeutic maintenance', in M. De Vries *et al.* (eds) *The Use and Abuse of Medicine*, New Haven, CT: Praeger.

Jordanova, L. J. (1980) 'Natural facts: a historical perspective of science and sexuality', in C. MacCormack and M. Strathern (eds) *Nature, Culture, Gender*, Cambridge: Cambridge University Press.

Kapferer, B. (1979) 'Mind, self and other in demonic illness', *American Ethnologist* 6: 110–33.

Laderman, C. (1991) *Taming the Winds of Desire: Psychology, Medicine and Aesthetics in Malay Shamanistic Performance*, Berkeley: University of California Press.

La Fontaine, J. (1981) 'The domestication of the savage male', *Man* 16: 333–49.

Leach, E. (1961) *Rethinking Anthropology*, London: Athlone.

Lee, R. L. M. (1981) 'Structure and antistructure in the culture-bound syndromes: the Malay case', *Culture, Medicine and Psychiatry* 5: 233–48.

Lewis, I. M. (1971) *Ecstatic Religion*, Harmondsworth, Mx: Penguin.

Murphy, H. B. M. (1982) *Comparative Psychiatry*, Berlin: Springer.

Newman, P. L. (1964) ' "Wild Man" behaviour in a New Guinea Highlands community', *American Anthropologist* 66: 1–19.

Ortner, S. B. (1974) 'Is female to male as nature is to culture?', in M. A. Rosaldo and L. Lamphere (eds) *Women, Culture and Society*, Stanford, CA: Stanford University Press.

Richards, A. (1982) *Chisungu: A Girls' Initiation Ceremony among the Bemba of Zambia*, London: Tavistock.

Scheff, T. J. (1979) *Catharsis in Healing, Ritual and Drama*, Berkeley: University of California Press.

Seligman, C. G. (1928) 'Anthropological perspectives and psychological theory' *Journal of the Royal Anthropological Institute* 62: 193–228.

Turner, V. (1969) *The Ritual Process*, London: Routledge & Kegan Paul.

Van Gennep, (1960) *The Rites of Passage*, London: Routledge & Kegan Paul.

Young, A. (1976) 'Some implications of medical beliefs and practices for social anthropology', *American Anthropologist* 78: 5–24.

Mythological and Ritual Theatre in Cuba

Inés María Martiatu Terry

Fernando Ortiz' book *The Dances and Theatre of the Blacks in Cuban Folklore*, first published in 1951, is one of the most brilliant and revealing works ever written on Cuban art. Of course, the subject had been treated by others before, but Ortiz discovered what other scholars had not seen or not fully comprehended. He demonstrated the intrinsic theatricality of the religious practices and popular festivals of African origin still celebrated in Cuba today. And at the same time as bequeathing us a legacy he presented us with a work of artistic anticipation. When Ortiz spoke of a primordial theatre, he talked about a theatre which, at that time, existed only in its profane form. But since the author apprehended Caribbean ritual theatre as it actually was, in all its splendour and vitality, he also foresaw what one day it would become.

Ortiz saw and described the transports, trances and, sometimes brilliant, performances of the 'mediums' in the ceremonies and rituals of the Regla de Ocha or Santería (of Yoruba origin), the Regla de Palo or Palomonte (of Bantu origin), the Regla Arará or Voodoo (from the Fon culture), the Abakuá Secret Society (from Calabar), the Bembé de Sao (which combines various elements taken from Santería, Palomonte and Spiritualism). However, it took many years before the histrionic potential of these performances was recognized by professional theatre artists and transferred to the stage. As an unprejudiced culturologist, Ortiz recognized the dramatic and spectacular character of these performances and called them 'theatre', without needing to add any adjective that would have placed it in an inferior position *vis-à-vis* the so-called western theatre. Quite the opposite was the case: his conception embraced a much wider vision than that offered by conventional theatre. He highlighted the 'total theatre' character of these performances, with their integration of music and poetry, dance and mime, acrobatics and trances, costume, make-up and masks, real 'installations' combining man-made elements (paintings, sculptures, drawings) with natural ones (flowers, fruits, stones, etc.). To the untrained eye, all these elements may seem like an extraordinary surrealist collage. But

• *Akanamba*, a performance based on a story from the Yoruba tradition and performed by Teatreros de Orilé, Centro de Teatro y Danza de La Habana, 1991. Videostill: Johannes Birringer

Performance Research 3(3), pp.53-59 © Routledge 1998

they are essential ingredients in the ceremonies where human beings establish contact with the supernatural world.

CARIBBEAN RITUAL THEATRE

In the sacred spaces where different religions of African origin, in syncretism with Catholicism, are practised and preserved, a ritual theatre is created, where mythological elements from a rich oral tradition are blended with scenic expression. Ritual is staged myth. From these complex and diverse ceremonies an important tendency has emerged, which finds expression in our sacred theatre today. The action, which dramatizes one or several myths, makes use of eloquent staging techniques loaded with meaning and is used to communicate with the gods and ancestors (Martiatu Terry 1992).

• Another ritual image from *Akanamba*, as performed, for the camera, by Teatreros de Orilé, 1991. Videostill: Johannes Birringer

It is within this context that a Caribbean ritual theatre movement, as foreseen by Ortiz, came into existence. I am using this term because it defines the character and functions of this theatre both in its 'sacred' (religious ceremonies), and 'profane' (presented in traditional and non-conventional spaces) forms. The adjective 'Caribbean' points us towards the cultural world where this theatre has its roots: Caribbean, hybrid of European and African components, Catholic and African religions, magic, carnival, music, dance, etc. The term 'Caribbean' fulfils at the same time two objectives: first, to differentiate this theatre from other types of ritual theatre cultivated in other parts of the world (including Cuba) and based upon other cultural or existential experiences; second, to point towards other types of theatre with similar mythological and ritual sources, characteristics and functions, which exist alongside ours (e.g. the Candomblé in Brazil, the Bantu-based 'Teatro Negro' from Barlovento in Venezuela, Voodoo in Haiti).

It is important to distinguish between 'Caribbean ritual theatre', deeply rooted within our traditions and living culture, and the western concepts of 'intercultural' theatre, 'anthropological theatre' or 'postmodern performance'. Ever since Antonin Artaud undertook his mental and actual journeys into the world of autochthonous theatre, actors and directors from the First World have been looking to distant lands in an attempt to recover a lost rituality, the essence of the spectacular, to find an answer to the old obsession with 'the other' or 'otherness'. 'Postmodern performance' is, according to the researcher Erika Fischer-Lichte, 'the product of a post-industrial society so weary of its own history and culture that it longs to obliterate itself and its traditions in an incessant wave of information and meaningless imagery' (Fischer-Lichte 1994). An 'anthropological theatre' with a strong intercultural vocation, focusing attention on the Hindu, Japanese, African and, more recently, South American and Oceanic cultures, has been practised by Jerzy Grotowski, Eugenio Barba, Peter Brook, Richard Schechner and others in an attempt to return to the myths, the rites

• (Above and below) Dancing by the initiates at a ritual honouring Shango, from the film *Mensajero de los dioses* [Messenger of the Gods] by Rigoberto López, Havana, 1988/89. Videostill: R. López

and the roots common to all cultures. Our ritual theatre, on the other hand, is not a return to ritual practices, but a blend of past and present, religious and social life. Myth and ritual are constantly present in our spiritual and material culture: in our eating habits, public gatherings, music, dances, clothes, etc. Our ritual theatre emerges from what Ortiz describes as 'transcultural': the sacred and the profane forms of theatre have each followed different evolutionary paths, but are still interrelated and influence each other because often they are produced by the same artists. These perform both in religious centres and professional theatres and give continuity to a unique praxis, which blends and articulates spiritual and artistic experiences. In the rites, they assume important religio-magical functions. When they transfer these into the professional theatre, they imbue the stage with a special power and establish a unique relationship with the audience.

A PROFANE THEATRE

When the catholic virgin, Charity, abandons her crown and sceptre, her secular clothing – rebuttal of all signs of sexuality; when she descends from the altar, where she could only enjoy the pleasures of incense and flowers and where all allusion to human love is sinful; when she comes down from the altar, half-naked and rattling with laughter to dance a ritual and tellurian dance with the men, a clearly erotic dance; when gods bestow on men the gift of love and flesh, with all its sweetness and violence; then, an improbable West-Indian syncretism is born, a stage picture and dazzling poetic image, which should mark an opening between us.

(Martiatu Terry 1992)

I am referring here to *Suite Yoruba*, a piece by the choreographer Ramiro Guerra, which was premièred at the National Theatre of Cuba in 1960. This coincided with the formation of the Cuban National Dance Company, founded by Guerra himself, and the presentation of *Bembé*, *Abakuá* and *Yímbula*, three spectacles sponsored by the folklore department of the theatre, directed by Argeliers León. Scholars such as Rogelio Martínez Furé, Miguel Barnet and Alberto Pedro Díaz took part, as did the musician Jorge Berroa, the film-maker Sara Gómez, and myself. This meeting of teachers and pupils resulted in a collaboration, which proved to be fruitful and which is still working today (Martiatu Terry 1987). It has evolved into a movement, which constitutes one of the most important aspects of the contemporary theatre scene in Cuba. It had repercussions not only in the spoken theatre, but also in other genres such as modern dance, folk dance, classical ballet and mime.

Unlike other movements of ritual theatre in the world, the Cuban variant is distinguished by the presence of an important textual element provided by many playwrights, some of whom are leading figures in the literary establishment of the country. This 'Cuban dramaturgy' is

sustained principally by the complex myths from various African religions practised in the country. These mythological sources offer poetical descriptions of the creation of the world, of the origins of humankind, of deeds and exploits of gods and humans. They are oral sources passed down from generation to generation. The most important one, the Oracle of Ifá, is the sacred book of the Yorubas and has often been used by writers as a source of inspiration. Although the legends, or *patakines*, from the Ifá were gathered into manuscript form by the *babalawes*, or Ifá priests, the tradition is essentially an oral one, where the manuscripts merely perform the task of retaining a documentary form of these stories. Some of the more important elements of the faith are transmitted only personally to the initiated following a long preparation process.

• Paying respect at an altar to the deity during an initiation ritual, from the film *Mensajero de los dioses* [Messenger of the Gods] by Rigoberto López, Havana, 1988/9. Videostill: R. López

Within this body of dramatic works typical of the 'Cuban dramaturgy', a few outstanding examples should be mentioned here. *María Antonia* (1967) by Eugenio Hernández Espinosa is a tragedy, where the elements of Santería play an essential role within its dramatic structure. *Chago de Guisa* (1989) by Gerardo Fulleda León, which won the House of America prize, is a kind of epic tale of initiation, which tells the story of a young fugitive and includes elements from the Yoruba and Bantu traditions. *Cefi y la Muerte* (1983) by Ramiro Herrero is based on the 'theatre of relationships', deeply rooted within the tradition of the Santiago de Cuba carnival. *Baroko* by Rogelio Maneses is more experimental and deals with various elements of Spiritualism and Santería. From among the women playwrights I should like to mention Fatima Patterson, whose *Repique por Mafifa* (1992) tells the story of Mafifa, a black bell-ringer from the conga orchestra of Los Hoyos in Santiago de Cuba, who does not wish to acknowledge the fact that she is as an incarnated spirit. Another woman playwright is Elaine Centeno, whose *La Piedra de Elliot* deals with the concerns of a youngster and his relation to God, religion, spirits and the mysteries of life.

All of these plays contain elements that challenge our preconceptions of dramatic genres. Caribbean culture attributes great importance to magical practices as a way of controlling reality, and to rituals as a way of influencing everyday life. Both, therefore, also affect the notions of tragedy or tragicomedy. Caribbean tragedies are different from classical tragedies in as much as their protagonists have a way of influencing fate and the will of the gods through magic. In *María Antonia*, for example, the heroine is able to save her life by means of her initiation into Santería.

POSSESSION AS PERFORMANCE

Possession plays an extremely important role within the different religious beliefs that are practised in Cuba. In all of the ritual ceremonies

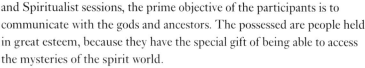

• During a ritual ceremony honouring Shangó, respect is paid at an alter to the deity. From the film *Un eterno presente: Oggún*, by Gloria Rolando with Pablo Milanés, Havana, 1991. Videostill: G. Rolando

and Spiritualist sessions, the prime objective of the participants is to communicate with the gods and ancestors. The possessed are people held in great esteem, because they have the special gift of being able to access the mysteries of the spirit world.

Trancing has also become a special area of study and practical experimentation within Caribbean ritual theatre. Recently, this has led to theatrical performances, where possession is 'staged', as we say in Cuba and as Ortiz also describes it in his book. Interesting work has taken on an educational slant, and new approaches to performance are developing with good results. They offer the actors an existential concept and path to self-realization and furnish them with techniques for finding resources within their personal and ancestral self-experiences. This, in the long run, changes not only their lives, but also their ideas about theatre and its uses.

Rogelio Meneses has been investigating for many years the techniques used by spiritual mediums and the members of the Bembé de Sao sect. He makes use of these techniques in his work as an actor and director of the Theatre Department in Santiago. In Havana, Mario Morales works with Spiritualism and Santería in his Orilé Theatre Group. Also in Havana, Tomás González has developed a system for his Transcendental Performance work, combining techniques of possession, the Oracle of Ifá and other ritual elements. He also founded the Teatro 5, where actors assume the roles of fortune tellers, work with the 'spectators' in divination sessions, and leave the order and length of the 'shows' up to to chance and fortuitous events (Manzor Coats and Martiatu Terry 1995; Martiatu Terry 1994). His work has been very successful and has found recognition both in Cuba and abroad.

As we have seen, this Cuban theatre has undergone a peculiar evolution that is in keeping with the character of the people and the mythological and ritual sources it draws upon. We have witnessed the rescue of a traditional technique, in which actors find emotional contact and reflect an ancient living culture that precedes and surrounds them. This vindicates the main function of ritual as an instrument of knowledge and mastery of reality. Both the artists and scholars, who have followed the process all these years, are faced with a series of challenging questions. The plays have developed themes rooted in the oral traditions, especially from the Yoruba background, with regular borrowings from the Ifá Oracle and its *patakines* (legends). From the first stage of development, where the characters were gods and the stories revolved around their exploits, we have moved to a more intimate and contemporary setting, where philosophical, existential, or religious problems are dealt with in a more immediate fashion.

As far as 'staged possession' is concerned, much research still needs to be done, especially on trance and its differing degrees of profundity, on consciousness-expanding techniques as proposed by some actors

and teachers, and on the two most common methods of arriving at this state: meditation (as favoured by the Spiritualists), or exhaustion through dance and music (as at Santería festivals).

However, artists are not only concerned with working with the energy generated through trance and possession. They also seek to transgress the conventional forms of representation. Within the dramatic structure of a *Güemilere*, a *toque de santo*, or Spiritualist session, the fixed framework leaves plenty of room for improvisation and direct contact with the audience (who should rather be called participants here). A whole range of new philosophical issues is raised regarding reception theory, the dramaturgy of non-text-based performance, the definition of role and character, the dividing line between the sacred and profane, the relationship between rehearsal and performance, between actualization and representation, and so on.

TOWARDS A THEORY OF CARIBBEAN RITUAL THEATRE

Having described some of the forms and traditions of Cuban ritual theatre, I should like to conclude with a few thoughts on the place of this tradition within the context of other scholarly approaches to contemporary ritual theatre. There is clearly a need for a theoretical base that is flexible and capable of adapting to new developments which it serves to explain. But in order to achieve this aim, it is necessary to deconstruct terms and concepts that have their roots in dominant ideologies and scientific discourses.

The heirs of the dominant culture have become owners of the dominant cultural discourses and insist that they are the only legitimate ones. They take the whole so-called 'western' culture as a 'universal' yardstick and place it in a privileged position above the dominated cultures. Claude Lévi-Strauss rightly said: 'There is not, and cannot be, a world civilization in the absolute sense of the word. . . . World civilization could only be the coalition, on a world scale, of cultures preserving their own character' (Lévi-Strauss 1963). However, in practice, the word 'universality' tends to identify the universal with the values of western society. It takes from the non-dominant cultures those forms of expression which it considers compatible with western standards and assumes the right to include in or exclude from the 'canon', according to what it finds useful or convenient for its own cultural agenda.

'Folklore' is a pejorative description and an abusive generalization, which treats the most heterogeneous forms of music, handicrafts and dances of the Third World in the same, condescending manner and separates them from the lofty realms of 'high culture', just as it refuses indigenous religions access to the elevated status of 'universal religions'. Similarly, the concept of 'popular culture' is little more than

• (This page, opposite and p. 57) Scenes of communal dancing during a ritual ceremony honouring Shangó. These are taken from the film *Un eterno presente: Oggún*, by Gloria Rolando with Pablo Milanés, Havana, 1991. Videostills: G. Rolando

a stereotypical interpretation, which diminishes the cultural value of what it designates as being 'different' from the aesthetic norms of the dominant culture. To this we can add the expressions using the prefix 'ethno' in order to indicate the inferiority of 'the other': ethno-music, ethno-theatre, ethno-literature, etc. The corresponding disciplines and academic professions in the 'First' World do not need such prefixes. German music is music, not 'ethno-music', and is studied by musicologists, not 'ethno-musicologists', though the Germans are an ethnic group just like the Yoruba or the Mongolians.

Caribbean ritual theatre, as it is developing in Cuba in its sacred and profane aspects, needs to be studied not only from the anthropological angle, but also from the viewpoint of theatre studies, employing the broadest possible concepts in order to fathom its depth, complexity and inherent peculiarities. It should also occupy its place, alongside other forms of theatre, in the disciplines of performance studies and ethnoscenology. For it to do so, a more comprehensive, in-depth, interdisciplinary and comparative study of the ritual elements in religion and theatre, in the social and artistic spheres, is necessary, employing methods of analysis that are free of ethnocentric prejudices, pseudo-scientific language and preclusive 'universalities'.

[Translated by Günter Berghaus]

REFERENCES

Fischer-Lichte, Erika (1994) 'La performance postmoderna: ¿Regreso al teatro ritual?', *Criterios* (Havana) 32 (July–December): 221–32.

Lévi-Strauss, Claude (1963) *Structural Anthropology*, trans. C. Jacobson and B. G. Schoepf, New York: Basic Books.

Martiatu Terry, Inés María (1987) 'Teatro, danza e identidad', *Tablas* (La Habana) 1: 37–45.

Martiatu Terry, Inés María (1991) 'Baroko: el rito como representacion', *Revolución y Cultura* 5–6.

Martiatu Terry, Inés María (1992) 'El Caribe: teatro sagrado, teatro de dioses', *El Público* 92 (September–October): 96–115.

Martiatu Terry, Inés María (1993a) 'La rappresentazione degli dei', *Teatro in Europa* 11–12 (July): 62–92.

Martiatu Terry, Inés María (1993b) 'Mayoría étnica y minoría cultural', *Tablas* (La Habana) especial XI Congreso de la ASSITEJ (Association Internacional de Teatro para Niños y Jóvenes).

Martiatu Terry, Inés María (1994) 'Taller de Actuación Transcendente: ¿El naciemiento de un método?', in *Taller de teatro en la escuela de América Latina y el Caribe*, Lima: Pontificia Universidad Católica del Perú.

Mazor-Coats, Lilliam and Martiatu Terry, Inés María (1995) 'A festival against all odds', *Drama Review* 146 (Summer): 39–71.

Ortiz, Fernando (1951) *Los bailes y el teatro de los negros en el folklore de Cuba*, La Habana: Editorial Letras Cubanas; 2nd edn 1981, 3rd edn 1985.

A Sense of Wonder

Gordon MacLellan

Images:

– a lone figure on a hilltop. The sunset sinking away over the plain and the mountains, the clouds burning, and the sky swelling turquoise. The Crow Man dances a prayer to the end of the day in a flare of leather and feathers and bells.*

* Personal dance, Bickerton Hill, Cheshire, lots of occasions.

– friends in a garden, a circle welcoming in all the world as witness, its presence marked by word and action and music. Promises are exchanged, food is shared, love flows. Celebration.†

† Private hand-fasting ceremony, 1996.

– an adventure into Faerie. A familiar place transformed: a once in a lifetime excursion. No longer the safe place of dog-walks and Sunday afternoon strolls, the woods are alive, trees stalk the visitors and boggarts in swarms riddle, sing, challenge and feast. Dark eyes watch from glowing toadstools. Smoke and fire flash and curl away over the ponds. Visitors are threatened, tempted, turned into frogs, enticed into a delight in the world, a chance to dance with the Faeries and to go home clutching the unspoken answer to the first riddle, and the last, the answer that will grow for them their own world of enchantment and wonder:

'. . . a round brown box without a lid, yet inside a whole world is hid.'‡

‡ 'The Risley Wassail': animated trail devised and performed by seventy children for an 'audience' of some two hundred victims, 1997.

This is what Creeping Toad does. We try to celebrate wonder, working with people to explore the relationships between themselves and the world we all live in. This is an adventure and in our work we try to find ways to give that journey shape. What we do, we remember – so we will dance our

• Crow Dancer. Photo: J. Woods

Performance Research 3(3), pp.60–63 © Routledge 1998

discoveries in pond and field, weave stories of stone, wood and water in an old quarry, or create wild and peculiar celebrations of wildlife, people, place and folklore that remind us of the enchantment in the old, worn-out, everyday places we know and ignore.

Sometimes, this work is called 'shamanic', other times it is 'ritual theatre': for us it does not particularly need a title. Too often a handy title seems to constrain rather than describe, trying to limit the work by fitting it within a definition. For me, a shaman is a person who walks between the human and non-human worlds, working to ease the movement of each through the life of the other, and in that sense I think that what Creeping Toad does is shamanic. 'Shamanic', not because it is part of a long, unbroken lineage with established teachers and recognized patterns of ritual and ceremony, but because it seeks to bridge the distance between people and the wider world. For me, in western society, you are a 'shaman' when you do the job: working at the behest of both human and non-human worlds.§

§ This argument is developed at greater length in the chapter 'Dancing on the Edge' in G. Harvey and C. Hardman (eds) Paganism To-day, London: Thorsons, 1995.

Creeping Toad is a hybrid between environmental education, community artwork and the perpetration of celebration. Work is inspired by the fusion of people and land: images come from across this range; from people and from other worlds. From people looking to explore familiar places in new ways, or to celebrate achievements, or to fire up the energy to launch a new initiative: power for people to claim a thought, a word, or a deed for themselves. The impulse to act also comes from outside the human world – from the dream of a wood, from the spring glow of snowdrop and crocus, the reflected shimmer of a branch in the water, the cold wind that blows over stone, from the voices of the people who speak through the hissing grass.

Our work is about communication, often without words, but touching . . . you listening to your own dreams, touching your own delight; reaching out to share experiences; the celebration, grief and glory that unite groups of people, and the joy that moves between people and places and feeds the fire in the hearts of both.

This is not to serve some proselytizing propaganda: that 'communication' remains the property of the individual. We may work as groups, whole companies, or on our own but all that a person does grows from that person's ideas: not from Toad impositions. The adventure of discovery is more important than some predetermined end-product or any personal agendas we may cherish of environmental and social transformation. We unleash people upon themselves and then hope.

The journey is still one of transformation. Not immediate, revelatory conversion but turning the soil, nourishing the seedling, the slow growing of an individual flower in the heart. The shape of the flower is governed by the individual, not by external, imposed dogma. We work with powerful tools – nature, emotion and inspiration – and while our work is full of laughter, light-hearted humour, mischief and strange moments, it also challenges all sorts of things.

> – but I don't know anything about nature
> (What do you need to *know* in order to *enjoy*?)

> – but I can't draw – paint – sing – write – dance
> (Yes, you can! You just have!)

> – but I don't count. I'm only a child – one person – not very bright – stupid.
> (Yes you do, we are all listening to your vision, it is part of what we are all producing. Your story is as valid and as potent as anyone else's. It is yours. Treasure it.)

But who does it? This is not work designed to preach to the converted. We work with those

• Mashs from Risley Wassail. Photo: G. MacLellan.

sensible people who do not read journals of personal change, or new-age wonder or old-age paganism. Actually, readers of all those sort of things get involved as well, but so do swarms of noisy children in inner London and noisy children in rural Yorkshire, wildlife trusts, city farms, play-schemes, families, grannies, grumpies and stray dogs.

Creeping Toad work sets out to be accessible: it does not assume previous knowledge or skills (or ever having heard of shamanism or ritual drama!). Whatever you bring we try to use but all that is asked for is enthusiasm and a readiness to jump.

Many projects revolve around community celebration and ceremony rather than 'ritual drama' – if 'drama' is often seen as something prepared and presented to an audience. Our work grows and changes as it goes, often unpredictably, 'Do not be afraid when a dragon eats your plans',* and

* Irritating phrase from Creeping Toad briefing sheets.

any final product is more often participatory than observed. You don't get away with being an 'audience' in a Toad performance!

In our culture, it feels as if most community 'ritual' marks changes (rather than provoking or empowering them as in more formal magical settings): rites of passage like coming of age, baptism, marriage and so on, community achievements – our team winning the local cup! – and seasonal change, as in harvest festivals. Some have survived from much older times without our always understanding or believing in their purpose – Soul Cakes, Bonfires, Hoddening Horses – but we still feel the importance of them and protect them for reasons that often we cannot explain. We are rarely involved with ceremonies that drive the change: seeding the furrows with blood, wassailing the orchards. Maybe personal and communal prayer is one of the few agents for change that is turned to by large numbers of people?

There are, of course, exceptions to this – some of us still weave corn-dollies from the last stook, and welcome the Dead home again at Hallowe'en, but it is important to recognize that people are still involved in rituals in the normal course of their lives. It seems to be one of those accepted truths that our society has lost its ritual 'focus' – those events that bond people together and connect them to where they live in place (ceremonies of harvest, seeding and growing) and time (respecting the ancestors, the Gods), but we need to recognize what we still have and what people still do.

People do want to find new ways of relating to their world – they keep booking Creeping Toad for a start! Looking at what people are already doing is a good start to exploring what they might want to do. Ritual gives frameworks for communities to work together and share experiences and inspirations that are accepted as both physical and spiritual. Finding the structure within familiar events gives us shapes to build new celebrations upon and gives people confidence to go back and review those familiar things again. Celebratory structure gives us keys and doors to imagination and inspiration and when those doors are opened all sorts of things spill out. Old traditions are given new impetus, new ideas are spawned from modern imaginations:

hanging prayers in a tree by a pool

a new annual procession to the well on the hill

wassailing a new orchard against all perils

wassailing any new feature for the sake of being loud and cheerful!

finding the stories that shape school and students

waking a green man to hold our hopes and dreams for this new wood

setting our dreams a-sailing down the rivers of our lives in skeletal boats

finding natural friends to support and encourage us in the world that grows around us

O, we are strong. We live and work in a land that can fill our dreams and imaginations with delight. The essence of Creeping Toad work lies in helping people find personal vision, exploring and expressing their feelings for the living world and their own place within it, breaking the isolation, a culture of separation. Connect and celebrate. 'A sense of wonder.'

Ritual and Crisis: Survival Techniques of Humans and Other Animals

Günter Berghaus

Rationalist philosophers of the eighteenth and nineteenth centuries believed that religion and ritual behaviour were typical traits of primitive societies and would disappear with the advance of civilization. However, exactly the opposite has taken place. An order that had previously been provided by the Church, by social hierarchies and political figureheads, has become eroded by capitalism. The industrial revolution led to mass migration from the countryside to the cities. It uprooted millions of people and severed their traditional bonds with nature and their ties to family and social groups. The rapid disappearance of structured living environments and the experience of alienation in the economic and social spheres provoked a growth of secular religions and new ritual practices to provide a sense of stability and equilibrium to the uprooted individual of the modern metropolis.

We can observe a continuity of this trend, if not actually an increase of ritual practices, in our secularized, postmodern and post-industrial societies. Aesthetic, social and religious rituals cater for the atomized individual of the western world, whose loss of personal security and transcendental certainties has created needs and desires that technology and secular entertainment cannot satisfy.

Theatre, which has supposedly progressed far

beyond its ritual roots, is also rediscovering that underneath the rational, word-centred discourses the embers of a ritual fire are still smouldering. The history of modernist theatre is inextricably linked to the rediscovery of ritual practices: from the Symbolist concept of a new festival culture, via the neo-primitivism of Stravinsky's *Le Sacre du Printemps*, Mary Wigman's *Hexentanz*, or Hugo Ball's *Gadji Beri Bimba*, to Artaud's reception of Balinese, Cambodian and Mexican ritualism. Nor is postmodern performance devoid of ritual elements: see, for example, the rebirth of Dionysus in Viennese Actionism, the paratheatrical journey of Jerzy Grotowski, the neo-Shamanism of Joseph Beuys, Alastair MacLennan, or Rachel Rosenthal, to name but a few.

We may find a possible explanation for this phenomenon by reviewing some of the psychological, social, anthropological and biological factors that shape ritualism as an ordering device and survival technique, particularly in times of crisis. Drawing on the hypothesis of a coevolution of genes and culture and of a constant feedback between the two, as well as neurobiological examinations of the role of rituals in regulating change, we can place contemporary ritualism in a wider framework of human evolution and interpret it as an existential need rather than a cultural choice. At the same time, it is necessary to emphasize the principal differences between the genetic

• Semana Santa procession in Seville, Spain. Photo: Berghaus

Performance Research 3(3), pp.64-73 © Routledge 1998

transmission of ritualization in the biological evolution of animals and the cultural transmission of rituals in human societies. Humans possess a unique learning capacity and complex communication systems (language, symbolic expressions, artistic creations), which allow them to develop their adaptive, formalized behaviour beyond mere ritualization and to produce complex and varied rituals, where ontogenetic learning processes outweigh phylogenetic programming (Wilson 1975; Chagnon and Irons 1979; Lopreato 1984).

RITUALIZATION AMONG ANIMALS AND THE PALAEONTOLOGY OF HUMAN RITUALISM

Rituals are a pervasive phenomenon in the animal world and have taken on a wide variety of forms, depending on the species concerned and its state of evolutionary development. Human rituals can be counted among the most complex of these, but, as palaeoanthropology reveals, a fundamental qualitative change from animal to human ritualism took place only some 60,000 to 130,000 years ago: in relative terms, at the last minute in the long day of the evolutionary development of our primate species. Or termed differently, the more primitive roots of ritualism still form the basic core and rationale behind the more sophisticated forms, which we would recognize as specifically human rituals today.

The comparative study of ritualized behaviour in the animal world has a long history and has been the key focus for many world-renowned scholars such as Tinbergen, Huxley, Lorenz, Eibl–Eibesfeld, etc. 'Ritualization' is now commonly understood by ethologists to be an adaptive mechanism for co-operation and social action in groups. It substantially increases the chances of survival in a hostile environment with limited food resources and allows co-ordination of food-gathering, complex hunting strategies, effective protection from other predators, etc. It is clearly a communicative behaviour with an ordering function, defining and facilitating the relations (1) between individual and group, and (2) between group and environment.

Animal ritualization with its stylized, exaggerated, formalized and repetitive features bears many similarities to human rituals, but there is also a key difference: biologically (genetically) programmed behaviour patterns are complemented by learned and culturally transmitted activities.

Just as animal communication developed into human language, rituals developed from simple behaviour into elaborate and complex actions. But many of the ethological functions of rituals remained active in the evolutionary process from the ape-like primates evolving in Africa some twenty million years ago via *Homo habilis* and *Homo erectus* (from about two million years to 500,000 years ago) to modern *Homo sapiens*.

Social animals, including human beings, can survive only in groups and require mechanisms that regulate their interactions, define the roles of individuals and maintain a balanced state of social relations. Groups are subject to changes caused by birth of new group members, death of leaders, etc., and these transitions require an ordering device, which facilitates the transformation of an organic system, while at the same time preserving and maintaining its integrity (Shaughnessy 1973; d'Aquili 1979).

Not only the groups but also their natural habitats are in constant flux and subject to sudden or qualitative change. One of the key functions of rituals is to prepare for, and help to cope with, these vicissitudes of nature. They serve to control instinctual reactions to the changes of seasons, environmental disasters, alterations in the demographic-geographic balance, etc. If the external change cannot be accommodated, a transformation of the system is required. The main function of rituals is to ease this transition from an old state into a new one. They serve as a medium of equilibration, providing stability in change and allowing the preservation of complex organisms.

RITUALS IN TIMES OF CRISIS

One of the key functions of ritualism is to serve as an adaptive technique of individuals and social groups faced with a situation of crisis. Ritual practices provide

> an institutionalised way of coping with existential stress, a means of support and reassurance during identity-crises. . . . Ritual is about change, and the terrors and uncertainties which surround change, but which must somehow be 'accepted into the system', both corporate and personal. It is about mankind's fear of novelty, of unstructured situations and states of flux, in which the old way is over and done away and the new one has not yet really begun.
>
> (Grainger 1974: 87 and 115)

Human life is full of such crises and periods of change, which is why rituals are so pervasive in both the private and the social world. Performative anthropology has examined a whole range of rituals and has shown how some patterns occur again and again in similar situations (Grimes 1982; V. Turner 1986; Schechner 1988; Pradier 1990). According to Victor Turner, four key stages can be discerned in the development of such rituals: (1) the breach of norm; (2) crisis; (3) redressive or remedial procedure; (4) restoration of social peace (Turner 1969, 1974, 1982). Social dramas provide a motor for social development, and the rituals attached to them ensure that the change is not destroying the dynamic order of society. Through the rituals the communities act out their collective dreams and fears, and vice versa: through the numinous quality of the symbols the rituals can act as formative agents in the creation and sustaining of communities.

Effective participation in ritual as an adult requires the learning of ritual practices in the early phases of life. Freud has posited a structural parallel between the patterns of development of the individual and those of the whole human race. The entry into the world is the first major crisis in the life of each individual; adapting the demands of the pleasure principle to the requirements of the reality principle leads to whole series of further crises. As a result, the adult psyche is, under the best circumstances, a balance between an infinite number of potential crises. Through unusual pressure from outside, the balance can be overturned and the crisis may erupt again. Jung stresses that the layers of human culture are extremely thin in comparison with the basic store of the primitive psyche (Jung 1964: 12). Human civilization is, psychologically speaking, still in its infant years. In a crisis situation, the individual, overwhelmed by the chaos, relives the experience of impotence as a young child and regresses to primary instinctual behaviour: ritual action.

Rituals and their symbols are a reflection of the collective subconscious. The desires and anxieties are also objectified in other forms, e.g. dreams, myths, fairy-tales. But in rituals they are acted upon. Rituals regularly employ practices that have a strong neurophysiological effect on the brain (e.g. dancing, drumming, auto-suggestion, hypnosis, drugs, etc.). Consequently, rituals lead to trance or possession states, which allow the individual to break through the normal state of consciousness and go through a cathartic experience that serves as a safety valve releasing the psychic tensions that have accumulated in response to the crisis (Scheff 1979; d'Aquili 1979; Csordas 1994; Laderman and Roseman 1996). Rituals transform libidinal energy, which otherwise might prove harmful to individual and society (Jung 1960). In the end, ritual performances produce a new equilibrium in the psychic household of both group and individual.

REVIVAL OF RITUALISM AND THE *FIN-DE-MILLENIUM ZEITGEIST*

The rapid changes brought about by the industrial revolution released the human being from the bonds of tradition, social hierarchies and natural environments. The experience of alienation and atomization in an unfolding capitalist society put the modern individual into a chronic state of crisis. The natural reaction to this insecurity and the disappearance of binding networks was the growth of secular religions and ritual practices. Examples for the early modern period are political mass movements, national ceremonies, communal rites, cultural group activities, new religious movements, etc. (Moore and Myerhoff 1977; Berghaus 1996).

Many of the fundamental traits of modern society persist in the postmodern period and have been supplemented by other, equally debilitating, features. More than ever before, the human being is living a fragmented, isolated and insecure existence. Neither tradition nor habit, neither social position nor nature, serve any longer as determinants of human action. Post-traditional society no longer operates with models that were binding in the past. There are no longer generally accepted value systems. The individual is free of communal restraint, but also of communal support. Increased mobility has caused the break-up of biological family networks and parent–child relationships. Marriage is no longer a social institution. Apartments for single occupants have replaced communal housing. As a result, most forms of traditional social cohesion have vanished, and the attainment of autonomy and self-fulfilment has led to life in a solipsistic vacuum.

Nothing is obligatory, and an immense range of options gives the individual the choice of modelling his/her own identity. But a world no longer attached to the binding forces of nature and the obligations to society is also unstable and insecure. In the early modern era, most people had a clear sense of past and future: the past meant social cohesion and a well-defined place in the physical environment; the future promised progressive release from the ties of tradition and habitat. But now, belief in such linear development has been shattered. Many of the problems that had been suppressed by the modern mentality are coming to haunt us, especially the destruction of the environment, the rise of anti-social behaviour, the loss of meaning and purpose in life. The euphoria of new technologies is waning, because they have solved few of the human problems and created many new ones.

At the end of the twentieth century, people react to the crisis of postmodernity by searching for a

• Handfasting (wedding) ceremony at a holy altar in Avebury. Photo: Berghaus

spiritual dimension in life. Christianity is being superseded by an array of new gods catering for new needs and desires. The phenomenon is in many ways similar to developments in response to the first industrial revolution, when theosophy and spiritualism influenced modernist art and experimental theatre. The counter-cultures of hippies, ecologists, eastern transcendentalists, etc., have contributed markedly to contemporary ritualism as a popular, romantic religion of the New Age. In a copious volume assessing 'the religious situation' in the 1960s, the philosopher Huston Smith arrived at the conclusion that 'institutionalized religion is losing its influence in certain areas of life where its presence used to be more evident. But institutionalized religion isn't all of religion, and the fact that the sacred is withdrawing from certain spheres doesn't mean it isn't moving into others' (Smith 1968: 599).

People disillusioned with mainstream religions seek new spiritual paths. It appears that the secularization of religion goes hand in hand with the spiritualization of ecological concerns. Earth religions, Nature worship and eco-spirituality are fast developing into the new religion of the twenty-first century. Peter Beyer has examined the burgeoning of religious environmentalism and its accompanying theo-ecological literature and has identified this as the most significant new religion of the global metropolis (Beyer 1994).

However, the trend is still competing with a vast array of cults and religious sects, which have emerged in the last quarter of the twentieth century (Needleman and Baker 1978; Robbins 1988; Hardman and Harvey 1995; York 1995; Heelas 1996). A large and still expanding spiritual supermarket is catering for the postmodern individual. People flock to ceremonial gatherings and ritualistic events in search of the numinous. Institutional religions are in a state of decline, crisis, or collapse. The functional breakdown of the Church has led to the emergence of a wide array of 'churches', where ritualism forms a core feature and serves as a basis for a reconstituted community and spirituality.

New Age and neo-pagan groups are among the most successful responses to the spiritual crisis of postmodernity. Both are concerned with healing and rebuilding a holistic culture, both stress self-transcending or self-actualizing techniques, both search for authenticity, identity and experience rather than dogma. Both cater predominantly for a population of upper middle-class extraction, who have become disillusioned with the myths of scientific progress, materialist consumer culture, political parties and religious orthodoxy. Tanya Luhrman in an article on 'Modern magic' found that most people joining alternative religious groups come from comparatively high socio-economic strata of society, are educated and enjoy successful careers as civil servants, businessmen, or computer analysts (Luhrman 1988). Her survey showed that ritual practices are at the centre of their activities, and although they choose mythic figures from Greek, Egyptian, Celtic, or Christian religions as their deities, they principally pursue a spiritual nature religion. Paul Heelas's study also revealed that the New Age is strongly associated with the middle to upper-middle professional classes (Heelas 1996: 121, 195). No reliable figures are currently available on the exploding neo-pagan movement, but impressionistic studies by a variety of authors indicate that technicians/scientists, civil servants, teachers and writers predominate, with income less significant than education.

A common feature of all those new religious movements is that they form part of a much wider therapy market, covering psychological, spiritual and medical practices. A wide variety of 'healers' offer their services to impatient individualists who enjoy successful professional careers, but are in need of a 'spiritual fix'. Concern with personal health produces a proliferation not only of stress clinics and trim gyms, but also of centres for alternative medicine or psychotherapy, religious 'self-actualization' through spiritual or occult practices. Most of these organizations are geared towards non-traditional 'bright-collar workers' dissatisfied with their vacuous existence and thoroughly rationalized life- and work-spheres. For them, healing rituals promise a 'symbolic creation and socialization of a new way of viewing the self in

• Ritual gathering at Avebury to celebrate the annual death and rebirth of the Sun God and his fertile relationship with the Earth Goddess. Photo: Berghaus

relation to the world' and produce 'a powerful sense of connectedness with others and with the natural environment' (McGuire 1989: 64).

A number of reports emphasize the paramount significance of ritual for the creation or the reinforcement of community feeling, social bonding, group solidarity and commitment to the belief system (Kanter 1972; Needleman and Baker 1978; Robbins 1988). Yet, it is ironic that although the desire for social cohesion fuels much of the ritualism in New Age and neo-pagan groups, it is essentially an individualistic pick-and-choose mentality that leads to the formation of the groups. A blend of Christian/Jewish, oriental and pagan mysticism is liberally laced with shots of Native American, Australian, or African trance techniques. Not being organically grown, these groups suffer from instability and sectarian division. Disaffiliation, denomination-switching, 'exiting', etc., are typical traits of the market consumerism in

new-religious, magical and occult circles. Detailed examination of the religious convictions of these alternative movements reveals a most heterogeneous hotchpotch of beliefs, due to a rejection of hierarchical structures, authorities and doctrines. Creeds are rather incidental in comparison with the paramount importance of ritual practices. What matters is not what is believed, but what is done. The common denominator is what Greenley observed in the 1960s hippy movement, namely 'an attempt to reassert meaningful community in ecstasy in a rationalistic hyperorganized world' (Greenley 1985: 160). Margot Adler's examination of ritualistic practises in the neo-pagan movement arrives at a similar conclusion, namely that their main purpose is 'to end, for a time, our sense of human alienation from nature and from each other' (Adler 1986: 162).

To achieve this aim, cult leaders employ the tried-and-tested method of 'inventing a tradition'.

What John Toland and Henry Hurle did to druidry, Edward Williams to the eisteddfod, Gerald Gardner and Alexander Sanders to Wicca, Aleister Crowley to the Golden Dawn, etc., has become a common practice in the new religious movements (Green 1997). 'Neo-pagans, generally, see themselves as modern-day heirs to the ancient mystery traditions of Egypt, Crete, Eleusis, and so on' (Adler 1986: 11). They adapt the old to the new and make religious practices from East and West conform with contemporary needs. Nostalgia for a past which represents identity, roots, social cohesion, and ecological balance produces rituals and ceremonies that are pure fake and fantasy. As one leading druid confessed: 'We know so little about what Druids got up to in the past that we are free to concoct just about anything and call it Druidry today' (Shallcrass 1995: 66).

The same could be said about a whole range of similar movements, usually characterized by the epithet 'neo-'. People drawn to their cult centres are not seriously interested in what Druids, Shamans, witches, medicinemen, etc., were actually up to. What matters is the *idea* of reviving an ancient practice and of rebuilding the social network which lay at its basis. Such utopian and palingenetic thinking has characterized many millenarians of the past; what seems to characterize the secular religions of this current *fin-de-millenium* is their performative, para-theatrical nature.

This creative use of ritual practices has become common in the postmodern age (Gerholm 1988). The cosmopolitan city dweller is no longer anchored in *one* system of cultural transmission and therefore has no use for (and often does not understand the meaning and purpose of) traditional rituals. This adds weight to Victor Turner's theory of the liminal-liminoid, anti-structural, playful character of human ritualism, which goes beyond the biogenetic foundation of animal ritualization (Turner 1982, 1986), and Schechner's view: 'The future of ritual is the continued encounter between imagination and memory' (Schechner 1993: 263).

In the theatre, of course, such a plundering of the past in order to satisfy contemporary tastes is entirely acceptable, and not only in our postmodern world. The modernist followers of the cults of Isis, Mithras, Orpheus, or Dionysus contributed little to our understanding of ancient mystery religions, but they helped to overcome the realist mode of late nineteenth-century theatre. Many of the great reformers of twentieth-century theatre had only superficial knowledge and understanding of the ancient and often non-European traditions which inspired their thinking. Yet, and possibly because of it, the effect of the *imagined* past was profound.

The theatrical leaders and masters of the 1960s and 1970s were probably more serious in their studies. Grotowski, Barba, Schechner, Brook, etc., did know what they were talking about. But what people come into contact with is predominantly the work of their epigones and acolytes. For them, the *idea* of a holistic tradition is the key attraction, but the rigour and dedication this requires are tacitly ignored. They form associations, where communal living and working practices are the norm, and where ritual techniques have replaced conventional rehearsal methods. These theatre communes offer a home to distressed urban souls much in the same manner as Monte Verità, Laban's dance farms, or Copeau's Burgundy retreat did in the early part of this century. In fact, they are little more than a profane counterpart to the modern cult centres of Hara Krishnas, Moonies, Wiccans, or Nichiren Shoshus, to which the non-theatrically inclined redemption seekers of our current era feel attracted.

SUMMARY

Although rituals are a common feature of all social organisms and an essential tool of human survival, a particular intensity of ritualism can be observed in periods of crisis. The cyclical nature of capitalism has produced three major crisis periods in western history: the late nineteenth century; the years after the First World War; the end of the millennium. From the plethora of rituals invoked to counteract the effects of crisis a few particularly conspicuous practices can be cited: spiritualism, occultism, political consociation, palingenetic mass movements, fascism, Christian fundamentalism,

• Celebration of the 'Children of Aunt Neva' (*Crianças de Tia Neve*) in Vale do Amanhecea outside the Brazilian capital Brasilia. Most members of this New Age sect are of upper-middle-class background and work as civil servants in the state bureaucracy. Their ceremonies are a concoction of ancient mystery cults and science fiction soap operas, held in the open air or in churches modelled on Portuguese colonial architecture and Indio buildings. Photo: Berghaus

neo-paganism, eco-spirituality. However, prevailing conditions of alienation in an economic, social and psychological sense produce a protracted, chronic loss of identity, which results in a continuous undercurrent of ritual practices to counteract this debilitating feature of all industrial societies. This accounts for a certain continuity of ritual practices in capitalist, urban societies.

Similar developments can be observed in the art world, where aesthetic rituals have always played an important role, but never more so than in periods of crisis. Well-known examples of this are the rise of theatre festivals in late nineteenth-century Europe; the body culture, youth movements and Expressionist cult theatres of the 1910s; neo-primitivism and the growth of theatre collectives in the 1920s; and a wide spectrum of ritual art performances outside conventional theatre spaces in the last quarter of this century.

REFERENCES

Adler, Margot (1986) *Drawing down the Moon: Witches, Druids, Goddess-Worshippers, and Other Pagans in America Today*, Boston, MA: Beacon Press.

Berghaus, Günter (1996) 'The ritual core of fascist theatre: an anthropological perspective', in Günter Berghaus (ed.) *Fascism and Theatre*, Oxford: Berghahn Books.

Beyer, Peter (1994) *Religion and Globalization*, London: Sage.

Chagnon, N. A. and Irons, W. (eds) (1979) *Evolutionary Biology and Human Social Behavior: An Anthropological Perspective*, North Scituate, MA: Duxbury Press.

Csordas, Thomas J. (1994) *The Sacred Self: A Cultural Phenomenology of Charismatic Healing*, Berkeley: University of California Press.

d'Aquili, Eugene G. *et al.* (eds) (1979) *The Spectrum of Ritual: A Biogenetic Structural Analysis*, New York: Columbia University Press.

Eibl-Eibesfeld, Irenäus (1970) *Ethology: The Biology of Behaviour*, New York: Holt, Rinehart & Winston.

Gerholm, Tomas (1988) 'On ritual: a postmodernist view', *Ethnos* 53: 190–203.

Grainger, Roger (1974) *The Language of Rite*, London: Darton, Longman & Todd.

Green, Miranda J. (1997) *Exploring the World of Druids*, London: Thames & Hudson.

Greenley, Andrew M. (1985) *Unsecular Man: The Persistence of Religion*, 2nd edn, New York: Schocken.

Grimes, Ronald L. (1982) *Beginnings in Ritual Studies*, Lanham, MD: University Press of America.

Hardman, C. and Harvey, G. (eds) (1995) *Paganism Today*, London: Thorson.

Heelas, Paul (1996) *The New Age Movement*, Oxford: Blackwell.

Huxley, Julian (ed.) (1966) 'A discussion on ritualization of behaviour in animals and men', in *Philosophical Transactions of the Royal Society of London*, series B, 251: 247–526.

Jung, C. G. (1960) 'On psychic energy', in *Collected Works*, Vol. 8, London: Routledge & Kegan Paul.

Jung, C. G. (1964) 'The role of the unconscious', in *Collected Works*, Vol. 10, London: Routledge & Kegan Paul.

Kanter, Rosabeth M. (1988) *Commitment and Community: Communes and Utopias in Sociological Perspective*, Cambridge, MA: Harvard University Press.

Laderman, Carol and Roseman, Marine (eds) (1996) *The Performance of Healing*, New York: Routledge.

Lopreato, Joseph (1984) *Human Nature and Biocultural Evolution*, Boston, MA: Allen & Unwin.

Luhrman, Tanya M. (1988) 'Modern magic', *Religion Today* 5(1–2): 1–3.

McGuire, Meredith B. (1989) 'The new spirituality: healing rituals hit the suburbs', *Psychology Today* (Jan.–Feb.): 57–64.

Moore, Sally F. and Myerhoff, Barbara G. (1977) *Secular Ritual*, Assen: Van Gorcum.

Needleman, Jacob and Baker, George (eds) (1978) *Understanding the New Religions*, New York: Seabury.

Pradier, Jean-Marie (1990) 'Towards a biological theory of the body in performance', *New Theatre Quarterly* 21: 86–98.

Robbins, Thomas (1988) *Cults, Converts and Charisma: The Sociology of New Religions*, London: Sage.

Schechner, Richard (1988) *Performance Theory*, London: Routledge.

Schechner, Richard (1993) *The Future of Ritual: Writings on Culture and Performance*, London: Routledge.

Scheff, Thomas J. (1979) *Catharsis in Healing, Ritual and Drama*, Berkeley: University of California Press.

Shallcrass, Philip (1995) 'Druidry today', in Charlotte Hardman and Graham Harvey (eds) *Paganism Today*, London: Thorson, 65–80.

Shaughnessy, James D. (ed.) (1973) *The Roots of Ritual*, Grand Rapids, MI: Eerdmans.

Smith, Huston (1968) 'Secularization of the sacred: the contemporary scene', in Donald R. Cutler (ed.) *The Religious Situation: 1968*, Boston, MA: Beacon Press, 583–600.

Turner, Victor (1969) *The Ritual Process*, London: Routledge & Kegan Paul.

Turner, Victor (1974) *Dramas, Fields and Metaphors*, Ithaca, NY: Cornell University Press.

Turner, Victor (1982) *From Ritual to Theatre*, New York: PAJ Publications.

Turner, Victor (1986) *The Anthropology of Performance*, New York: PAJ Publications.

Wallis, Roy (1984) *The Elementary Forms of the New Religious Life*, London: Routledge & Kegan Paul.

Wilson, Edward O. (1975) *Sociobiology: The New Synthesis*, Cambridge, MA: Belknap Press.

York, Michael (1995) *The Emerging Network: A Sociology of the New Age and Neo-Pagan Movements*, Lanham, ML: Rowman & Littlefield.

GRACE LAU

Photographers are frequently accepted solely in their role of documenting events, of recording 'real life'. The "real life" image is subsequently either consumed by an avid audience, or critically deconstructed by photo-historians and academics, or, in some cases, iconized to represent a significant moment in history. In all cases, though, it is the product – the photograph – that is significant. The process by which the photograph came to be made is too frequently disregarded as irrelevant.

The Camera as Catalyst:

In my photographic practice I am acutely aware of my role as photographer, of the effect my camera has as catalyst in the "real life" performance that is acted out in front of the lens. Having worked as an independent photographer for Skin Two magazine since its inception over ten years ago, I have become acquainted with a great many people engaged in S/M activities. S/M rituals are masquerades with structured role-playing according to fixed rules. Highly intricate codes and symbolic forms of communication connect the players in their performances, their use of costumes, props and theatrical environments.

Photography as a Form of Ritual Theatre

The stage on which the ritual is performed is, typically, a home-made dungeon in the suburbs. Converted cellars or lofts serve as "playrooms", where the principal roles of the dominant maîtresse (or, in fewer cases, master) and the submissive "slave" are acted out. There are numerous variations to this basic formula of an "adult wonderland"; the main qualifications required from the actors are imagination and control.

When photography comes into play, a further dimension is added. I, as photographer, participate in the ritual, not only as actor, but also as director, voyeur and, most important of all, facilitator. It has taken me over ten years to learn my role and to perform my "script" in a manner that is appropriate to the process of creating the final product, the photograph. My performance has several functions. The primary one is to heighten the tension of the play by my presence as voyeur. This role encourages the ritual to evolve along its own course and, at the same time, directs some of the action. The mechanical recording of the camera lens adds further impetus to the main actors' fantasy game, accelerates the pace or slows it down. The camera acts as a catalyst in this elaborately constructed fantasy world. My role is one of silent but conspicuous complicity. I have to ensure that the submissive partner is aware of my presence through the sound of the shutter release, timed to accentuate the ritual at crucial moments. Although the "sub" cannot see me, he needs to know that I am recording his experience, that I am part of his fantasy, that I am witness to his pain. The photograph prints provide evidence, or proof, of the performance for retrospective consumption.

S/M is a ritual performed without prior rehearsals, but develops according to pre-arranged rules, which orchestrate the actions of three players with equally important parts. Total control and concentration are essential throughout the performance. There is a full and intimate agreement between the three of us.

The sub-text to this ritual exists in the form of another masquerade. Although the client appears submissively grateful, he has paid for the service of the dominatrix and of the photographer. So, who is wielding true power?

I have not fully resolved the question.

Maṇḍala Meaning and Method

Ritual Delineation of Sacred Space in Tantric Buddhism

Martin J. Boord

In the allegorical system of the Vajrayāna, a *maṇḍala* is the dwelling place of sacred wisdom, the abode of Buddhahood represented as a palace of gods. Buddhist tantric texts and their commentaries describe a countless number of *maṇḍala*, of both peaceful and wrathful types, together with a complex cycle of inner meditations known as '*yoga* of the steps of generation' in which these palaces are meditatively constructed from philosophic emptiness by the transformation of seed-syllables and symbolic implements, etc. Accompanying these generation stage meditations are a number of elaborate and demanding rituals that dramatize the meditations with arcane theatre. These may take several days to perform, with many elements of the performance being repeated again and again, so the outline presented here is merely the briefest sketch of such activities.

PREPARATION OF THE SITE

The first essential is to choose an especially auspicious environment in which to perform the rite. According to ancient Indian tradition, the sign that the four great elements *(mahābhūta)* are stable and in harmony in any place is for an open expanse like a watery *(ap)* lake to be seen in the east, a flat-topped hill of earth *(pṛthivī)* seen in the south, a pointed hill like flames *(tejas)* seen in the west and folded ridges like billowing clouds of wind *(vāyu)* seen in the shape of the mountains to the north.

Signs of the instability of the elements, on the other hand, are visible when a curved row of sharply pointed mountain peaks juts up in the formation known as 'fangs of the lord of death', denoting the hostility of the sky, or when holes are to be seen in rocks, showing that the rocks are hostile, or when the waving of a solitary clump of trees acts like a beckoning hand, displaying the enmity of wood. Such places may prove counter-productive to the purpose of one's practice and thus the wise do not linger in them long.

Sites in which mischievous spirits such as *yakṣa* and *rākṣasa* have made their abodes should also be avoided as far as it is possible to do so. Such sites are recognized by identifying on the ground the clawmarks of these demons and by the presence there of violently spilled blood. The landscape in those places will also exhibit the forms of terrible sharp weapons and there will be burnt cinders, deep cracks and potholes, and many poisonous biting insects in the earth. The moans of ghosts and so on will be audible at the places where two pathways cross and one may see the laughter of malicious *nāga* in the patterns made by the torrents of water swirling in the streams. Furthermore, it should also be kept in mind that goblins *(bhūta)* like to make their dwelling in neglected and abandoned shrines. One should keep away from all such places.

• Photos: Martin Brauen.

Performance Research 3(3), pp.78-84 © Routledge 1998

REQUESTING FROM THE LOCAL SPIRITS PERMISSION TO USE THE SITE

Then one prays for success and makes offerings of food and drink and other material necessities to the worldly spirits in order to pacify their hostility.

> Oh, you gods and demigods,
> All you powerful serpent deities
>   and other forms of demon,
> Whatever spirits there may be who dwell
>   within this place –
> With one knee placed upon the ground
> I press my palms together and invite you here.
> May you rejoice in the success of this rite!

And the *mantra*: OM Eat, eat, all you hosts of spirits. Accept this *bali* offering, protect this great occasion (*samaya*) and grant me all success. Eat, drink and savour as much as you like. Do not transgress against me! Act as my helpers in all ways and bring about an increase in perfect happiness! HŪṀ HŪṀ HŪṀ PHAṬ SVĀHĀ.

MAKING PAYMENT BY LINING THE ARMPIT OF THE 'LORD OF THE SOIL' (*KṢITIPATI*)

The selected site should be marked out as a square, one side for each of the four seasons, aligned to the four cardinal points of the compass and subdivided into eighty-one smaller squares. Dwelling within this 'site of supreme repose' is the great chthonic *kṣitipati* in the form of a mighty serpent (*mahoraga*) representing the eight *nāga* kings: his head is empowered by the *nāga* king Ananta, his ears by Padma and his neck by Takṣaka. Upon his shoulders he carries Mahāpadma and in his heart Vāsuki Śaṅkhapāla makes up his navel, Karkoṭaka his genitals and Kulika resides in his tail.

As the sun makes its annual circuit of the twelve signs of the zodiac, the whole bodily alignment of the *mahoraga* slowly swings around in a clockwise direction beneath the ground. By careful calculation, one must discern his position and mark out

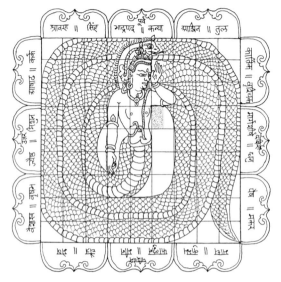

• The chthonic serpent basking on the site of supreme repose. To pay for use of the site, precious gifts should be buried within the shaded area beneath his armpit

the place of his armpit. One then digs a hole in that position, to a depth of at least 1 cubit, and offerings of precious gems and grain, etc., should be buried within it as gifts. The texts warn that if the calculations are incorrect and the serpent is inadvertently struck on the head while one is digging into the soil, one's wife and children will die for the offence. If the serpent is wounded in heart or belly, one's wealth, prosperity and enjoyments will vanish. Sickness will follow if the serpent be struck on the anus and death if he be pierced through the tail. If he be struck on 'the knee', prolonged absences from home will result. Furthermore, all the auspicious good fortune which may be expected to follow the presentation of gifts to the front of the serpent will undoubtedly disappear if the offering pit is dug behind his back. For these reasons, therefore, care should be exercised in establishing the serpent's position beneath the soil.

The ground should again be made good except that any sharp stones, thorns, or other inauspicious debris which had been taken out when the hole was dug, should not be replaced.

ESTABLISHING THE CIRCLE OF PROTECTION (*RAKṢĀCAKRA*)

One should then fix a boundary around the sacred enclosure by nailing it down with a *vajra* spike. This may be accomplished with a hand gesture (*mudrā*), or actual wooden spikes may be used. These *vajra* nails are to be implanted in ten directions around the outer perimeter of the chosen site. While implanting them, one imagines establishing there fierce guardians whose function it is to protect the site from invasion by external troubles. Reciting a *mantra* such as OṀ VAJRAKĪLI KĪLAYA MAHĀYAKṢA KĀLARŪPA SARVAVIGHNĀN BANDHA BANDHA HŪṀ PHAṬ, 'OṀ Adamantine spike, you must nail down! Great *yakṣa*, black in form, fix! Fix all obstacles! HŪṀ PHAṬ', one should nail down all obstructors with the fierce blows of a *vajra* hammer and think that they become immovable.

ASKING FOR THE BLESSING OF PRTHIVĪ, GODDESS OF THE EARTH

Next the *yogin* forms a small mound of earth in the centre of the chosen site and worships it as the actual manifestation of the goddess herself. This is done in accordance with the usual procedure of visualizing her presence within the mound, and then activating this presence by invoking her wisdom essence from the sky to merge with the visualized form. The *yogin* then recalls the way in which she bore witness to the enlightenment of the Buddha Śākyamuni (*Lalitavistara* XXI, 88):

> This earth, the support of all beings, is impartial,
> Equally disposed towards everything
> Be it animate or inanimate.
> She is my judge that in me there is no deceit.
> May she testify here as my witness!

The goddess is then praised and presented with offerings, and her permission is requested for the construction of the *maṇḍala*:

> OṀ Come, come, oh great goddess of earth,
> Mother of the world.
> You who are replete with jewels
> And adorned with divine ornaments.
>
> You whose necklace and anklets tinkle
> In the service of Vajrasattva –
> Having accepted this libation of water
> May you fulfil the rites of the *maṇḍala*.
> HRĪṂ HĪ HĪ HĪ HĪ HAṀ SVĀHĀ.

The ground is then once more made smooth and level. The small mound of earth in which Pṛthivī has temporarily taken her abode is carefully removed to an elevated place nearby which overlooks the site and from where she can act as witness to the rite. The level ground is now sprinkled with perfume and flowers in order to sanctify it for the manifestation of the *maṇḍala*.

The chosen site must be levelled off and tamped down to make it firm and hard. It is then plastered with the five sacred products of the cow mixed with perfume. When it is dry, it should once again be sprinkled with sanctified scented water as the master recites 'OṀ Homage to the all-pervading pure nature of the Buddhas everywhere, unequalled, as vast as space, purifying the *dharmadhātu*. Praise!'

• Visualizing the divine palace in the sky, its plan is drawn out upon the ground with a length of chalk-covered string and the site is purified with scented water

The *yogin* then appropriates the *maṇḍala*-holding earth by generating himself as the deity seated in the very centre of the site. Arising, he dances around the site with *vajra*-steps in order to protect and stabilize the earth itself. Imagining the sole of each foot to be transformed into a single-pronged *vajra* by the sound of the syllable HŪM, the *yogin* moves across the site in such a way as to trace the figure of a single-pronged *vajra* upon the ground. He should then repeat the process whilst visualizing a three-pronged *vajra*. Once more he dances with the image of a five-pronged *vajra* in his mind, and then again, with the soles of his feet in the form of a *viśvavajra*, he dances the form of a *viśvavajra* upon the ground. With firm divine pride, the *yogin* rejoices, offers prayers and praises, and vividly contemplates the *maṇḍala* that is to be constructed.

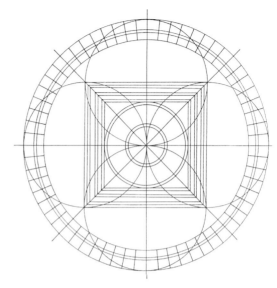

• A stage in the unfolding of the maṇḍala plan

MARKING OUT THE GROUND WITH STRING

Clearly imagining the divine palace of the gods in the sky, one should draw its outline as a plan upon the ground by marking out the area with a length of string, commonly refered to as the 'adamantine thread' (*vajrasūtra*), covered in powdered chalk. By holding the two ends of this piece of string and pulling it taut, one can strike a neat straight line by tweaking the string. The plucked cord will deposit chalk dust along its length and this is the 'working' or *karma* line. Circles can also be inscribed by holding one end of the string at the centre of the circle and moving around this with the required length of string held taut.

When one has finished drawing the white chalk lines that mark out clearly the intended form of the *maṇḍala*, these lines of activity *(karma)* must be blessed with knowledge *(jñāna)*.

As it is said:

> The five Buddhas, the great kings,
> Are the string with which the *vajra maṇḍala* is laid out.
> This indeed is the most wonderful secret
> Of all the Buddhas.

This string is made up of twenty-five threads. Vairocana is the patriarch of the Tathāgata family and his *maṇḍala* is spun of five threads, of which the chief one is white. Akṣobhya's *maṇḍala* of the Vajra family has five threads, of which the chief is blue. Ratnasambhava's Gem family has a yellow thread as its ruler and the Lotus family of Amitābha is governed by red. The five threads of the Activity family of Amoghasiddhi have a green thread as the foremost among them and, when these five *maṇḍala* are spun together, there results the wisdom thread (*jñānasūtra*) of twenty-five strands in five different colours. This is the string which is used to pitch the knowledge lines in the sky which bless the activity lines on the ground. It is not covered with chalk, should not be permitted to touch the ground and it leaves no mark. Its function is to empower the *maṇḍala* of relative form with the nature of the absolute truth of all the Buddhas.

LAYING DOWN THE COLOURED POWDERS

Powdered colours of rare and exotic pigments are then carefully manipulated into place by allowing them to dribble in a fine line from the narrow opening of a tapered copper funnel. This is controlled by the gentle vibrations set up in the funnel by means of a serrated ridge along its uppermost edge which one strokes with a small flat stick. As each tiny speck of coloured powder alights upon the consecrated ground, the *yogin* must have the firm conviction that another Buddha has descended from the sky in order to become manifest in the very fabric of the drawn *maṇḍala*. In this way the entire structure is made of Buddhas and has enlightenment as its very essence.

Radiating with five primary colours and countless secondary hues, the *maṇḍala* palace is blue, white, yellow, red and green. These colours are assigned to the centre and the four cardinal directions of the *maṇḍala* where they consolidate a whole range of associations. In each direction stands a Buddha as the utterly purified embodiment of one of the five aggregates (*skandha*) of human experience and whose primordial wisdom is said to be nothing other than the transformation of a root poison (*kleśa*) of the unenlightened mind.

In the centre of the floor of the palace stands the blue dais of the lord of the *maṇḍala*. It is the colour of deepest space and yet shines with a radiant intensity that is awe-inspiring and profoundly blissful as it transforms the aggregate of consciousness (*vijñānaskandha*) into the actuality of the greatly compassionate Vairocana. The beautiful blue light-rays that emanate from the very centre of this *maṇḍala* spread out to pervade the entire universe and they bless it by granting all beings the opportunity to gain the state of Buddhahood with the wisdom which has the pure nature of the sphere of fundamental reality (*dharmadhātuviśuddhijñāna*). They liberate the mind from ignorance and invite all beings to enter the *maṇḍala* of highest knowledge.

The pure white rays that radiate from the east pacify the sickness and troubles that have arisen in the world due to the misguided behaviour of its inhabitants. They still the ferociously devastating tidal waves of aggression, bitterness, resentment, hatred and fear, so that a tranquil lake is formed. Upon the calm surface of the waters of this lake, the clarity of the mirror-like wisdom (*ādarśajñāna*) dawns and the aggregate of form (*rūpaskandha*)

arises as the body of the Buddha Akṣobhya. Those who have access to this wonderful reservoir can use it gently to moisten and soothe the pain of all beings scorched in the hell of vicious torment (anger) with unending tears of great compassion and the milk of human kindness.

The rays of golden yellow that shine from the south enrich the earth and encourage all beings in the development of their own inherent good qualities. Overturning the suffocating false pride of ego's arrogance, these rays transform the aggregate of feeling (*vedanāskandha*) into the Buddha Ratnasambhava having the wisdom of fundamental equality (*samatājñāna*) which recognises the sameness of self and others. It also recognizes all objects and their causes and conditions as being equal due to their sharing the nature of *śūnyatā*. Material generosity and emotional tolerance open the doors to an immense storehouse of the treasures of mutual understanding and togetherness so that

• Photo: Martin Brauen

wealth and precious spiritual experience grow stable and firm. Genuine communication is made possible by the natural empathy that results from this primordial wisdom of impartiality through which the *yogin* is enabled to renounce all prejudice. Thus he comes to accept that the hopes and fears of all beings render them equal in suffering the impersonal vicissitudes of *saṃsāra*. With increased joy the *yogin* is empowered to offer unbiased assistance to all sentient beings, knowing that the seed of Buddhahood lies ready to unfold in every single one. Ultimately, the yogic faculty of 'one taste' *(ekarasa)* is achieved in the southern quarter of the *maṇḍala* through knowledge of the single value of all illusory phenomena.

From the western quarter of the *maṇḍala*, a powerful red light with the colour of blood and fire overpowers and transforms the sins of lust and greed. The mind of attachment that desires to grasp and possess the particular objects of its fantasy is cut loose, liberated as the wisdom that recognizes the special potential for benefit in every situation. This clear discriminating wisdom *(pratyavekṣaṇjñāna)* recognizes the unique value of every object and circumstance, and it complements (but does not contradict) the wisdom light of the south that knows the way in which all things are the same. This wisdom which sees how things are uniquely different is the energy of desire totally purified of selfishness and thus freed to act for the benefit of others. With the blessings of this red light from the west, the aggregate of perceptions *(samjñāskandha)* arises as

the Buddha Amitābha and an ultimate feeling of all-pervading bliss is experienced.

The light that radiates from the north is green. It swirls and billows and penetrates throughout the universe in the manner of air. It counteracts the wind of jealousy that so easily blows the *yogin* off course, and it destroys the accumulations of aeons of evil *karma* by uncompromising acts of altruistic endeavour. This green light carries with it primordial knowledge of the appropriate activity to deal with whatever arises *(kṛtyānuṣṭhānajñāna)*. Within its radiance the Buddha Amoghasiddhi is revealed as the transformation of the aggregate of creative will *(saṃskāraskandha)*. It is energetic and strong with a stamina that perseveres and endures through any situation, accomplishing great goals until all beings have gained entry to the pure *maṇḍala* from which it emanates.

One then draws rings of lotus-petals, *vajra* and fire around the *maṇḍala*, all the while honouring it with banners and music and dance and song. When the deities are all present in the *maṇḍala*, the *yogin* makes copious offerings of water for bathing the feet and rinsing the mouth, and they are offered flowers, incense, butter-lamps, perfume, delicious food and drink, delightful music, soft clothes, precious jewels, flags, parasols and all manner of other wonderful items. The deities are praised and requested to maintain a continuous presence in the *maṇḍala* throughout the ensuing rituals of its utilization.

When all is over, the deities are dismissed back to their own abodes with dance gestures and music. VAJRA MUḤ.

When the *maṇḍala* has been utilized for its intended purpose, the powders are swept up and a great procession accompanies them as they are carried in a bejewelled golden urn to the nearest spring, river, or lake in order to be entrusted to the care of local *nāga*.

Grotowski's Art as Vehicle: the Invention of an Esoteric Tradition

Lisa Wolford

In a recent text, Georges Banu describes director and performance theorist Jerzy Grotowski as 'the Great Absent Figure' at the end of the twentieth-century theatre history (1996: 245). Referring to Grotowski's decision to stop creating public performances after the première of the Laboratory Theatre's production of *Apocalypsis cum figuris* in 1968, Banu suggests that Grotowski's abscence, his choice to pursue his ongoing work in a relatively private context, can be read as a radical critique of contemporary structures of theatre production (1996: 243).

While I would not wish to deny the significance of Grotowski's accomplishments as a stage director or the extent of his influence on contemporary performance, I would suggest that Banu's formulation is somewhat misleading insofar as it (over)emphasizes the centrality of theatre as a defining element in evaluating the significance of Grotowski's ongoing lifework. Despite his significant contributions to twentieth-century performance and actor-training, Grotowski is not so much a person of the theatre as one whose interests, for a certain period of time, passed through theatre, but always with an orientation toward elsewhere. Grotowski's goal, as Richard Schechner recently observed, is and has always been to approach 'a definite and particular kind of spiritual knowledge' (1997: 463), using performance as a framework, a necessary structure for the performer's inner search.

Indeed, Grotowski relates that it was almost by chance that he chose a career in theatre at all. When the time arrived for him to enroll for university studies, he considered three different fields which he thought offered more or less equal opportunities to pursue his primary interests with relative freedom in the repressive atmosphere of communist Poland: Sanskrit studies; psychology; and theatre (in which, as Grotowski observes, the censors attempt to control the content of the final performance, but are relatively inattentive to what goes on in the private forum of rehearsals). The entrance examination for the State Theatre School in Cracow was scheduled first among the three, and when Grotowski (contrary to his own expectations), was accepted he chose to enroll. Scholars such as Jennifer Kumiega and Halina Filipowicz have noted that from the earliest phase of Grotowski's work, he seems to have regarded theatre as a means rather than an end.

Grotowski himself finds nothing shocking or self-contradictory in the unusual course of his creative journey:

In appearance, and for some people in a scandalous or incomprehensible manner, I passed through very contradictory periods; but in truth . . . the line is quite direct. I have always sought to prolong the investigation, but when one arrives at a certain point, in order to take a step forward, one must enlarge the field. The emphases

Performance Research 3(3), pp.85-94 © Routledge 1998

shift. . . . Some historians speak of cuts in my itinerary, but I have more the impression of a thread which I have followed, like Ariadne's thread in the labyrinth, one sole thread. And I am still catching clusters of interests that I had also before doing theatre, as if everything must rejoin.

(Thibaudat 1995:-29)

Grotowski sees the various phases of his work as being unified by certain consistent desires and questions, underlying interests that have fascinated him since childhood, long before he ever thought of pursuing work in the field of theatre. He suggests that the underlying impulses of his work would have remained much the same even if he had chosen to pursue a career in another field.

TECHNIQUES OF THE BODY

Following his so-called 'exit from the theatre' in the late 1960s, Grotowski has maintained an active and continually evolving exploration of the range and boundaries of performative phenomena. This research has coalesced in the form of four distinct projects: Paratheatre or Theatre of Participation (1969-78); Theatre of Sources (1976-82); Objective Drama (1983-6); and Art as vehicle (1986-present).

The three most recent phases of Grotowski's research, while by no means identical in terms of their goals and objectives, are united by a shared emphasis on performative behaviours derived from the ritual traditions of various cultures. Grotowski posits that certain performance elements (e.g. particular songs or ways of moving) can exert a tangible impact on practitioners, affecting the physical, psychological and energetic state of the doer(s) in precise and measurable ways. Through extensive fieldwork and applied practice, Grotowski has sought both to identify such elements and to understand the process by which they function.

Since early childhood, the investigation of ritual techniques and so-called paranormal phenomena has been a consuming fascination for Grotowski. '[F]rom the very beginning,' he observes, this special field of interest 'was not a matter of any precise religion or even of different religions, but

much more of something, I can say, technical. It was also not cut off from the body or refusing the body' (1997: 254). Yet it was only in 1976, with the initiation of his Theatre of Sources project, that this interest in embodied ritual technique was overtly addressed in the frame of Grotowski's professional work. Grotowski emphasized that the focus of his research in this period was not concerned with the sources of theatre, but rather with various techniques that have been developed in different cultural contexts which he perceives to be capable of functioning as tools for the internal evolution of practitioners.

In conducting research on culturally traditional techniques and ritual performance practices, Grotowski's usual pattern was to travel alone to a designated field site in order to make contact with practitioners in that region, then request permission to return with a small group of his collaborators in order to study the embodied practices of the contact group.* His intention was never to stage these rituals, never to imitate the practices in an aesthetic context, but rather to determine whether the efficacy of the performative element as ritual tool could function objectively, which is to say, could it create a discernible, consistent and predictable psychic and/or physiological effect, when employed by practitioners from a different cultural background. Part of Grotowski's agenda during this period of intensive fieldwork was to determine whether there were certain principles of psychophysical technique, precise ways of using the body, that recurred in different traditions and could be said to *underlie* cultural differentiation – something as simple as a way of walking or a way of tilting the spine forward while dancing, which appeared as a foundational element or 'morpheme' of ritual/performance behaviours in diverse traditions, and which was used in different contexts for similar purposes or to obtain similar effects. Grotowski wanted to explore the impact of these elements on the physical and energetic state of

* See *Tecniche originarie dell'attore*, a collection of lectures delivered by Grotowski at the University of Rome in 1982–3, for a fascinating discussion of the principles that informed his work during this period.

participants, without regard to culturally conditioned structures of belief, and also outside any framework of spectator-oriented performance Many of Grotowski's journeys during this period took him to India, though it is interesting to note (in light of speculation about the influence of Indian performance genres on his method of actor-training) that Grotowski's object of study in these travels never focused on a culture's aesthetic performance traditions, but rather on structured meditational and esoteric practices: 'techniques of the body' in the sense invoked by anthropologist Marcel Mauss. 'I believe precisely,' wrote Mauss, 'that at the bottom of all our mystical states there are body techniques which we have not studied, but which were studied fully in China and India, even in very remote periods' (Barba and Savarese 1991: 231). Alongside his investigation of Hindu yogic practice, another element of Grotowski's research which began to take on importance during the Theatre of Sources period was an emphasis on performance materials (both songs and codified dance forms) connected to African and Afro-Caribbean ritual practices, a line of investigation which continues to the present day.

Grotowski's research involving culturally traditional materials carried forward into his subsequent project, Objective Drama. In 1982, during the period of martial law in Poland, Grotowski requested political asylum in the USA. He accepted a position on faculty at the University of California-Irvine in 1983, where he began to develop a research program with the collaboration of a small group of 'technical specialists' from Bali, Taiwan, Korea and Haiti, as well as North and South America. Objective Drama, according to an early grant proposal, was concerned with

> those elements of the ancient rituals of various world cultures which have a precise and therefore objective impact on participants, quite apart from solely theological or symbolic significance. Grotowski's intention is to isolate and study such elements of performative movements, dances, songs, incantations, structures of language, rhythms and uses of space.
>
> (Focused Research Program in Objective Drama 1984: 1)

While Theatre of Sources focused on locating ritual/performative elements so simple that Grotowski believed they could be said to precede differentiation into culturally specific codifications, Objective Drama dealt with the developed forms of diverse embodied techniques, including a more explicit emphasis on materials connected to performance per se, and an investigation of how such elements could function when juxtaposed to one another in the context of collaborative, intercultural performance pieces. Work continued to focus heavily on an investigation of Afro-Caribbean ritual/performance materials, and of the specific psycho-energetic states induced in practitioners who worked with these materials over extended periods of time.

ART AS VEHICLE

Since 1986, Grotowski's main focus of attention has been directed toward a project he calls 'Art as vehicle', a program of practical research conducted at the Workcenter of Jerzy Grotowski and Thomas Richards in Pontedera, Italy. According to Grotowski, Art as vehicle focuses on 'actions related to very ancient songs which traditionally served ritual purposes, and so can have a direct impact on – so to say – the head, the heart and the body of the doers' (Thibaudat 1995: 29). Almost all of the songs used in this research are derived from African and Afro-Caribbean ritual practice. Grotowski's work is founded on the premise that these songs, which he refers to as 'ancient vibratory songs', can serve the practitioner as a tool for activating a process that creates a transformation from one quality of energy (gross) to another (subtle). He speaks of this inner process as a type of 'itinerary in verticality':

> Verticality – we can see this phenomenon in categories of energy: heavy but organic energies (linked to the forces of life, to instincts, to sensuality) and other energies, more subtle. The question of verticality means to pass from a so-called coarse level – in a certain sense, one could say an 'everyday level' – to a level of energy more subtle or even toward the higher

connection. . . . There, there is another passage as well: if one approaches the higher connection – that means, if we are speaking in terms of energy, if one approaches the much more subtle energy – then there is also the question of descending, while at the same time bringing this subtle something into the more common reality, which is linked to the 'density' of the body.

(Grotowski 1995: 125)

In speaking of this 'itinerary in verticality' and of the transformation of energy from heavy to subtle, Grotowski implicitly alludes to a complex system of practices and beliefs related to interior evolution which can be traced in the esoteric traditions of various cultures, but which is particularly well developed in Hindu yogic practice – a body of teachings with which Grotowski is intimately familiar, and in which it is possible to find very precise analogies to the fundamental premises of his current work. Art as vehicle is an unusual type of performance practice which explicitly shifts the locus of meaning away from its conventional place in the perception of the spectator, relocating it (and it is precisely in this aspect that Grotowski's recent work most closely corresponds to traditional ritual practices) in the experience of those who do. The basic impulse of the work is autotelic, concerned with performative elements as a tool by means of which the human being can undertake a work on her/himself. Grotowski attempts to (re)constitute a type of performance which he describes in terms of 'art as a way of knowledge' (Sullivan 1983: 42), a form of art that is in itself an initiatory practice. Grotowski explicitly refers to his current work as 'a type of yoga', noting that while, in one sense, Art as vehicle is very much concerned with elements of performance craft, the interior goal of the work is analogous to that which is sought in meditative disciplines.

It is neither accidental nor insignificant that Grotowski's closest collaborators in this research are not only skilled performers, but also individuals with developed knowledge of the respective source traditions from which Art as vehicle borrows. Thomas Richards, whom Grotowski identifies as his essential collaborator, is an American of Afro-Caribbean descent, who had studied traditional African music and dance forms before he ever encountered Grotowski's work. Mario Biagini, who has been involved with Art as vehicle since the inception of the project, is pursuing an advanced degree in Sanskrit studies.

Grotowski speaks of his work with traditional song in relation to the discipline of *mantraṣastra*, suggesting that specific sounds affect an individual's psycho-energetic state in physically objective ways:

The mantra is a sonic form, very elaborated, which englobes the position of the body and the breathing, and which makes appear a determined vibration in a tempo-rhythm so precise that it influences the tempo-rhythm of the mind. The mantra is a short incantation, effective like an instrument; it doesn't serve the spectators, but those who practice it. The songs of tradition also serve those who practice them. Each of these songs, which were formed in a long arc of time and were utilized for sacred or ritual purposes . . . brings different types of results. For example, one result is stimulating, another brings calm (this example is simplistic and crude; not only because there are a great many possibilities, but above all because among these possibilities there are those which touch a much more subtle domain).

(1995: 127)

Grotowski observes that although mantras and songs connected to ritual tradition can exert similarly precise effects on the practitioner's internal state, the latter are more productive for his research. The recitation of a mantra (a devotional practice known as *japam*) often requires immobilization of the body, an aspect which clearly limits the potential application of such a practice in a dynamic performative situation. '[I]n the song of tradition, it is no longer a question of the position of the body or the manipulation of the breath, but of the impulses and the little actions. Because the impulses which run in the body are exactly that which carries the song' (Grotowski 1995: 128).

Richards, who leads the day-to-day work of practical research in Art as vehicle, describes the process of energy transformation at the core of this practice in a way that attests to the profoundly embodied nature of the doer's experience:

> The melody is precise. The rhythm is precise. The person who is singing begins to let the song descend into the organism. . . . The syllables and the melody of these songs begin to touch and activate something I perceive to be like 'energy seats' in the organism. An energy seat seems to me to be something like a center of energy inside the organism. . . . In my perception, one energy center exists around what we call the solar plexus, around the area of the stomach. It relates to vitality, as if the life force is seated there. In some moment it's as if this begins to open, and is as if receiving through the stream of life impulses in the body related to the songs . . . it's like some force is collecting in the plexus. And then through this place, this very strong energy which is collecting can find its way, as if entering a channel in the organism, toward a seat slightly above it, for me related to what in my intimate world is 'heart'. Here, what is in the vital pool begins to flow upward into this other resource and transform itself into a quality of energy much more subtle. When I say subtle I mean more light, more luminous. Its flow is completely different, its way to touch the body – because these energy pools can be perceived as touching the body. From this pool related, let's say, to the 'heart', something becomes open which is helping this upward, and it's as if this begins to touch a level of energy around the head, in front of the head, behind it. I don't mean this to be a general formula which should be the same for everyone. But in someone's perception it can be all connected, like a river which is flowing from the vitality to this subtle energy someone might perceive as being behind the head and above, even above, touching something that is no longer related to the physical frame, but is as if above the physical frame. As if some source, when touched, begins to be activated, and something like a very subtle rain is descending and washing every cell of the body. This journey from one qualify of energy, dense and vital, up and up toward a very subtle quality of energy, and then that subtle something descending back into the basic physicality. . . . It's as if these songs were made or dis- covered hundreds or thousands of years ago for waking

up some kind of energy (or energies) in the human being and for dealing with it.

(Richards 1997: 12)

THE PARADOX OF CATEGORIZATION

The name by which Grotowski refers to this body of investigation is taken from a talk delivered by Peter Brook in 1987, 'Grotowski: art as a vehicle'. Brook observes that Grotowski is looking for 'something which existed in the past but has been forgotten over centuries and centuries; that is that one of the vehicles which allows man to have access to another level and to serve more rightly his function in the universe is – as the means of under- standing – the performing art in all its forms' (1988: 34). Brook articulates Grotowski's concern with performance as a means, in a manner analogous to the way in which certain monastic orders have historically used music or the making of liqueurs to give form and structure to their inner search. Brook asserts that the hidden work of the laboratory exerts a strong and vital influence on other forms of theatre work, even if this influence appears indirect. In stating his conviction regarding the 'living, permanent relationship . . . between the work of research that is without public witness and the immediate nourishment that this can give to the public work' (1988: 33), Brook suggests that the relation of Grotowski's Workcenter to the broader realm of theatre is analogous to that between the monastery and the Church.

The day-to-day activities of practical work in Art as vehicle concentrate primarily on the develop- ment and execution of performance pieces, what Grotowski and his collaborators call Actions – repeatable, precisely scored works that are fully analogous to a theatrical production in terms of structure and detail. Working under Richards' direction (and, at recurrent intervals, under Grotowski's supervision as well) members of the research team in residence at the Workcenter develop a set score of physical actions, which support the work on the vibratory songs; the songs, derived almost exclusively from Afro-Caribbean ritual tradition, provide the axis of the structure. The Actions developed at the Workcenter are perhaps more easily apprehended as a variety of dance theatre than as narrative performance, although a fragmentary story is discernible in certain Actions, and passages of text (derived from scriptural) rather than dramatic sources) are interspersed with musical materials. These rigorously rehearsed performance structures are developed over relatively long periods of time, sometimes several years.

Both Richards and Grotowski emphasize that in the practical, day-to-day work of Art as vehicle, there is no discussion of qualities of energy or the question of a 'vertical itinerary'. The language of daily work is a language of craft, overtly directed toward developing participants' acting skills. The more subtle elements of the ritual songs are never addressed directly; the attention of the practitioners, especially in early stages of work, is focused much more explicitly on the external structure of the performance, elements that comprise an 'acting score' in a fairly conventional sense of the word.

The work of Art as vehicle is not made accessible to random spectators – it is not possible to go to the theatre in Pontedera, buy a ticket and arrive at the door – but neither is this practice entirely cut off from pubic view. Grotowski and his colleagues frequently present their work in a format of barter, or work exchange, with other theatre artists, ensemble groups, both well known and obscure, who are invited to the Workcenter for relatively brief periods. The visiting groups present examples of their own work, witness, as spectators, the performance structures developed at the Workcenter, and then engage in a dialogue with Grotowski and his collaborators. Richards, discussing the benefits of such exchange for both the Workcenter research team and the visiting groups, emphasizes a common basis in performance craft: 'Our basic elements are the same as the basic elements of acting. And on one level, the level of craft, the work is the same for the actor in public theatre and the person who is doing this work. It's in some way the

same field' (1997: 30-1). More than 150 theatre groups have visited the Workcenter since Grotowski and his collaborators initiated this form of meeting. More recently, Grotowski and Richards have begun to present their work in the context of large-scale, international symposia, inviting small audiences composed of both practitioners and scholars (usually about 15-20 at a time), and meeting collectively to analyse and respond to the work. At an event held in October 1996 in São Paulo, Brazil, approximately 150 people witnessed a live presentation of Action, while more than 600 participated in related symposium events.

Although the external structure of the work conducted at the Pontedera research center can be apprehended as a performance, the creation of a performance event for the sake of its reception by random spectators lies outside the primary goals of Grotowski's and Richards' current work. Richards relates the practice of Art as vehicle to the traditional performances of the Bauls, yogin-bards of India, whose spiritual practice takes the form of songs and dances that can be appreciated on an aesthetic level. Richards suggests that the Bauls, by means of their ritual songs, accomplished 'something that was like performing, but it's not just that they were doing theatre – they did have some precise doings with these songs, some way of behavior with these songs, which was artistically on a high level – but what they were doing really was related to the work with their teacher, to this something "inner"' (1997: 60-1). Richard clarifies that Action, the structure developed around the ritual songs, 'is in some way a performance':

> It can be seen. But is it just for – to be seen? No. Because the moment it's – just for to be seen, just for this, it would lose the contact with its original intention, with the reason for doing. Action is on that edge-point, which is like what I can imagine, from my orientation, as 'primary performance.' It's finding its value in the act of doing, and that act of doing exists in a structure which accepts the fact that someone is there watching, and also that there is not someone watching.
>
> (Richards 1997: 62)

In an interview with Jean-Pierre Thibaudat, Grotowski used the term 'laic [or lay] ritual' to describe the practice of Art as vehicle. He suggests that this expression is 'both tactical and true', noting that during the early period of his work in communist Poland he had to 'pass between Scylla and Charybdis, that is in some way between the atheist state and the Polish Church', without simultaneously antagonizing both forces (Thibaudat 1995: 29). Such a process required an acute tactical sensibility, a strategic mindset which has remained with Grotowski even in situations when external circumstances do not necessarily seem to warrant excessive caution. The term 'lay ritual' positions Grotowski's current praxis at the threshold between sacred and secular realms, belonging fully to neither. Grotowski suggests that the description is also true in so far as 'what is verifiable in practice "precedes" cultural, philosophical and religious differences. And this thing, verifiable in practice, is comprehensible even if one is conditioned by different roots' (Thibaudat 1995: 30).

If one allows Grotowski's ambiguous definition to prevail, then Art as vehicle is not mysticism, in the sense of a sectarian or doctrinary practice. It is also not not mysticism in so far as Grotowski accepts, and even on occasion promotes, Brook's monastic analogy (1988: 34) as a description of the work. Conversely, the work is not theatre. Speaking of the Afro-Caribbean ritual songs that provide the basis of investigation in Art as vehicle, Richards maintains that 'they simply were not made for doing a "public performance" as we can conceive of this term now' (1997: 25). And yet it is not not theatre: when witnesses come to view the activities of the Workcenter, Richards acknowledges that 'they're observing a group of actors working in a precise performative structure. . . . So is it theatre? Is it not theatre? On a certain level, you can say, yes, they are witnessing something, they are seeing something done' (1997: 26-7). Thus, in Grotowski's and Richards's definition, Art as vehicle is neither: not theatre and not not theatre, not mysticism and not not mysticism. And at the same time it is both, or at least such appears to be the meaning they attempt to convey.

Art as vehicle explicitly combines African ritual elements and Hindu esoteric practices with an overtly Stanislavskian approach to performance craft. As Schechner observes,

> Grotowski's rhetoric is spiritual while his practice combines 'ancient ritual techniques' (or ones foreign to most Europeans and Americans) with theatre exercises long known to students of Konstantin Stanislavski or Vsevelod Meyerhold.
>
> (Schechner 1993: 248)

The performative framework of Art as vehicle is by no means extraneous to the interior agenda of the work, but functions as an essential component of the practice. Having explored the paradoxical positioning of Grotowski's practice at the threshold of performative and esoteric disciplines, I must finally conclude that Art as vehicle cannot be contained in a classification of either/or, but is rather a matter of both/and. The work of Art as vehicle, specifically as realized in the performance structure *Action*, is simultaneously a performance and a form of embodied esoteric discipline. The latter aspect, however, can be realized only if the former is well accomplished. If the performer does not have mastery of craft, if she or he is unable to discover and activate the precise vibratory quality of the song as ritual tool, nothing can be accomplished; thus the 'itinerary in verticality', the interior element of Art as vehicle, is dependent on mastery of the performative framework for its actualization. The two elements cannot be separated, and any attempt to assess the validity of Grotowski's current praxis by privileging one over the other – whether labeling the work purely as mysticism or, conversely, purely as performance – will be incomplete and potentially distortive.

THE MATTER OF GENERATIONS

Grotowski speaks of his work in Art as vehicle in relation to a 'process of transmission', saying that a deep and systematic research cannot be accomplished in a single lifetime, but is rather a matter of many generations (Thibaudat 1995). He speaks of his lifelong research as 'a tangible thread and a practice' that he himself received from other hands:

It's as if my heritage comes from distant generations; it passes through many generations and even several races. And, at the same time, it's not a question of syncretism, of a melange, but of the objectivity of the impact of certain practical approaches, even if they've appeared in different contexts.

(Thibaudat 1995: 30)

He seems deeply concerned that this practice (of which he does not consider himself the originator) should neither disappear nor become frozen at the moment of his death, but rather should continue to develop under the guidance of other practitioners.

As Eric Hobsbawm and Terence Ranger have suggested (1983), it is the nature of an invented tradition to find its genealogy in the past, to suture itself onto a base of purportedly ancient custom in order to legitimize its efficacy and importance. Ideally, if a tradition perpetuates itself over an extended period of time, the aspect of 'invention' may become so naturalized as to be nearly invisible, and the acts of hybridization and transplantation which were necessary to create it recede from view, perhaps giving an illusion that the invented practice is the result of an uninterrupted transmission through the ages. Hobsbawm theorizes that the process by which a tradition comes to be 'invented' is most clearly exemplified and most visible in those instances where a particular practice is 'deliberately constructed by a single initiator' (1983: 5). This is arguably the case with Art as vehicle, despite the important contributions made by Grotowski's collaborators. The tradition of which Grotowski is now the creator/keeper was not transmitted to him whole, not given to him, complete, in the framework of master and disciple, but rather assembled through long years of practical research and collaboration with ritual specialists of various traditions. Grotowski did not seek out these specialists in order to create a syncretic *mélange* of their disparate traditions, but rather to investigate certain principles of objective or psychophysiological impact which could be seen

to recur in different embodied techniques. This tradition finds its 'home', its site of embodiment, in a dislocated interculture that is not African, Indian or Polish, and most certainly not Italian in any sense, despite the fact that the physical building where this work is accomplished is located in a rural Tuscan village. To borrow a phrase from Joseph Roach, the practice of Art as vehicle constitutes a type of 'displaced transmission' (1996: 28), a practice assembled from fragments of living tradition still surviving in diverse locations and cultural milieux.

It is precisely this issue of the cultural positioning of Grotowski's current research – the relation between the invented tradition of Art as vehicle and the specific cultural practices, both living and extinct, which are assembled in his work – that has prompted the most intense criticism from scholars and observers. As Schechner observes,

Grotowski's fundamental assumption is the belief in a kind of archeology of performance, whereby the modern layer, present practices, can be scraped away, or dug down under, so that older, more authentic, deeper layers can be recovered and practiced. Flying against today's call for cultural specificity, the denial of 'universal' human cultural traits, Grotowski's method, from Theatre of Sources onward, has been to sift through practices from different cultures for what is similar among them, searching for the 'first,' the 'original,' the 'essential,' and the 'universal.'

(1997: 490)

Schechner is suspicious of this tendency, asking 'why, for Grotowski, does old = good?' and articulating his answer in terms of an alleged desire on Grotowski's part for a sort of pre-lapsarian, Edenic wholeness (Schechner 1997: 491).

The tendency to privilege the ancient, or to look to African, Indian and other non-white cultures in search of a supposedly ancient font of wisdom, has somewhat troubling implications insofar as it is linked to the exoticizing practices of high modernism, which historically tended to position non-western populations as the bearers of sacred tradition located in the mists of a distant, allochronic past. Speaking of the Afro-Caribbean songs that constitute the main focus of work in Art as vehicle, Richards explains that Grotowski conceptualizes these songs as having been passed down over a very long arc of time. 'We can find them now in the Caribbean, he says, but what is their source? The slaves in the Caribbean had brought them from Africa. . . . But Grotowski continues in his analysis to say that he feels that even before [they appeared in] West Africa, these songs can be traced back to the ancient Egyptian tradition, or even before, to what might have existed before that Egyptian tradition' (Richards 1997: 9). This conception of the Afro-Caribbean songs as having passed down through centuries, even millennia, implicitly frames the material as part of the common heritage of humankind, effectively downplaying the specificity of their current appearance in African and the African diaspora traditions.

On the other hand, Grotowski (who was himself a political refugee, having fled Poland during the period of martial law) is by no means naïve regarding the dynamics of oppression and forced relocation that have ineradicably shaped the lives of diasporic peoples. He notes that the particular type of syncretism that characterizes Afro-Caribbean and Afro-Brazilian religious practices could have arisen only in a sociocultural context in which African rituals and belief systems were brought into contact with Euro-Christian iconography in the context of extreme colonialist oppression and slavery.

Rather than viewing tradition as something static, frozen in the past, Grotowski acknowledges the dynamics of hybridization and adaptation which unavoidably shape the transmission and practice of traditional techniques. Tradition, Grotowski has said, would surely die if one's attitude toward it were passive; tradition can survive and grow only if it is approached with an attitude of exploration, an element of research. By foregrounding the relation between tradition and research, Grotowski articulates a notion of tradition-as-process that is in keeping with recent paradigms of ethnographic scholarship, a

conceptualization that foregrounds agency in the transmission/production of ritual practices and allows for adaptation, invention and change.

In a symposium held in São Paolo, Brazil, in October 1996, dedicated to the work of Art as vehicle, Mario Biagini (1996) articulated his understanding of the word 'tradition' in relation to this practice:

> In some place, it is said that in this whole world, everything goes downward like a great and heavy waterfall. Everything falls. Something special happens in human relations and immediately after, something starts to deteriorate, like an almost inevitable process. . . . Imagine this very big waterfall, everything falling down, and imagine that inside this waterfall, there is a very little, invisible stream of water that is fighting upward, that is going in the other direction. It means that this is a very very dangerous situation. It means that in any moment, because of any kind of mistake or external situation, this fighting, fragile stream, can just go with the rest of the waterfall. In India they say that this very little stream is hidden even from the gods. They don't like it. They like that everything goes in the other direction.

Drawing on a background of extensive fieldwork and practical research, Grotowski has created a ritual practice, an invented tradition, that is simultaneously ancient and new. It is not an imitation of existing rituals from other parts of the world, but rather a distinctive performance/ritual that functions in accordance with principles that can be traced to long-standing disciplines of esoteric practice. Like the sacred performances of the Bauls, Art as vehicle is not a mimetic enactment of ritual performance; *it is ritual*, even if one is able to discern the seams where Grotowski's practice is grafted onto the roots of supposedly ancient traditions – even if one can argue that those roots have been tampered with: transplanted, excavated, hybridized . . . partly imagined.

These are complex issues, and I have to acknowledge that my own involvement with this work – my 'complicity' with Grotowski's practice – is too intimate and too intense for me to be able to articulate a detached or unconflicted response.

Hobsbawm suggests that invented traditions tend to proliferate in those historical moments when 'a rapid transformation of society weakens or destroys the social patterns for which "old" traditions had been designed' (1983: 4). While I would by no means wish to deny the importance of examining the underlying premises of Grotowski's research, I am fully convinced that Art as vehicle is a concrete attempt to come to terms with a world in which 'the centre has not held', an attempt to create a site, in which individuals who feel the need to (re?)forge a connection with some element of the sacred or the numinous can do so – in a tangible, embodied manner. I cannot discount the value of what I take to be Grotowski's central aim.

ACKNOWLEDGEMENTS

This article was originally presented as a guest lecture at the Interdisciplinary Humanities Institute of the University of California at Santa Barbara (November 1996). A condensed version was subsequently presented at the third annual Performance Studies conference in Atlanta, Georgia (April 1997). I extend thanks to Tracy Davis for her comments on an early version of this text, and to Carla Pollastrelli, administrator of the Pontedera Workcenter and organizer of the symposium in São Paulo, Brazil, for the many forms of assistance she has provided over the course of my research.

REFERENCES

Banu, Georges (1996) 'Grotowski – the absent presence', in *The Intercultural Performance Reader*, ed. Patrice Pavis, trans. Susan Basnett, New York and London: Routledge, pp. 242–6.

Barba, Eugenio and Savarese, Nicola (1991) *A Dictionary of Theatre Anthropology: The Secret Art of the Performer*, ed. Richard Gough, trans. Richard Fowler, New York and London: Routledge.

Biagini, Mario (1996) Presentation given at a symposium sponsored by the Centro de Pesquisa Teatral do SESC, focusing on current research at the Workcenter of Jerzy Grotowski and Thomas Richards, 16–18 October 1996.

Brook, Peter (1988) 'Grotowski: art as a vehicle', in *Workcenter of Jerzy Grotowski*, Pontedera, Italy: Centro per la Sperimentazione e la Ricerca Teatrale, pp. 31–5.

Filipowicz, Halina (1991) 'Where is Gurutowski?', *TDR: The Journal of Performance Studies* 35(1): 181–86.

Focused Research Program in Objective Drama (1984) *Research and Development Report*, Irvine, CA: University of California.

Grotowski, Jerzy (1995) Appendix, 'From the theatre company to art as a vehicle', trans. Thomas Richards and Michel Moos, in Thomas Richards, *At Work With Grotowski on Physical Actions*, New York and London: Routledge.

Grotowski, Jerzy (1997) 'Theatre of sources', in *The Grotowski Sourcebook*, ed. Richard Schechner and Lisa Wolford, New York and London: Routledge.

Hobsbawm, Eric and Ranger, Terence (eds) (1983) *The Invention of Tradition*, Cambridge: Cambridge University Press.

Kumiega, Jennifer (1985) *The Theatre of Grotowski*, London: Methuen.

Richards, Thomas (1997) *The Edge Point of Performance*, Pontedera, Italy: Centro per la Sperimentazione e la Ricerca Teatrale.

Roach, Joseph (1996) *Cities of the Dead*, New York: Columbia University Press.

Schechner, Richard (1993) *The Future of Ritual*, New York and London: Routledge.

Schechner, Richard (1997) 'Exoduction', *The Grotowski Sourcebook*, ed. Richard Schechner and Lisa Wolford, New York and London: Routledge.

Sullivan, Dan (1983) 'A prophet of the far out', *Los Angeles Times* (2 October): 1, 42.

Thibaudat, Jean-Pierre (1995) 'Grotowski, un véhicule du théâtre', *Liberation* (28 July): 28–30.

The Performance of Pain

Ted Polhemus

A photograph taken around 1850 shows a North American Sioux Indian hanging from a tree by means of two hooks which have been pierced through the flesh of his chest. Our initial perception might be that he is the tortured victim of inter-tribal warfare, but in point of fact this image represents the last recorded example of an ancient practice – the Sun Dance or O-Kee-Pa – which was widespread among the indigenous populations of the American Northwest. Whether for personal enlightenment or to gain knowledge for the sake of the tribe, the male participant (alone or perhaps accompanied by a friend) would go forth into the wilderness, prepare himself by fasting and sexual abstinence, insert the appropriate hooks, thorns, or eagle's talons into the flesh of his chest or back and suspend himself until he succeeded in ripping his flesh free to fall back to earth. In the process, with luck, a higher state of consciousness might be achieved or he might leave his body to soar high about the mountaintops in order to spot herds of buffalo or an enemy's advance. Made illegal by the American government later in the nineteenth century on the grounds of barbarism, the Sun Dance would be revived only a hundred years later by white American 'Modern Primitives' seeking spiritual enlightenment and the heightened physical sensations of extreme 'Body Play'.*

* Body Play is also the magazine founded by Fakir Musafar (Menlo Park, CA: Insight Books).

In 1983 two white Americans, Fakir Musafar and Jim Ward, went out into the Wyoming wilderness to attempt an experimental re-creation (and, since direct instruction from native American practitioners was impossible to obtain, a reinterpretation) of the Sun Dance ritual.

While the original Sun Dance rituals were either unobserved private affairs or seen only by other participants (and/or by tribal deities), Fakir Musafar and Jim Ward recorded their experience and edited this into a film – *Dances Sacred and Profane* – which has been distributed for viewing by Fakir Musafar. This is significant because (although it seems clear that Fakir Musafar and Jim Ward did what they did for their own personal fulfilment) the screening of *Dances Sacred and Profane* establishes a situation in which body ritual can become (for the non-participating viewer) pure performance, a spectacle, even, perhaps, an entertainment. Even if techniques of body manipulation and entire ritual structures may be translated accurately from ancient, traditional cultures to our own, it must be borne in mind that the presence of a non-partici-patory audience (whether in a cinema, a theatre, an arts institution, or a night-club) fundamentally alters the nature of the event as private or community-based rituals become public performances.

This distinction between, on the one hand, personal or community-observed private ritual and, on the other hand, audience-observed performance events requires consideration in light of the recent, phenomenal rise of experimental theatre/film/video/performance art that incorporates those forms of bodily manipulation ('play' in Fakir Musafar's term) involving pain which ultimately derive from traditional societies, where the viewing of such physical rituals was/is limited to an audience of those intimately involved in the event.

In particular, performances by Ron Athey, Franko B, Bob Flanagan and Fakir Musafar have revolution-

Performance Research 3(3), pp.97-102 © Routledge 1998

ized the possibilities of our performative experience. At long last breaking free of a logo-centric semiotics, such performers have placed the body back at the centre of expression and, in so doing, have rekindled communicative powers long lost. But both performers and audience must be aware that the re-creation of such powerful rituals within the context of culture, where distinctions have traditionally been made between 'the stage' and the auditorium, the professional performer/actor/artist and the audience, imposes new limitations (as well as offering fresh possibilities).

To push this point to its logical conclusion, we might also consider the case of those sword-swallowers, fire-eaters, human pincushions and 'blockheads' who performed their acts of painful (and often dangerous) bodily manipulation in sideshows and circuses.*

While such venues

* For a fascinating discussion of the art of sword-swallowing and fire-eating see the interview with 'Captain Don' in (1989) *Modern Primitives* (Vale and Juno 1989: 68–75).

have been in decline in the second half of the twentieth century, new opportunities have arisen for speciality acts in fetish clubs and sex clubs, at pop music festivals, and in a new breed of circuses (for example, the French Circus Archaos). Is there a fundamental difference between, say, on the one hand a 'human pincushion' or man who performs feats of attaching great weights to piercings in his nipples, tongue, or genitals (for example, the *Chaos Clown* Peter Mastin) and on the other hand an 'art' performance by, say, Ron Athey or Franko B involving blood-letting? One could argue a difference based upon whether the performer sought a consciousness-raising experience or simply a profitable money-making, but (as I have already suggested) the mental state and expectations of the audience must also be put into the equation. If, as some performance artists are discovering, 'art' audiences are coming to demand greater acts of corporal brutalism, then such artists may have to consider whether their continued employment and success depend upon their effectively recategorizing themselves as an 'entertainment' more suited to the side-show than the prestigious arts institute (which should not, I hope, be seen to imply any disrespect to 'daredevil' performers like a sword-swallower or a pierced lifter; rather, I would like to see such entertainers brought within the legitimate sphere of 'performance art').

However, as well as distinguishing between private/community-based rituals and public, audience-directed performance, it is also important that we distinguish between the different kinds of *motivations* that may precipitate any manipulations of the body involving physical pain. Two of these – consciousness-raising/spiritual enrichment and financial profit – have already been touched upon. Two others – body decoration and erotic stimulation – will be considered now.

Just as a parameter can be identified stretching between the purely private and the purely public, so too can a gradation be identified between physical alteration that is purely for decoration – the product (for example, a nipple piercing achieved under an anaesthetic) – and one that is purely for the ritual of its execution – the process (for example, a temporary piercing of the nipple done within an S/M ritual, which will be allowed to heal over).

Both in traditional societies and in our own, bodily modifications and decorations which require an element of pain in their execution (tattooing, piercing, scarification, etc.) are rarely significant purely as product (that is, as decoration). For the 'Modern Primitive' as for tribal and peasant peoples, the process of acquisition is increasingly appreciated for its ritualistic experience, which may serve to mark a rite of passage from one state to another. It cannot be pure chance which has led so many of our ancestors to incorporate painful and therefore testing and significant body decoration into their communal rituals – especially those which mark the transition into adulthood and membership of the society.

Equally, the world-wide spread of such painful rituals of bodily modification attests to their profound significance and value to traditional social systems. While missionaries and modern 'Third World' governments have done much to eradicate such practices, some remain even today. Examples of this may include:

- in Bali, the filing into sharp points of a young man's or woman's teeth on reaching adulthood
- in parts of the Amazon, the piercing of a young man's lower or upper lip and then the gradual stretching of this piercing to accommodate larger and larger discs
- the extensive scarification of young women in parts of Africa.

In all such societies, the pain involved and the permanence of such decorations serve useful (arguably, vital) sociocultural functions: in the first instance challenging, testing and developing the stoicism and determination of the individual and, in the second instance, underlining the lifelong nature of tribal membership and of cultural commitment. They also, of course, provide an occasion of significant ritual and (in the fact that the application of such decorations may be witnessed by significant others within the tribe) of performance. Again, as with tribal uses of rituals of physical pain and endurance such as the Sun Dance, the audience at such rituals of painful body modification is strictly proscribed. (For example, amongst the Nuba a young woman's scarification rituals may be witnessed only by other, older women who have themselves experienced such scarification.)

In our own society too, the performative aspect of such rituals of body modification was traditionally afforded only to a limited community of like-minded (and like-decorated) individuals. Thus a group of sailors on leave might witness one or more of their circle receive a tattoo; or an initiate into a motorcycle club receiving a tattoo 'badge' may be viewed by all the other members of that club. Likewise, among 'Modern Primitives' (and others) the act of receiving a body-piercing may be structured into an occasion of ritual significance with appropriate music and lighting and with a highly restricted audience whose presence and whose viewing of the act underline its significance.

Gradually, however, the possibilities have grown for (in some instances) extending the range of such an audience beyond the confines of participants and intimates. For example, at tattoo conventions it is now commonplace for different tattooists to set up stalls where anyone present at such a convention can witness the act of someone's being tattooed. A friend of mine received a large ritual scarification on his abdomen on stage at a fetish club in London watched by hundreds if not thousands of clubbers. The cult film *Robert Having His Nipple Pierced* offers anyone with the price of a ticket a front-row seat on the occasion of Robert's body modification. And, of course, dozens of TV documentaries on tattoo and piercing have included footage of acts of painful body modification. Thus have once purely intimate rituals become more openly public and therefore performative – the experience transformed by the nature of the audience. (Whether this is for the better or for the worse is not for me to say. My point is simply that the fact that such an act is seen by an 'outside' audience inevitably – like Sartre's voyeur in *Being and Nothingness* who realizes that he is *himself* being observed – propels all participants into a knowingly performative role.)

Finally I should like to consider the sphere of painful body ritual that is motivated primarily by sexual impulse. Here (and here only) is it appropriate to label such activity as 'S/M'. The concepts of sadism and masochism are western in origin (specifically deriving from de Sade and Sacher Masoch) and are inappropriate to categorize ritual practices in traditional societies. It is absurd, for example, to label a Sioux practitioner of the Sun Dance or a Nuba woman undergoing scarification as 'masochistic'. Likewise I see no justification for applying this terminology to those 'Modern Primitives' who seek to revive such rituals and permanent body decorations unless, of course, they are doing so specifically and explicitly within an

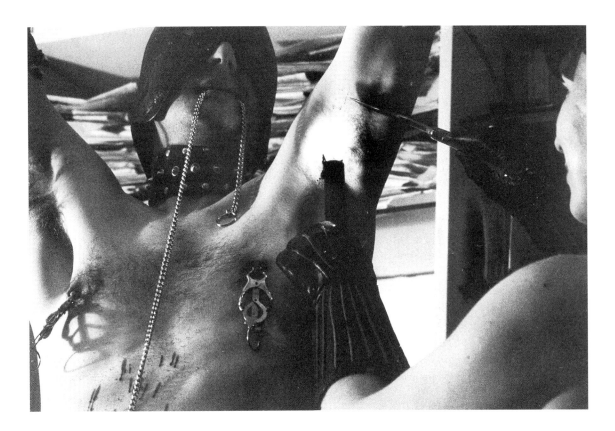

S/M context. It should also be appreciated that S/M as it is practised consists of highly ritualized 'scenes' between consenting partners, who respect each other's limits and needs. (It is not, in other words, wanton violence perpetrated on unwilling victims.)

While reasons for participating in S/M acts go far beyond the scope of this essay, it is appropriate that we emphasize that it shares with the other subjects discussed here the organizing of physical pain within ritual structures. And, furthermore, that these rituals may take place either within a private (or community-based) context, or within a context of public performance. As has been said previously, the question of whether there is an audience to witness the ritual act and, if there is an audience, its nature significantly affect the nature of the act itself.

We need only consider a couple enacting an S/M ritual alone in their own home. Indeed, within the private domain, the blindfolding of the submissive participant offers total visual privacy to the dominant partner – thereby totally removing his or her performative responsibilities. S/M or 'fetish' clubs, on the other hand, offer options for both categories of observation previously considered: in the 'playroom' one might find the same couple as before enacting the same S/M ritual (say, a 'scene' involving bondage in an uncomfortable position, or a whipping), but now encircled by an audience which, in this situation, would typically consist of others who themselves belong to the S/M community (and many of whom may themselves enact their own ritual 'scenes' within this club environment). Such S/M performances tend to be spontaneous (at least in the sense that the couple has not been 'booked' to appear) and are not professional (in the sense that the club does not pay them to perform).*

Such clubs, (both 'straight' and gay), however, may also present S/M performances on a

* It can happen, however, that a female dominant is a professional hired for the occasion by her submissive partner.

stage utilizing pre-booked and often paid participants. Here, even though the rituals performed might be similar or identical to those witnessed in the 'playroom', the context (where clubbers may have come to dance rather than participate in S/M activities) subtly changes the nature of the phenomenon such that (even if extremely painful S/M activities are involved) it must be (and is) categorized as a 'show' and evaluated in terms of its performative capabilities. Nevertheless, because such clubs almost invariable operate a 'dress code', whereby to gain entrance to the club one must be suitably attired, even such a staged performance takes place within some boundaries of a sense of community. If, however, the same 'scene' is filmed and sold as a video which anyone can purchase, then S/M rituals (like those considered previously) enter the theatrical territory where (as has been the case for centuries in western theatre) the voyeur's only requirement is monetary.

In summary, I am suggesting the following.

1 The meaning and significance of a performed act depend, ultimately, upon the nature of (and the existence of) an audience.
2 The relocation of 'primitive' or 'private' rituals involving physical pain within western traditions of 'theatre' and 'art' requires us to completely reconsider our culture's imbedded distinction between stage and auditorium, professional actor/artist/performer and audience.
3 We cannot presume that the content of performance is independent of its structures.
4 And vice versa.

The human body is the ground zero of our being. This has been true throughout human existence and yet we so often forget it. In any society in times of chaos and anomie the only antidote to such formlessness is a return to physicality. Not, of course, to the 'natural body' (for no such thing exists for human beings), but some envisioned, strange, mythic form, which we create in our mind's eye and then realize in some customizing of our own flesh. As throughout human history, we must mould and bend and cut and scar and bleed and compress and paint the flesh

into some form that makes sense to us, and in so doing sketch out a form and structure which we can project upon the screen of our daily lives. If the sphere of activity that we label 'performance' has any value and validity, then it must participate in this project. But to do so, it must either re-think itself (its structure, its role, its criteria of validity) or it must admit its impotence and recognize that it is only *intimate* (private or community-proscribed) rituals which today (as so long ago) offer that intensity of experience and that plasticity of form with which we can fashion a future.

Everywhere around us extraordinary performances are taking place: Sun Dancers ripping themselves free, Modern Primitives sculpting themselves into icons of another age, leather-clad explorers of the outer limits of sensation. If theatre and art cannot embrace them, then theatre and art no longer warrant our attention.

Photo credits: Copyright Claude Alexandre.

REFERENCES

Musafar, Fakir (ed.) (current) *Body Play & Modern Primitives Quarterly*, Menlo Park, CA: Insight Books.

Polhemus, Ted and Randall, Housk (1994) *Rituals of Love*, London: Picador.

Polhemus, Ted and Randall, Housk (1996) *The Customized Body*, London: Serpent's Tail.

Tompson, Mark (ed.) (1991) *Leatherfolk: Radical Sex, People, Politics & Practice*, Boston, MA: Alyson Publications.

Vale, V. and Juno, Andrea (eds) (1989) *Modern Primitives*, San Francisco: RE/Search.

Wood, David (ed.) (1996) *Torture Garden, a Photographic Archive of the Body New Flesh*, London: Creation Books.

HOMEM 'TÁ COM MÁSCARA NA
CABEÇA

ANASTÁCIO MAIA
CAXINAUÁ

The Serpent's Song

Ritual Performances of the Kaxinawá in the Amazon Forest

Cláudia Neiva de Matos

THEATRE, PERFORMANCE, POETRY

The ritual origins of western theatre have been the subject of many studies ever since Aristotle located the beginnings of Greek theatre in Dionysian cults and established a direct line of development from dithyrambs to Attic tragedy. How much of this is true nobody will ever be able to say, since much of this history 'is mythical, and the connections are obscure, or at least hypothetical' (Barthes 1982: 64). However, there can be no doubt that among the Greeks, as well as in other ancient cultures, there existed practices (ritual and/or theatrical), which involved multi-expressive channels of communication, such as gestures, voice and music. Dance and song, music and poetry, stage sets and costumes – all these elements can be seen to mobilize and metamorphose the human body and spirit, and are characteristic of the communicative activity which we call performance.

This behaviour can be ritualistic or theatrical, but is not necessarily restricted to artistic performances on the stage. For Paul Zumthor, performative activity is fundamental to oral communication and always includes 'as an irreducible element the idea of corporeal presence' (Zumthor 1990: 41–2). In order to 'introduce into the study of literature the concept of sensorial perception, or in other words, the living body' (Zumthor 1990: 29), Zumthor

underlines the connection between poetry and theatre and sets out his proposal for an extension of the concept of performance:

> I am convinced that the idea of performance should be considerably extended; it should incorporate the whole complex of activities embraced by the word 'reception', but relating these to the decisive moment, in which all of these elements crystallise in and through an act of sensorial perception – that is, by means of a physical engagement. . . . Until now, the term and the idea of performance tended (at least in the Anglo-Saxon meaning of the word) to cover all kinds of theatrical activities. But is not all literature fundamentally theatre?
>
> (Zumthor 1990: 19)

Contrary to most academics, Zumthor concentrates his attention on the body of the listener and/or spectator in the process of aesthetic communication. When emphasizing the active role of this 'receiver', the analyst displaces and enlarges the stage: the fundamental action of the performance takes place inside the spectator, opening up and fostering a personal link with the 'emitting source', be this a text, an author, or an actor. The effect of this aesthetic transaction Aristotle tried to describe with the concept of catharsis. However, 'performance is the only live form of poetic communication and . . . a heterogenic phenomenon, which is impossible to define in simple and general terms' (Zumthor 1990: 37).

In the first instance, this concept applies to

• "Homem 'tá com máscara na cabeça" – The man has a mask on his head. Artist: Anastácio Maia Kaxinawá

Performance Research 3(3), pp.104–113 © Routledge 1998

poetic forms transmitted by the voice. But Zumthor takes it a step further and introduces the body into the act of reading and literary reception. This is particularly the case with literature not purely concerned with transmitting information in a codified fashion, but rather with employing 'non-informative elements with the intention to provide pleasure, which . . . for the reader constitutes the main and often only criterion of poeticity' (Zumthor 1990: 27). In this case, the performance does not depend on the physical presence of the author, or on the concrete presence of a voice. Rather, it takes place in the world of reception, by the suggestive power of the poetic word.

I DREAMT JUST ONE DREAM: THE CIPÓ AND I

The above observations are part of the theoretical framework which I am using for my research into the performative aspects – poetry, drama, and ritual – of a particularly important element of the indigenous Amazonian culture: the psychedelic journey provoked by the drinking of Cipó.

'Cipó' is a generic name given to various types of vine found in the Amazon forest (in Peru they are called 'Ayahuasca'). It is a hallucinogenic drink consumed by many tribes of the Amazon basin, including the Kaxinawá, who have been the subject of my investigations. The Kaxinawá call themselves *huni kuin* (real people).* There are 3,500 of them in the Brazilian states of Acre and Amazonas and a further 1,000 in Peru. Their first contact with white people dates back to the nineteenth century, when the rubber industry began to flourish and the whites invaded the land of the native population of the Amazons. Following the murder, expulsion and exploitation of the Indios, the Kaxinawá are not in a bad situation nowadays, at least compared with other tribes in Brazil, considering that they have been able to preserve their language, culture and identity.

The power of the Cipó did not escape the attention of the whites and became part and parcel of the psychedelic culture of the 1960s. In its mystical connotation it was introduced through and developed into an important element of a religious sect in Brazil, mainly composed of white people, called Santo Daime.[†] The drink is prepared with various types of Cipó and other leaves and produces a chemical mixture[‡] that affects sensory perception, particularly vision, and provokes optical illusions, or what the followers of Santo Daime call '*miração*' (inner vision). The Indians occasionally use the same Portuguese term, but they also have other words to describe the effects of the drug. In Rãtxa-Kuin, the language of the Kaxinawá, the term *pae*, meaning strength or energy, is used. The name of the drink of Cipó is *nixi pae*, but it is also called *huni* (human being).

Cipó is generally drunk in a group of men, which includes an elderly man invested with shamanic authority. He acts as a singer and helps the travellers on their journey, invokes the magic energy and controls its excesses.[§] It can happen that there is more than one singer present and that two, three, or more of them sing different songs at the same time. However, when the Cipó is drunk for a healing purpose, the ritual may involve only two participants.

Although the practices linked to the use of Cipó among the Indians are determined by tradition, they are not as formalized as in the Santo Daime ceremonies. For the Kaxinawá, the great magic power experienced and celebrated during the trance state is attributed not to a formally defined sacred being, but to the spiritual essence of Nature, called *yuxin*. It is to be found in every particle of creation, including the human being. Propelled by

* 'Kaxinawá' (Bat's People) is a term given by the whites. For more information about this people see Aquino and Iglesias (1994).

† The Santo Daime sect was founded in the early part of the twentieth century, when Raimundo Irineu Serra came into contact with the Kaxinawá and experienced the power of Cipó. The belief of the Santo Daime cult is a mixture of Christianity and elements taken from the Nature religion of the Indios. A series of hymns, inspired by the Cipó journey, is part of the sect's repertory of songs. See MacRae (1992).

‡ Details about the drink's composition and its ingredients can be found in Lagrou (1996: 204–5).

§ The meaning of the term 'shamanism' as a reference point in anthropological research becomes richer when aspects of performance and aesthetic representation are taken into account. See, with regard to the Kaxinawá, the essay by Elsje Maria Lagrou, 'Shamanism and representation among the Kaxinawá' (1996).

the power of *dami* (transformation), it links matter
and mind, the plant and animal worlds, the cosmic
and human universes, in a process that expands the
sensorial perception of the concrete world and
creates both a mystical and aesthetic state. Such an
experience forms the basis of some of the
Kaxinawá's most significant artistic creations.

Among the Kaxinawá, the experiences and representations of the spiritual forces of nature, when
the doors open for the *yuxin* spirits to appear, are
contained in what one may call the 'Jibóia complex'.
This is a group of practices, myths and beliefs that
are interlinked through their common origin – the
snake Jibóia (*Yube*).*

* Lagrou refers to a different snake called *sucuri*, but I prefer to call it Jibóia, as this is the name my Kaxinawá informants used during our conversations.

The legend of the snake
stands at the centre of
the cultural system and
world-view of the Kaxinawá. It is also the main
character of their myths as well as of their visual arts
(*kene*): drawing, painting, crafts, ceramics and body
painting. It was Jibóia that one day 'taught Muka
Bakanku, an old woman, the art of jenipapo
drawing,† the design of

† Jenipapo is a small fruit, whose black/blue juice is used as ink to paint bodies and other surfaces with decorative patterns.

hammocks, baskets and
ceramics' (Lagrou 1996:
199).

Kene, the graphic art of the Kaxinawá, is mainly
produced by women. Among the men, the Jibóia's
powers manifest themselves through the drinking
of Cipó (*huni, nixi pae*) and in the songs (*huni meka*)
that accompany, stimulate and express the effects of
the drug. The Jibóia is also the central theme of the
stories and songs connected with the hallucinogenic
journey. The lyrics follow a traditional aesthetics
and use highly characteristic forms:

> To sing as we used to do before, ha ia e, e,
> The Cipó I have already drunk, ha ia e, e,
> And the force is becoming stronger, ha ia e, e,
> I am singing to find a release, ha ia e, e,
> Every son inside the force, ha ia e, e.‡

‡ All songs reproduced in this essay were taken from the Kaxinawá language. As far as possible, the English translation attempts to preserve the syntactical structure and hazy imagery of the original. Many verses are made up of incomplete sentences and have no verb. They are distinctly different from ordinary language and communicate primarily through visual and multi-sensorial imagery.

• Body painting executed with the juice of the jenipapo fruit amongst the Asurini in the Xingu-Tocantins region of the Amazons. Photo: Renato Delarole

The origin of *nixi pae*, according to a myth told
to Lagrou by two Kaxinawá, begins with a man
going to hunt *anta*, a wild mammal that lives in the
Amazon forest and the central region of Brazil. As
soon as he is in the forest, a serpent comes out of a
lake and transforms herself into a beautiful woman,
who has the whole of her body decorated with
jenipapo designs. They fall in love, and the serpent-
woman's relatives teach him how to drink *nixi pae*,
to overcome the moments of fear and sickness, and
to gain access to the world of 'hallucinatory vision'.
When he returns to his people, he teaches them
how to make the drink of the Cipó:

> The men brought all types of Cipó until they found the
> right ones. The same happened with the leaves. Then he
> explained how to prepare the drink and afterwards to let
> it cool down. In the night, he drank it with the other adult

men of the village. The man sang the songs he had
learned from the serpent. He sang all night, all next day,
another night and day, and at the end of the third night he
fell dead. . . . Through this adventure . . . he learned and
brought to his people the secret of the drink that gives
access to the invisible worlds of the spirits of water, sky
and forest.

(Lagrou 1996: 204–5)

The *huni meka* have an important place among
the various types of ritual songs in the Kaxinawá
culture. Contrary to most indigenous songs, they
do not require any choreography, although their
lyrics mention dance quite frequently:

Walk, walk, my Ixã,
Dance on the wave of strength,
Soar highly while dancing
And keep growing, my son!

Apart from the songs related to subsistence
(fishing, agriculture, etc.) and festivities, the production and reception of *huni meka* seem to be more
concerned with the exploration of subjectivity and
inner imagery.[§] This
probably explains why
so often one person
sings to help the others

§ According to Lagrou, most of the
rituals relating to 'yuxin-ness' are collective, as is the case in the Santo
Daime cult.

on their spiritual journey and to get the best of the
energy (*pae*) which Nature offers to them. In this
type of dreamlike poetry, the words have an intimate,
contemplative touch. But for this contemplation to
reach its full revelatory power, the singer's presence
as poet, interpreter, shaman and performer is absolutely essential. The song captures the 'almost cine-
matographic dynamic of the psychodelic journey'
and acts as 'a means of expressing the male experience' (Lagrou 1996: 206). In fact, the masculine
quality is always present in the erotic lyrics:

Far way another firm soil
Far way another firm soil
She follows, commanding,
Into the middle of the male body
Into the centre of a locked force.

Kene and *dami* have the same mystical origin, the
Jibóia, 'a happy shaman and ambiguous being, who

lives in the earth, in the water and in the air; who is
male and female, young and old, and who created
the water and the butterflies' (Lagrou 1996: 206).
The journey and songs integrate the male and
female worlds and provide a matrix of images,
which fill the dreams of men and make them alert,
watchful, ready for action. Here, the Apollonian
side of the performance comes to the fore, integrat-
ing song and dream and translating the experience
of the inner visions into *kene* (drawing).

She was very near, to me, to me,
The dreamt force was coming closer, to me, to me,
The hidden Jibóia waits and looks, to me, to me,
The rainbow comes down from the sky, to me, to me,
The force she drank went up, to me, to me,
Within, the force is kicking, to me, to me,
From the sky the songs would come, to me, to me,
From the sky the drawing voice, to me, to me,
In this way I can go inside myself, to me, to me.

In this imagery, an important role is played by
the air and the sky, and many winged beings confer
a special dynamism on the contemplated scene:

There above, high up in the sky
The lower vulture of the sky
The enchanted vulture of the sky
Under your curved wings
You keep on gathering the force
The force is always gathered
Inside the locked force
Haira haira, haira haira, e, e, e, e, e, e, e, e,
Haira haira, haira haira, e, e, e, e, e, e, e, e.

The *huni meka* are drawn-out songs, which can
go on indefinitely as they accompany the journey.
They are structured in a repetitive manner and may
or may not have a refrain. Often the refrain is
executed as what the Indios simply call 'sound';
that is, rhythmic sequences of non-signifying
syllables creating hypnotic and enchanting effects.
The verses work mainly with visual references.
They alternate and combine cyclic and linear
movements, which mirror the phases of the hallucinogenic journey. Parallel to descriptive and

• "Dashúati". Artist: Tuin Yrumapa Kaxinawá

narrative passages, which reinforce the visions of the person who drank the Cipó, there are comments regarding the action of drinking, and sections which celebrate the integration of body and spirit, vision and sound.

> When the sound fills this vision, hai e, hai e,
> Morning rises hearing the sound, hai e, hai e,
> Come out, spirit of the dream, hai e, hai e,
> Turn around, spirit, and come, hai e, hai e,
> Big body big dog, hai e, hai e.

The texts are formulated either in the first or second person singular, as if spoken by or to the protagonist of the journey, and often both versions are used in the same song. For example:

> You carry on always singing, hai e, hai e,
> You have already turned off the force, hai e, hai e,
> Inside the hollow belly of a man, hai e, hai e,
> I poured the Cipó of the dance, hai e, hai e,
> I already drank this force, hai e, hai e.

This oscillation between first and second person singular shows the symbiosis between the man who dreams and the man who supports the others while they are absorbed in their dreams. It suggests a transcendence of individuality and a transformation of 'self' into 'other'. This process is typical of the force of *dami*, the energy of psychic and physical metamorphosis, and, according to Lagrou, 'serves as a key symbol in the shamanic cosmo-vision of the Kaxinawá' (Lagrou 1996: 207). In the altered state of consciousness, everybody is a sort of shaman. That is why the singer is able to incorporate every person into the ritual, sharing their dreams, and giving them a voice and a form.

CELEBRATION OF UNITY: NATURE AND CULTURE, BODY AND SOUL, I AND THE OTHER

The production of images – in this case, individual and internal images – under the effect of the Cipó drink, but also under the suggestive power of the songs, brings to mind Nietzsche's theory of the origins of theatre and literature in *The Birth of Tragedy*. In this seminal work he proposes a

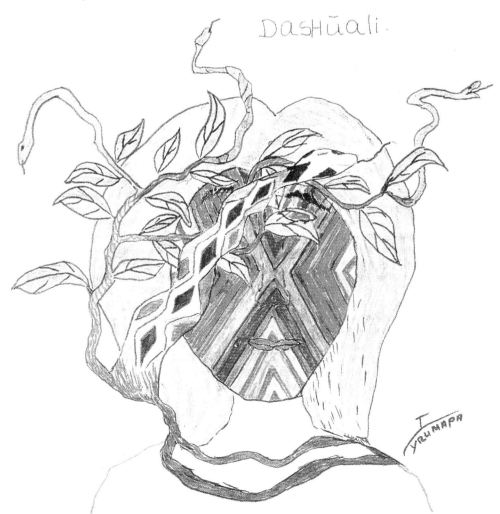

Dashūali.

connection between artistic expression, sensual apprehension and transformation of the world, experienced by individuals and groups from the times of the Dionysian cults until the constitution of Attic tragedy. The rise and decline of classic Greek theatre, especially of tragedy, are connected to the transformation of the relationship between individual and collective, and of the roles involved in the performance.

Nietzsche saw the origin of art in the marriage of Dionysiac and Apollonian forces: arts directed to the ears and the eyes, unfolding and recomposing the senses, putting together sound and image. But this association takes place only in the union of poetry and drama in tragedy. The generating power of poetic language is centred in the Apollonian *epos*; but in the songs of the Dionysian ritual the ancestral lyricism and the enchanting power of the words produce a profound movement in the human being's body and soul. The word is never a silent

• "Adam and Eve". Artist: Tene Kaxinawá. A shaman is caring for a sick person, by drinking the cipo himself and calling forth its strength by singing a ritual song

abstraction; but it needs to be embodied and incarnated in the human voice. It is here that the intellectual (Apollonian) element of the word is united with the physical (Dionysiac) element of the sound.

The power of poetic-dramatic expression has its origin in the chorus. What is the place occupied by the chorus? In the beginning, the large chorus of the dithyramb, which did not know of actors or characters, was a spectacle in itself. The sole reality of the chorus was a 'vision generated from within itself' and expressed with 'the symbolism of dance, sound, words' (Nietzsche 1993: 44). The introduction of characters happened gradually, but always referred back to the basic principle of the person's transform-ation. Initially, the chorus represented the god Dionysus, incar-nated in the form of satyrs, then as a chorus of satyrs, and finally as humans.* The primal discharge of Dionysian energy and the shock it produces makes a person abandon his or her individuality and enter another character.

* Silenus, son of god Pan, leads the chorus in the satyr plays. To Nietzsche, the satyr was the 'archetype of man, the expression of his highest and most intense emotions, an inspired reveller enraptured by the closeness of his god, a sympathetic companion in whom the god's suffering is repeated, the harbinger of wisdom from the very breast of nature, a symbol of nature's sexual omnipotence' (Nietzsche 1993: 40).

> Enchantment is the precondition of all dramatic art. In this enchantment the Dionysiac reveller sees himself as a satyr, and it is as a satyr that he looks upon the god: in his transformation he sees a new vision outside himself, the Apolline complement of his state. With this new vision the drama is complete.
>
> (Nietzsche 1993: 43)

The receptor, the person who hears and sees and through the songs receives the force of the spirits, is in reality the one who occupies the centre-stage position, even in moments of intro-version and silence. The relationship between the songs and the Cipó journey highlights certain aspects of Zumthor's concept of performance, and also of Nietzsche's notion of transformation in the original Dionysian rituals. It refers to the moment

when the ego transcends itself, when personal and collective dreams come together, when the psycho-neurological properties of the drink merge with the effect of the poetic language of the songs. Here, the human being confronts himself or herself in his or her most profound depth and stands at the same time in and outside of the self: everywhere everything is *yuxin* (spirit), *huni* (human), *pae* (strength) and *dami* (transformation).

The most prominent feature of this performative situation of the Cipó journey is the presence of the voice. Even in other types of indigenous vocal and musical performances, where choreographic elements play an important role, it is still the language of the songs that takes prime position in the set-up and development of the performance. Using the basic formula words + music + movement, where each element influences the others, the ethnomusicologist Hélza Camêo supposes for indigenous artistic expression the existence of a central stimulus, an initial impulse, a generating power, which comes through the voice: 'Consider the song as a result of an emotional exal-tation of the word, which in the intensity of its ejection acquires a musical content, becomes expressive, and highly impressive' (Camêo 1977: 12).

The poetic words emitted by the singer's (performer's) voice organize, in a psychological and cultural way, the trance of the 'travellers'. In this condition, the physical and metaphysical realms are fused by means of the *dami*'s power: 'Nature is transformed into human being and human being into Nature' (Lagrou 1996: 214).

The performance of the voice, the vocalization of the words in chanting or singing, unites in the Cipó journey the human spirit with the energy of Nature, not only as an individual sensation, but as a collective experience of the world. The perform-ance brings into relief the importance of *communitas*, meaning not just the physical presence of a community, but also the actualization of a culture deeply rooted in the collective unconscious. As Hymes says, the performance works with a 'non-redundant repetitiveness', or, to use Zumthor's phrase, 'the performance and what is transmitted through it are linked in as much as the nature of performance affects what is known. The performance, somehow, modifies knowledge' (Zumthor 1990: 35).

It is through the songs that the Cipó's natural magic is inserted into the community's traditional culture. The forces of nature and culture are joined in the experience of ecstasy. The Cipó journey is an existential rite of passage, where the individual is released from a state of isolation, and reactivates, in a concrete practical and an imaginary inner fashion, the figure of the chorus, which everybody carries inside himself or herself and projects into the infinite space of the world:

> Ancestors present, to me, to me,
> Different within and dancing, to me, to me,
> The drink rises and flies around, to me, to me,
> From high above pulling the sun to me, to me.

The Cipó journey, as portrayed in the serpent's song, acts as a means of connecting sender and addressee, voice and vision, body and soul, nature and culture, individual and collective, eternal return and continuous advancement. Through the Latin prefix *per*, 'movement through', it seems also to give new meaning to the term 'performance'.

[*Translated by Günter Berghaus*]

ACKNOWLEDGEMENT

I wish to express my gratitude to Joaquim Maná Kaninawá, Josimar Tuin Kaxinawá and Daniel W. Guimarães for their help in translating the verses into Portuguese. This work has been made possible by the generous help of the Comissão Pró-Indio do Acre, whose paedagogic programme includes the documentation and publication of indigenous songs (e.g. the collection *Nuku Mimawa*, listed in the References; see Kaxinawá 1995).

REFERENCES

Aquino, Txai Terri Valle de and Iglesias, Marcelo Piedrafita (1994) *Kaxinawá do Rio Jordão: história, território, economia e desenvolvimento sustentado*, Rio Branco (Acre): Comissão Pró-Indio do Acre.

Barthes, Roland (1982) 'Le Théâtre grec', in *L'Obvie et l'obtus*, Paris: Seuil, 63–85.

Camêo, Hélza (1977) *Introdução ao estudo da musica indígena brasileira*, Rio de Janeiro: Conselho Federal de Cultura/Departamento de Assuntos Culturais.

Kaxinawá, Joaquim Maná Paula (ed.) (1995) *Nukti Mimawa (Livro de musicas)*, Rio Branco (Acre): Kene Hiwe/Setor de Educação da Comissão Pró-Indio do Acre.

Lagrou, Elsje Maria (1996) 'Xamanismo e representação entre os Kaxinawá', in E. Jean Matteson Langdon (ed.) *Xamanismo no Brasil: novas perspectivas*, Florianópolis: Editora da LTFSC, 197–231.

MacRae, Edward (1992) *Guiado pela lua: Xamanismo e uso ritual da Ayahuasco no culto do Santo Daime*, São Paulo: Brasiliense.

Nietzsche, Friedrich (1993[1872]), *The Birth of Tragedy out of the Spirit of Music*, trans. Shaun Whiteside, Harmondsworth, Mx: Penguin.

Zumthor, Paul (1983) *Introduction à la poésie orale*, Paris: Editions du Seuil; English-language edn (1990) *Oral Poetry: An Introduction*, Minneapolis: University of Minnesota Press.

Zumthor, Paul (1990) *Performance, Reception, Lecture*, Quebec: Le Preambule.

Diary of an Imaginal Navigation – Maria de Marias

When there is something that can be contemplated there is something that creates union.
(21. Shih Ho/Biting Through, Book III, The Commentaries, *I CHING or Book of Changes*, Tr. Wilhelm Reich)

September 1990. `La Nave', an old factory in Poble Nou, one of the oldest industrial districts of Barcelona. *Nave*, in Catalan, means ship, but also industrial plant. I find myself in an industrial Ship of Fools, a theatre. A large black curtain, left behind from a previous stage production – object and symbol of the purest spectacular tradition. The `factory' sets the scene for a *telluric temple* veiled by the *Image-Relic*: inside a glass cage, the corpse of a deer foetus is propped up by an iron structure, which shines through the decaying tissue.
Rosemary is burned and blends with the smell of artificial strawberry coming from a smoke machine.

My clothes have been shed. I am naked, denuded to the bottom of my being. I am asked to walk towards the urn. My gaze falls across unfathomable surfaces of viscera in a state of advanced putrefaction. Simultaneously I am transfixed by the *Image*. I feel awe and tender devotion towards the being, who lived within the warm walls of his mother's uterus, never in the outside world. I recognize a kind of pure virtue – subliminal virginity – in the one who was never seen, never *imaged*, alive. The reverie of this supreme innocence (or perhaps was there a visitation from the little deer's Recording Angel, who keeps track of all good and bad deeds?) enraptures my gaze: the Image of Death. Organic material engaged in pure motion. In another dream I see the fearful Mask of Change.

I have to stay in the factory-ship-theatre all night because the precinct remains closed until 5 a.m. I sit on a small platform. `Push it,' I am told, `push it!' It feels like a heavy birth. The genesis of a dreadful beast which one day may swallow me up. My face and breast are covered with blood – theatre blood – then, semen. I try again. I push and push. At one point, something yields and gives way: my body shapes the figure of a telluric daimon. I remember the relentlessness of this unexpected event. Much later do I realize how it has changed the course of my life.

The *image* and the *process* are recorded through the lens of a video-camera. The beholder is Albert Vidal. He comes to me, opens his arms, kisses me on both cheeks and offers me biscuits, because I have been a good girl.

Maria de Marias

ON THE SPIRIT OF THE DOLL

(Text for a live installation at the XXV International Festival of Puppets & Visual Theatre, Barcelona, Autumn 1998)

Mid-February 1998
Madam Durga's Playroom
A Transient Settlement in London Offering Shelter to Cultivate Fields of Thought & To Reshape Plots

I Fix my Camera
to Record
– Still Frame –
My Own Act of
Metamorphosis
Naked Transvestism
Epiphanies of Motion
When Novel Orders of
Subtlety Disclose
The UnIntelligible
Materia
For the Body
to Signal the Radiant
Existence
Of an Imagined Ethos
The Kinematic
Numina
Inscribed in
Callisthenic Stanzas

On my Waist
I hold a Dummy
Of Colonel Marcos
From Chiapas
Positioned to Fit into
the Frame
– Now an Electronic
Live Canvas –
The Doll
The Wavelength Keeper
Of this Hermitage

THE DOLL
Like a **Torimono**
Magical Object
of Worship
Vehicle of the Life Forces
Used by Japanese
Trance Dancers
To be Possessed by
The Figures of the
Nether World
**Even before the Great
Zeami Merged The
Ritual Practices into
an Art Form**
Further
Down
A Vital Cultural Autism
Silenced Interludes
To Pervade the
Interstices of Code
Profane Rhapsodies
Where the
Re-Enactment of
Possession is Played
anew
To Authenticate
Human's Ludic Stance

The Transparent I
Surfs on the Waves of
the Void
Imaginal
Synchronicities
Of Cultures, Genres
& Ages
The Frequency of the
Pulsating Energy Field
Creates Form
&
The Doll Dwells
in my Womb
Mirroring
a Thousand Souls

o

THE
THOUSAND SOULS
OF THE
DOLL

Book Reviews

The Future of Ritual (the final chapter)

Richard Schechner
London: Routledge,

283 pp. ISBN: 0415-046904 (pb): 0415-046890 (hb)

The Future of Ritual conjures up thoughts of the past and present of ritual, a scheme that is in itself curiously Aristotelian, with its beginning, middle and end. Yet Schechner himself is hardly an Aristotelian theorist or critic, nor is he the person most likely to write one of those dread volumes on 'drama and the dramatic', despite the early essays (on Euripides, Ionesco, etc.) which show a conventional interest in plays past and present. The future has categorically disappeared from Schechner's marginal if recurrent concern for dramaturgy, and this displacement creates for us a further, possible triad: drama as the beginning and middle, and ritual as the end.

For the Carleton-based *Drama Review* the transition to the future was initially a shock, as Schechner replaced Corrigan, but the integrity of the theatre rather than the future of either performance or ritual was the initial rallying-cry. The claim was, relatively quickly, that the new-look *Drama Review* had 'forged an existence out of old ambitions by avoiding old habits' (*Drama Review* 8(2): 9) and I recall a rather bizarre ambition to 'restore virginity to the theatre' in another, early *Drama Review* 'Comment'. Perhaps this is how we should see it now, some thirty-five years later (count that number, and assure yourself it is correct): there is a ritual for the restoration of theatrical virginity, and you may find it performed three times a year in the pages of America's habit-breaking review of performance studies.

But despite the Aristotelian ironies, it is far more convincing to connect this prophetic strain with another, profound triad of writing in and out of modernism, and recall Schechner's apocalyptic vision of the avant-garde in *The Decline and Fall of the (American) Avant-Garde.* I have it on authority, after all, that the apocalyptic vision 'depends on a concord of imaginatively recorded past and imaginatively predicted future, achieved on behalf of us, who remain "in the middest"'. Even more trying, if we like prophecy and the apocalypse, and regard it as our millenarian birthright, is the following arid observation: 'Men in the middest make considerable imaginative investments in coherent patterns which, by the provision of an end, make possible a satisfying consonance with the origins and the middle.'

So, discarding Kermode as a 1960s seer on the grounds that we are already still living with stacks of them, we could ask instead what ritual means to Schechner. Now I might answer that myself by reference to another question which seems more pressing: if we asked what performance is, we could readily conclude that it is a term that is subject to a great deal of slippage. As a colleague said to me, it is easy to get dewy-eyed about performance until you hear the phrase 'performance-related pay', and think unnervingly of Lyotard and the corporatist performativity we do not discuss. Schechner sees this slippage as characteristic of ritual, and he is right, because this particular quality has from the beginning underpinned his notion of performance and granted it validity. You might say that 'performing' links both ritual and theatre, but you might also turn that round: if ritual can be shown to be like theatre, then 'performing' and 'performance' will assume a general validity as concepts. This necessity is present in Schechner's writing from the beginning to the end (if it is appropriate to speak of an end). I shall return later to the diagrams which initiate and close this discursive manoeuvre, but the middle we all know pretty well, because it lies in the *Essays on Performance Theory* and related works.

The early part of 'the future of ritual' displays a set of familiar discursive gestures in service to the central tenet. So it is no surprise to read that 'ritual is ordinary behavior transformed' (228), and, quite naturally, animal behavior equates to human behavior, in the lovely phrase 'nonhuman primates . . . behave in some respects very much like

Performance Research 3(3), pp.117-129 © Routledge 1998

humans' (229). Yes indeed, we cry, thinking warmly of chimpanzee Mike and his kerosene cans, and it is then inevitable that 'theatre, dance, music, some kinds of painting' are accordingly 'behavior arts', and so dissociated from the human characteristic of speech (ibid.). The conclusion is also familiar, from this re-rehearsal, to readers of *Performance Theory*, *Performative Circumstances* and *Between Theater and Anthropology*: 'Both animal and human ritual actions are very close to theatre' (230).

They are such entrancing phrases: 'very much like . . .' and 'very close to . . .' The mode of conjunction and association is pronounced in the second phase of the essay, which moves to authorities through a concern for violence, which Schechner links to sex. The selective allusions to Girard here are puzzling, because Girard's theory is one of drama, most notably, and it is, as Schechner acknowledges, an Aristotelian one: indeed, it begins even to be Platonic, because the dramatic character is a substitute for the surrogate victim, and so is, in Schechner's apposite formula, 'a representation of a representation' (235). But the essay begins to be taken over by authorities, and if violence is seemingly a confused preoccupation it gives way to the involvement of ritual in what appears to be a doctrine of artistic inspiration. This Schechner formulates as a 'porosity' in relation to the unconscious, which Freud is adduced to confirm, and once Ehrenweig arrives to join them the congruence is almost alarming. So 'Ehrenweig's theories fit very nicely with those of Girard and Freud' and, only a little later, 'Ehrenweig sounds like Girard' (238).

I have it in mind, in this connection, that a cat's yowl can sound very like a baby's cry, but not to the baby's own mother, which is a more natural way of putting it than to remember Wittgenstein's warning against the phrase 'is really', as in 'x is really y'. But one can put that another way: if neurosis = art in a doctrine of inspiration such as Schechner is suggesting here, then are these concepts (for such they surely are) coextensive? 'Very much like' and 'very close to' are associative, and boost our sense of similarity; but similarity has a 'very close' relationship with difference, and so is another of these matters which is subject to slippage. The result is, of course, a compromise: art and neurosis are 'closely linked' (ibid.). There is nothing futuristic about much of this, and the general theory of artistic inspiration seems uncompromisingly romantic in its individualism: 'what art manipulates on an individual basis, ritual does collectively' (ibid.). This seems to me like Nietzsche, without Nietzsche's tension between the two terms.

There is, in performance theory, a need for ritual, and a significant contribution in this regard came from Victor Turner, who liked liminality, and wanted to find it in modern life. That is a rather flat statement, but it summarizes a considerable degree of regret, aspiration and faith to which Turner's writings give voice. The third part of the meditation by Schechner on the future of ritual is really framed by Turner's final search for the location of universals of performance in the brain, which causes Schechner some trouble. If the need for ritual is located in the brain, this is awkward, because ritual is supposed by

Schechner to 'short-circuit thought' (239). Despite his opening advertisement of a resolution, Schechner plainly finds it hard to resolve the contradiction, and this part of the essay represents him at his most confusing and confused.

Reading it again I am aware that he loses himself, and leaves us in a relatively pointless perplexity. Is he tracking a postmodern phenomenon of ritualization here, of which he in some part disapproves, or is he attempting to evaluate its divergent claims to a kind of culturally displaced authenticity? The situation is complicated by the fact that the figures he discusses, one or two at length, vary from experimentalists and practitioners to neurologists and academics, with performance theory holding the middle ground. Goodman's workshops at the Cuyamungue Institute in New Mexico support a contention that the repetition or simulation of gesture reproduces the psychosomatic phenomena of ritual. The process becomes one of divination, a kind of future for ritual, but Goodman's work seemingly contains a major theoretical contradiction: the 'workshop-ritual-dance' produced is 'not like going to the theatre or performing in an ordinary play or dance', but it is apparently 'parallel to what occurs . . . in ancient classical Greek theatre' (245). How easy is it to separate the category 'theatre' or 'ordinary play or dance' from the ancient Greek theatre? For Turner, for example, these art forms were all 'liminoid', not liminal. Yet Schechner leaves us with this conundrum as he turns to Grotowski, about whose activity he is not particularly revealing, and which he can summarize only as 'the development of some kind of ritual performance' (248). It has to be said that however little we knew of Grotowski, we at least thought that we knew that.

Schechner fidgets. He is dissatisfied with Turner's and McLean's forays into the brain, and fairly scathing about some of the more crudely instrumental programmes offered to the consumer ('flim-flam': 254). He is not actually very happy either with 'Grotowski's Performer and with wisdom that exists before or behind cultures' (257), and there is no reason why we should not be happy with his dissatisfaction were it not for the fact that it leaves the future of ritual relatively uninteresting. There is a reflex action – 'The avant-garde is art's permanent revolution', and 'experimental art' is reliably subversive (259) – but that does not help ritual greatly, and the future is ultimately confined to 'the life of the imagination' (261) and to dreams. I have failed, even on re-reading, to find it a radical thesis:

> At some point in human history people began performing their dreams and elaborating on them. They were not facts nor were they imaginary. They were performances of events between fact and imagination. (263)

Perhaps I was wrong about that small volume on drama and the dramatic.

Schechner's politics in 'the future of ritual' are equally confusing. He can get quite indignant, if briefly, about 'expressions of Western hegemony, attempts to cull and harvest the world's cultures' (257), but chooses to rely on Girard, 'a dyed-in-the-wool advocate of differentiation' (234) and Freud, whom he describes as 'a social Darwinist' (236). So is the future of ritual just a

mess, or do we get upset about it, and make an attempt to insert our own values into its misty becoming? Is ritual part of a value-system, but its future not? Should we protest against these 'expressions of Western hegemony' while we are waiting for 'more equality of power, more actual multiculturalism' (257)? Should we refuse to sign up for workshops? Or do we just rely on the fact that the 'avant-garde is art's permanent revolution', and on those subversive qualities of 'experimental art' that we all know and love so well, and trust so implicitly?

A word about Schechner's diagrams: *The Future of Ritual* is a volume with photographs and maps and plans, but only one diagram (7.1: 229), reflecting the trend towards documentation that characterizes the book. This diagram shows us, right at the beginning, 'the ritual tree', which leads upwards from the root in 'ritualization' through increasingly sophisticated, animate life-forms to a branching at 'human ritualization'. From there three branches support 'social ritual', 'religious ritual', and 'aesthetic ritual' and spread themselves into 'everyday life, sports, and politics', 'observances, celebrations and rites of passage' and 'codified forms and ad hoc forms' respectively. It is, as Schechner describes it, a figure of the 'evolution of ritual'.

In the archetypal essay of the second edition of *Performance Theory*, Schechner had announced his theoretical programme with a rejection of the thesis of the Cambridge anthropologists, and implicitly of all developmental and evolutionary schemes for performance. The diagram there, Figure 1.1 (3), which represented the misleading Cambridge thesis, had its root in

'primal ritual', and of the 'rites' that were its branches (it resembled a shrub rather than a tree) two had falsely flowered as 'tragedy' and 'comedy'.

Displaced and disgraced as a source for drama in Schechner's figurative beginning, 'ritual' reappears in the end as a undeniable source of performance. So the 'future of ritual' becomes most apparent as the restoration and refiguration of its presence in theory.

Graham Ley

REFERENCE
F. Kermode (1967) *The Sense of an Ending*, New York: Oxford University Press.

Shamanism: Archaic Techniques of Ecstasy

Mircea Eliade
trans. W. R. Trask
Bollingen Series LXXVI
Princeton, NJ: Princeton University Press
1974 (1964)
610 pp.. ISBN 0 691 01779 4

In my paperback edition, the volume's index ends on page 610. That index, itself thirty-seven pages long, contains an entry for 'rite(s)/ritual(s)' on page 600. But here are listed only four pages: two under 'fertility', one under 'harvest', and one under 'initiation', although there are also 'see s.v.' references under 'hunting', 'Medicine', 'of passage', and 'of "roads"', which direct you to those index headings, comprising another eight pages of references among them. That's all. And there is no entry for 'performance'.

And yet I judge that Mircea Eliade's vast compendium on

shamanism, first published in French in 1951, has become for many readers decades later an incitement to – perhaps a manual for – the making of ritual. Partly this has to do with the popularity of shamanism as a recycled spiritual option among the unchurched religious seekers of the postmodern West. Partly it has to do with Eliade's role as uncontested authority on the 'archaic' essence of this fashionably 'earth-based' spirituality. It also has to do with another word in his book's subtitle: 'techniques'. In any case, this book, as a scholarly tome and a kind of sacred text, deserves periodic reappraisal – although I will not attempt a straightforward summary of its sprawling contents.

There were reports of what the West came to call 'shamanism' as early as the seventeenth century, when travellers returning to Russia from Siberia spoke of 'primitive' practices, repugnant but fascinating to a Europe on the brink of its rationalist Enlightenment, and attributed these to a figure whom one tribe, the Tungus, named as *saman*. Later, as the discipline of anthropology came into existence, in the nineteenth century, there were scholarly descriptions and assessments, with the western suffix '-ism' appended to the Tungus word for this pagan religious specialist.

By the mid-twentieth century, Eliade had a thousand sources to draw on as an 'historian of religions', who had never done fieldwork with the Tungus or any other indigenous people. In his view, stated in the opening pages of *Shamanism*, the history-of-religions approach to the texts and testimonies from the field could contribute a more comprehensive perspective on what he saw as a primarily religious phenomenon than anthropology, psychology, sociology, or history in the usual sense could supply by themselves.

Eliade was by all accounts an indefatigable researcher, and the sheer size of his study evidences the comprehensiveness he ventured: in addition to its 610 pages there is a 12-page foreword, after which there are fourteen chapters, an epilogue, and a 56-page list of works cited. Moreover, with his kind of scholarly training he could also look past the context of a particular culture's shamanism to see similar structures or patterns in other religious contexts around the world and in different historical periods. This 'comparativist' methodology, stressing shared traits among widely separated sets of spiritual practices, is one reason why Eliade's book is still in print at the end of the twentieth century.

Among non-scholars, apparently universal themes are spiritually appealing simply for their universality, and not seldom impel people toward some sort of ritual practice. The popular success of the ex-academic Michael Harner's workshops in neo-shamanism is reliant on this idea of what Harner calls a 'core' of cross-cultural elements common to most or all indigenous shamanisms, an idea he credits to Eliade (Harner 1982).

For his part, Eliade never gave workshops in neo-shamanic ritual and never referred to Harner's. But the emphasis on techniques in his big book seemed an invitation to drop the 'cultural trappings' and even the religious cosmology surrounding particular shamanisms so as to make possible the 'direct experience' of a supposed generic shamanism in weekends such as Harner's of ritualized drumming and guided imagery. Another term from Eliade's subtitle, 'archaic', once meant outdated, yet in the decontextualized practices of neo-shamanism the word has come to mean primal, originary, pure – especially when the privations of any specific shamanic culture and the beliefs and rigours entailed in an indigenous shaman's vocation are jettisoned.

Meanwhile, academics have not been unanimously kind to this eminent scholar, or to his masterwork on shamanism. An early review by the anthropologist Edmund Leach referred to Eliade's scholarship as 'sermons by a man on a ladder' (Leach 1966), while a more recent essay by the Russian ethnographer V. N. Basilov noted that his own fieldwork in Siberia scarcely verified Eliade's stress upon the shaman's upward trance-journeys (Basilov 1990). Additionally, performance studies scholar-turned-cultural historian Michael Taussig has complained bitingly about Eliade's concept of the shaman's magical flight as a satisfying narrative of ritual death always coming to closure in rebirth (Taussig 1989).

What these criticisms have in common is their impatience with an historian who undervalued historical contexts, a scholar of religions who seemed to be driven by his own unacknowledged commitment to a Christian mystical resolution, a celestial salvation – toward which he saw shamanism tending at a lower stage of religious evolution.

Knowing about such accusations I pursued my own investigation in writing my book *The Soul of Shamanism*, and learned by simple arithmetic that, despite occasional statements as to their equal validity, Eliade's actual references vastly privilege shamans' heavenly flights over their underworld journeys (Noel 1997: 34). Moreover, the latter realm is often portrayed as 'infernal', with ecstatic travel there only a prelude to ascension. I then wondered why Eliade the painstaking scholar could so skew the ethnographic material in his sources.

I was surprised to find that at the time when he was working on his massive shamanism volume he was also composing a long novel in Romanian, *Noaptea de Sanziene*, translated years later as *The Forbidden Forest* (Eliade 1978[1955]). In the imagery of this novel, Eliade's religious vision of a celestial Christianity is made plain as the shaping force within his work on shamanism. Accordingly, I had to conclude that although the information in *Shamanism* is often still useful – and some shamans do indeed ascend to the skies in their trances – Eliade's interpretation of his data lacks the authoritative objectivity promised by the scholarly text's seriousness, scope and popular reputation. The preoccupations of a religious imagination as much as of neutral 'scientific' research characterize the dry erudition of his sweeping overview.

And yet his book's popular reception continues to hold it as the absolutely authoritative account of the ritual practices of traditional shamanism. It is not that, as I have sought to indicate. To call it 'the bible' of neo-shamanism is closer to the truth, but only in the sense that the bible is a blend of faith with fact, and its authoritative status requires faith on the part of the reader. Although personal religiosity combined with patient research to create his text, such a requirement was undoubtedly not what Eliade had in mind for his readers.

One could also designate *Shamanism* as a devotional handbook for those who seek their own 'ecstasy' by ransacking and attempting to apply the techniques described in its pages. To stand outside of one's normal embodied self – the meaning of *ec-stasis* – and be 'out of the body', 'beside oneself' in dreaming or on drugs, in raves or rituals, cannot but be an attractive prospect for seekers, who confuse recreational romanticism, however sincere, with the genuine religious healing that has been so traumatically achieved by shamans in indigenous cultures that the West has tried (all too often with success) to obliterate. Now we want their rituals, sanitized and safe, to perform as our experimental pastime. Eliade surely never expected or intended that his book be used in this way either, but now it is taken to provide the imprimatur of scholarship, even of a kind of 'science', for neoshamanists who use its second-hand ethnographic descriptions as performance scripts.

Instead of such problematic implementation, as literal-minded as it is unwittingly colonialist, let us look again at this imaginative academic's 'exhaustive' narrative. Just to read through its 610-plus pages is a kind of initiation, to be sure, as was writing it, but it won't initiate us into indigenous shamanism – and neither will rituals inferred from its pages.

Even its tempting catalogue of techniques includes only one explicit reference to actual initiation rituals, where we read that rites marking the passage from one age-group to another, or admission to a tribal secret society, all involve a symbolic death and resurrection. Drawing upon five sources, Eliade lists six

typical features of these initiations: a period of isolation in the bush; the daubing of face and body with ashes or the donning of funerary masks; symbolic burial; symbolic descent to the underworld; hypnotic sleep or unconsciousness; and various difficult physical ordeals (64). We should note that even this concrete description of features is generalized, not an account of one tribe's ritual on one occasion. Moreover, on the next page he points out that 'morphologically the future shaman's initiatory ordeals are of the same order as this great class of passage rites and ceremonies for entering secret societies' (65). In other words, what he has just described as features of initiation rituals are not specifically shamanic at all, but are only similar as to general form. Indeed, he goes on to say there are no passage rites in Siberia or central Asia, the homelands of shamanism. And there is the critique of Michael Taussig to remind us that death and rebirth narratives – the core of initiation rituals for Eliade – are not necessarily congruent with shamanic experience, which can be chaotic and unresolved.

Consequently, the foundation provided by Eliade's 'authoritative' study of shamanism for performing authentic shamanic rituals turns out to be virtually non-existent. Of course, learning that that is the case, one could still press ahead to invent performances that are faux-shamanic, I suppose, postmodernist innovations that acknowledge their lack of grounding in indigenous practice. Such neo-Eliadean constructions might even usefully subvert Eliade's Christian mystical rendering of the ethnography of shamanism, operating mindfully in the domain indicated by his adjective 'symbolic' while relinquishing all claims to being authoritative – except as an authoritative invention of *fin-de-millenium* desire and creativity.

Interestingly enough, in a lecture entitled 'Waiting for the dawn', given not long before his death in 1986, Eliade spoke approvingly of the yearning for initiation that he observed in the western youth culture of the 1960s and 1970s. He cited the popularity of Carlos Castaneda's writings about a supposed Mexican Indian shaman as resulting in a 'para-shamanistic underground movement' which sought a 'spiritual preparation' for its hallucinogenic ecstasies. He also noted that 'professors of theatre like Theodore Kirby, rightly detected in shamanism one of the origins of drama. Moreover, shamanistic techniques are employed in experimental performances of the so-called "Alternative Theatre"' (Eliade 1985: 15). He did not elaborate on this last remark, nor did he ever suggest that his own book could or should be a manual for such performances. The focus on a desire for initiation, however, for personal *renovatio* or renewal, seems as good a diagnosis as any for why ritual-prone post-modernists might be lured into doing so. If the yearning is real, however, Eliade's text is a dubious means of satisfying it.

With all of the foregoing having been said, a final possibility remains. We could arguably abandon Eliade altogether as *substance* and still see his work as a handy *scaffolding* for constructing a neo-shamanic assessment of the movement of our own lives. We might find that the experience of living our ordinary western lives of suffering and survival already entails initiations we perform unmindfully every day. It only

requires the difficult work of making them conscious, re-imagining ourselves, in order to find a shamanism fit for western seeking. These could be rituals answering to our yearning, honestly distant from whatever really went on in Siberia or central Asia with the actual shamans whom Mircea Eliade saw, and showed us, only through the refractions of his enormous account.

Daniel C. Noel

REFERENCES

Basilov, V. N. (1990) 'Chosen by the spirits', in M. M. Balzer (ed.) *Shamanism: Soviet Studies of Traditional Religion in Siberia and Central Asia*, London: M. E. Sharpe.
Eliade, Mircea (1978[1955]) *The Forbidden Forest*, trans. M. L. Ricketts and M. P. Stevenson, London: Notre Dame University Press.
Eliade, Mircea (1985) 'Waiting for the dawn', in D. Carrasco and J. M. Swanberg (eds) *Waiting for the Dawn: Mircea Eliade in Perspective*, London: Westview Press, 11–16.
Harner, Michael (1982) *The Way of the Shaman*, New York: Bantam.
Leach, Edmund (1966) 'Sermons by a man on a ladder', *New York Review of Books*, 20 October, 28–31.
Noel, Daniel (1997) *The Soul of Shamanism: Western Fantasies, Imaginal Realities*, New York: Continuum.
Taussig, Michael (1989) 'The nervous system: homesickness and dada', *Stanford Humanities Review* 1: 44–81.

Anthropocosmic Theatre: Rite in the Dynamics of Theatre

Nicolàs Núñez
trans. Ronan J. Fitzsimmons
London: Harwood 1998 [1987]
188 pp. ISBN: 3718-657112 (pb); 3718-657104 (hb)

RITUAL AND TRANSFORMATION

Nicolàs Núñez's book *Anthropocosmic Theatre: Rite in the Dynamics of Theatre* (first published in Spanish in 1987) has recently been published by Harwood in a translation by Ronan J. Fitzsimmons. It offers some insights into the sources and shapes of the methods he employs in his workshops (e.g. in the UK at the CPR conference in Cardiff in 1993) and enables contextualization within the forms of other recent theatre practice.

Octavio Pax claims that 'Núñez and his colleagues have striven to re-introduce the sacred dimension into theatre'. Núñez's principal sources are the Tibetan Dance of the Black Hat (from Bon shamanistic tradition) and the Mexican/Nahautlan Shell Dance.

The book itself is patchy (it has some fascinating detail on the above sources at the beginning, unnecessary reproduction of tedious official speeches at the end). This is perhaps symptomatic of something more worrying. There are clear similarities in some of the work as described with aspects of Grotowski's para-theatrical practices; aims and approaches to some extent also recall Barba and Brook, and Artaud lurks in the background (so too does Carlos Castaneda, though he is not credited in the text).

The problem, we suggest, lies in the fact that, as with these other practitioners, although the intention is admirable and the results sometimes impressive, they do not seem to have a clear understanding of the full implications of the traditions and processes on which they are drawing. These traditions, existing as part of a cultural weave, have complex ways of understanding the methods they employ and the stages of any resulting change. Their aim is (in Schechner's sense) transformation: that involves physiological and psychological changes of functioning, both short- and long-term. Grotowski, for instance, borrowed (via Barba's mediation) from Indian methodology, and Barba himself has attempted to locate and analyse a 'pre-expressive' condition underlying or generating the dynamics of performance. Many attempts to account for what is going on here, however have either bogged down in semiotics (is it a 'subscore' or an 'underscore'?) or floated into ecstatic ineffability. There are two main reasons for this: (1) they have no clear sense of the precise conditions of consciousness (understood as a psycho-physiological pheonomenon) operative in and during these changes; and (2) they have no adequate terminology for or awareness of the levels of language that precede verbalization.

Núñez's book offers the chance to think about these things again, precisely because it presents on the one hand claims for an important dimension of performance/transformatory work, and has on the other notable gaps when it comes to describing in detail the processes and effects of that work. If, as many practitioners have implicitly or explicitly claimed, performance is or should be transformative, we need to look more closely at how it is so, and at how the traditions from which performance tools have been acquired themselves understand what is occurring.

Peter Malekin and Ralph Yarrow

Masked Performance: The Play of Self and Other in Ritual and Trance

John Emigh

Philadelphia: University of Pennsylvania Press 1996

xvii + 336 pp. 93 illus., 8 colour plates Bibliography, Index
ISBN 0-8122-3058-2 (cloth); 0-8122-1336-X (pbk).

Emigh's stated intention is to deal with the relationship of the mask to its wearer in ritual and theatre 'as a paradigm for the relationships of self and other (and self and self) that lie at the heart of the theatrical process' (xvii). To a large extent, the book provides descriptive material, focusing on performance traditions in Asia. Thus, the first chapter broadly discusses 'the range, modalities and psychological underpinnings of masked play' (xx) against the background of theatre and rituals from Papua New Guinea. Chapter 2 takes up trance performances in Orissa, India; and in Chapter 3 a performance by Balinese Topeng master I Nyoman Kakul is described and analysed in detail, followed (Chapter 4) by a transcript of that performance. In Chapter 6, the life and work of Hajari Bhand, a street performer who was formerly a Rajasthani court jester, 'provides a focus for further observations on the frequently mischievous play between self and other that is central to theatrical practice' (xx). Throughout those chapters, a rich variety of well-researched information is provided in clear, easily understandable language. Even those who have never witnessed the performance styles described, will get a vivid impression of the music and the movements, the preparation of performers, and the author's fascination with all those aspects. Numerous black-and-white photographs and some colour plates illustrate Emigh's descriptions.

The use of mask in Asian ritual and theatre is placed within the contexts of both their cultures of origin and predominantly western conceptualizations of ritual, theatre, performance, and related areas such as play, identity and consciousness. This contextualization is at the centre of Chapter 5, adapting Schechner's 'taxonomical model' to describe the 'interactions among "domains" that characterize theatrical forms' (171) with regard to Balinese Topeng. It becomes evident that most of the material presented in the book goes back to earlier essays published in the *Drama Review* and elsewhere: references, although relevant, tend to become dated, and the activity of recycling (a term Emigh uses in his introduction with reference to the book) has not included sufficient updating of the theoretical framework into which he chooses to place his excellent descriptive observations. As a result, the relationship of self and other, one of the issues which Emigh sets out to address, remains terminologically and conceptually vague. What is the self, what the other, how are they defined, on their own and in relation to each other? Which approach in philosophy, psychology, or any other discipline dealing with this vast subject should be used when addressing the self and the other in the context of ritual and theatre? Brief passages point in this direction, such as reference to Csikszentmihalyi's concept of flow (26–8), but they are far too occasional to be systematic.

Chapter 7 takes the form of an interview with Emigh, conducted in 1981 (or 1982; introduction and chapter disagree as to the date), and shows how Asian ritual and theatre influenced Emigh's own creative work as director and performer. The conclusion in Chapter 8 develops those personal ideas further and brings them up to date with a long section on recent intercultural theatre practice, highlighting productions by Suzuki, Lee Breuer, Jatinder Verma and Peter Brook. Emigh's insight here is striking: 'the process involved in producing intercultural works is very much like that of adjusting to a new mask: approaching a performative tradition with respect, appreciating the potential life residing within a form, and finding a meeting ground between "self" and "other" that will allow a new theatrical life to flourish' (285).

On the whole, Emigh's book does not successfully deliver on some of the targets it sets out to address. However, it offers well-presented, detailed and valuable insight into the use of masks in (predominantly Asian) ritual and theatre. It is highly recommendable on that account.

Daniel Meyer-Dinkgräfe

Les Chamanes de la préhistoire: Transe et magie dans les grottes ornées.

Jean Clottes and David Lewis-Williams
Paris: Editions du Seuil 1996.
ISBN 2–02–028902–4, Price FF 249
German-language edition:

Schamanen: Trance und Magie in der Höhlenkunst der Steinzeit.

Sigmaringen: Jan Thorbecke Verlag 1997.
ISBN 3-7995-9051-X, DM 79
American edition:

The Shamans of Pre-History: Trance and Magic in the Painted Caves

New York: Abrams 1999.
ISBN 0-8109-4182-1 (hb), Price $49.50

David Lewis-Williams has for many years been a leading proponent of the shamanism theory used to explain the meaning behind palaeolithic cave art. For more than twenty-five years active in documenting South African rock art, more recently he has been relating the results of his research to rock art studies in Europe, Australia and the Americas. His interpretation of palaeolithic rock art as reflecting the insights and experiences of shamans in trance performances draws on the ritual practices of the San people, on ethnographic studies of shamanism and on recent neuropsychological research into trance and altered states of consciousness.

His many papers and articles have caused considerable controversies in scholarly circles. Archaeologists have become extremely sceptical of the method of interpreting prehistoric art by analogy with ritual practices of more recent periods. Similarly, essentializing theories that presume a similar biological and psychological rationale behind ancient and modern art are viewed with great suspicion nowadays. Too many of the early studies abounded with wild generalizations, oversimplifications and plain wishful thinking, or what Paul Bahn called 'a wafer-thin layer of fact nestling in a thick sandwich of assumptions and subjectivity' (*Rock Art and Prehistory* [Oxford: 1991], 12). The shaky foundations of the attempts to relate palaeolithic rock art to hunting magic, fertility rites, bear cults, etc., have caused an understandable backlash and a general reticence about engaging with the meaning and function of this art at all.

David Lewis-Williams's publications have contributed markedly towards bringing the question of

meaning back on to the agenda of rock art studies. The present volume, written jointly with Jean Clottes, is an attempt to present to a more general public the main aspects of his shamanic theory. It is lavishly illustrated, is written in a popular vein and can be counted as a useful introduction to the subject for readers from outside the archaeological camp.

Readers of this journal are likely to be familiar with some of the key texts in shamanic studies and will therefore find the first chapter, with its highly selective description of shamanic practices from a variety of cultures, too general, if not superficial. Only the section on shamanic practices of the San people, gathered from ethnographic accounts and contemporary observation, contains some new aspects, because they offer an explanation of the ritual meaning behind African rock art and thereby present a perspective on similar works created during the European Stone Age.

Chapter 2 is a brief description of some of the key characteristics of Franco-Cantabrian rock art in the open air, under rock shelters, and in caves, executed as paintings, engravings, or modelled clay. The authors consider the main themes, their geographic-chronological distribution and stylistic variations. None of these discussions differs substantially from the picture presented in handbooks and other general introductions to the subject. The same can be said about the third chapter, which outlines the main schools of thought regarding the interpretation of palaeolithic art: art-for-art's-sake, totemism, hunting magic, fertility rites, structuralism. Some of the main arguments for and against these theories are rehearsed in the fashion of their main representatives and illustrated with photographs of examples regularly drawn on by these scholars.

So far, the book offers no surprises and only readers with next to no knowledge of rock art will gather new information from the text (the excellent photographs will be welcomed, I guess, by every reader, specialist or not).

It is only in the last third of the book that the authors enter into controversial territory. They present and substantiate their main reasons for suggesting a shamanic origin of many of the palaeolithic art works on rock surfaces. These last two chapters summarize a discussion that has been conducted in specialist journals and at various rock art conferences, and go a few stages beyond the suggestions previously made by Eliade, La Barre, Halifax, Lommel and Noel Smith.

As many authors have emphasized, the range of animals depicted in caves is only a small segment of the actual fauna of the period (and played no role, or only a subordinate part, in the nutritional habits of the people). This standardization suggests that the animals portrayed played a symbolic role in the religious concepts of the period. Clottes and Lewis-Williams go a step further and say that the images are related to shamanic vision quests. They leave it open whether the images were created during or after a trance experience, but are convinced that many of them fall into the three main categories of hallucinations, which are a neuropsychological constant among humans of all periods and cultures: geometric; animalistic; and mixed human/animal figures.

Clottes and Lewis-Williams believe that the geographic position of rock paintings may reflect different rituals of a shamanic nature: those in the open air, under a rock shelter, or at the cave mouth possibly relate to healing or divination rituals; those in the large inner halls to communal trance journeys; those in the distant recesses, to individual meditation and hallucination. While these assumptions are rather debatable, there is little doubt that the caves selected for decoration had special features that made them suited to ritual purposes. Artists seem to have explored very carefully the rock surfaces before deciding what to paint where. Some rocks had a shape or texture that suggested certain animals; some were suitable for being touched, others for being viewed from a distance by large groups of people; some were surrounded by cracks or recesses, where ritual objects could be deposited. In many cases, an intimate relationship between rock surface and image can be observed. This is especially so when an image is viewed with a flickering torch or oil lamp: the angle and nature of the light make the animal emerge, vanish and resurface in a magical fashion. The rock surface thereby appears like a membrane connecting the two worlds of humans and spirits. This impression is enhanced by the engraved images found in many caves. Here, the person on a vision quest literally cuts through the surface of the rock, creating a pathway for the spirits to emerge, or for the seer to penetrate the spirit world and establish contact with these beings on the other side of the membrane.

In Clottes and Lewis-Williams's theory, the caves were places of supernatural powers, which could be contacted and appropriated by means of paintings or engravings. The images themselves crystallized the visions of the shamans and were an integral element of the ritual process of securing the support of the spirit world. To what degree this interpretation is correct, nobody will ever determine. Some people will apply the above-quoted verdict by Paul Bahn and reject it as hypothetical and unprovable (as, in fact, Bahn himself does in his recent *Journey through the Ice Age* [London: 1997], 181–3). Others, however, will be inspired to reflect further on some of the aspects emphasized by Clottes and Lewis-Williams and hitherto undervalued (e.g. the relationship between geometric signs and figurative paintings, or between rock surface and painted/engraved image).

Scholars coming from the discipline of Performance Studies will find the hypotheses outlined and illustrated in this volume highly suggestive, because shamanism is now widely regarded as a vital link between ritual and theatre. Although this relationship is believed to be very old, ethnographic evidence for it is restricted to recent historic periods. Any visual records from earlier times, reaching back even to the prehistoric, are therefore extremely valuable. Clottes and Lewis-Williams's documentation and evaluation of these images are pointing us in a direction that warrants the attention of, and further examination by, anybody engaged in performance research.

Günter Berghaus

Adults in Wonderland
Grace Lau
New York: Serpent's Tail
1997.

ISBN: 1852-425520 (pb); £19.99

Photography is subversive, not when it frightens, repels or even stigmatises, but when it is pensive, when it thinks.
(Barthes 1981)

Grace Lau's retrospective, *Adults in Wonderland*, is a quest for erotic imagery for women, which, inspired by her curiosity and a love of her camera, introduced her to the 'forbidden' territories of fetish and S/M. In 1984 she became the photographer of the sub-cultural magazine *Skin Two,* while her many exhibitions have led to wide media coverage and established her work among critics, who have described her photography as having 'demarginalized pornography' and made it acceptable again for feminists (25). In 1992 Lau set up 'Exposures', a series of photographic workshops which promoted women's visual perspectives based on their own experience and history. Describing her own work Lau writes that her camera acts as a catalyst to animate her subjects, producing images that deconstruct traditional concepts, make new reference points and reveal and conceal identities.

In this time of fetishizing and commodifying the body, transgressive sexual imagery has become almost as familiar to our western society as the violence and horror in cinema. The fashion world, appropriating sub-cultural style and queer art, has upgraded fetish gear (and its association with devious sexualities) to mainstream via the cat-walk shows of designers such as Jean-Paul Gaultier, Vivienne Westwood and Alexander McQueen. Body art such as tattooing and piercing has similarly infiltrated popular culture, while body modification and the work of the modern primitive artists have called for a new focus on the body in radical, sometimes drastic searches to reclaim the body from the jaws of new technologies and science. Such body reconfigurations, in their contribution to and beyond the art world, have attracted much

healthy attention and opened up new possibilities for polysexual erotic imagery in the visual arts. However, until recently, because of unresolved debates around pornography, erotic photography has been left to fester and women, needless to say, have been the losers both in terms of the female body being such a taboo subject for erotic photography and as the receivers of erotic imagery themselves. While women photographers such as Cindy Sherman have done much to subvert the politics around the female body and Della Grace has helped to fill the void of sexual imagery for women, such work is still under-represented. Lau's work, taken over the last fifteen years, records the thrill of polymorphous perversity and fills a gap in this market.

Lau takes us by the hand and guides us through an adult fantasy world of fetishism, sexual deviance and sado-masochism to discover imagery that is testingly erotic. Worlds of dressing-up and toys, dungeons and castles, parties and balls recall the adventures of Lewis Carroll's heroine Alice, the only difference being that Lau's worlds are for adults. The photographs are layered with relevant quotations and accompanied by an autobiographical text, which is anecdotal and insightful. The inclusion of text unpacks the mystery of the photographs and makes the reader familiar and even comfortable with images that for some could be hard-edged and alienating. Lau's book is not masturbation material. You will not find the sensationalism of S/M magazines or the arresting glamour of Mapplethorpe, but rather will make discoveries of power and pleasure from her tactful feminist perspective.

Lau herself explains with honesty and involvement the very real

experiences in which she found herself during her years as a photographer, and in this sense the book is like a photo-journal. She sees herself as an extension of her camera and an active participant with her subjects, a far cry from the objective photographer. By adopting this method she has had continuously to question her own identity and subjectivity, and this is obvious in some of the images especially those where she is reflected in the mirror, beside her subjects.

The opening chapter shows her pioneering work on the male nude and features male dancers who were compliant subjects. Her portraits then reflect her interest in blurring gender boundaries, through her discovery of a third gender – powerful women body-builders, cross-dressers, transvestites, female-looking men and androgynous women. These photographs are discoveries and statements rather than erotic material for women, very staged in their presentation, and they work best in the colour shots, where their ironic artificiality is exaggerated.

Having discovered the concept of photo-male nudes for female viewers and learned that women found more erotic both a story-line around their male nudes and the sight of couples interacting, Lau broadened her horizons and moved out of her studio and domestic areas into the domains of 'pervs' – the participants of sado-masochism. Various friends, such as a financial consultant who had a penchant for cross-dressing, took her to clubs in London. Lau's work in this section reflects the risk she took in moving out of her 'natural' creative space, and also the inspiration that she found in such adventurous environments, which were at first so alien to her. The photographs are fluid, they are more collaborative and they capture the genuine pleasure of the subjects in whatever activity they are performing.

This was the world of the masquerade, fantastical costumes, where 'Alice' really started to play and Lau felt that she became a third in the slave/dominatrix duo. In justification of her involvement, Lau borrows a quotation from Susan Sontag (1980) describing the act of photographing, and writes that 'it is a way of at least tacitly, often explicitly, encouraging whatever is going on to keep on happening'. She admits to finding some of this work hard, and a feeling of fragmentation resulted from taking so many photographs that became absorbed into the masquerades and roles of their subjects. She writes: 'At times, I feel that all the world outside is indeed a stage and that the scene I am photographing is so intense and vividly real, the rest fades into insignificance' (45). An extraordinary site for one shoot was at a bed-and-breakfast bondage hotel, which had a fully equipped, heated and sound-proofed dungeon, where a couple had chosen to celebrate their tenth wedding anniversary. The photographs convey an ease that Lau genuinely experienced with most of the sadomasochistic practices she photographed, because of the participants' rules of consent, and speak of the trust between client and photographer, which Lau herself felt was partly to do with her being a woman; the end-result is a celebration of the pleasure in sexual deviancy.

The final chapter addresses the gaze and 'who's looking and at whom'. The photographs show audiences looking at male or female

strippers, the open, jovial, relaxed atmosphere of the female audience watching men strip juxtaposed with the clandestine, tense, hostile atmosphere of the male audience watching the female stripper (reflected in the absence of photographs of these unwilling participants). Through this work she moved into another area, 'the Readers' Wives' – that of top-shelf men's magazines where male readers submit personal photographs of their wives in supposedly erotic poses. Lau writes about her personal dilemmas when working with a man who wanted his wife to be photographed in a bath of tomato ketchup, while he directed her. She expresses her confusion as to why this might be erotic, and describes herself as feeling out of control when taking the photographs, like a voyeur without consent to do her job, because of the wife's submissiveness. This ambivalence is apparent in the photograph of this scene, which is taken from the shadows, and lacks the vitality and involvement of other images.

A book, whose approach and content are similar to Lau's is *The Lusty Ladies* by the American photographer Erika Langley (1997), which documents Langley's time working in a strip club, where in order to take non-objectifying photographs of female strippers and to collaborate properly, she became one herself. Both books avoid the tacky gloss of the commercial porn market – gay or heterosexual. They display their subjects as very real embodied people, who enjoy working with these women photographers. The main difference between the two books is that Langley's female nudes are assertive in their demystifying gutsiness, whereas Lau's are confrontational and take refuge behind

props. For Lau the female nude is as problematic a subject as ever, but she argues that when photographs are taken in mutually supportive environments, while questions about guilt, relationships, sex, communication and identity may not be resolved, 'issues are allowed to be raised and explored with a view to reducing their negative and dysfunctional facets' (111).

Josephine Leask

REFERENCES

Barthes, R. (1981) *Camera Lucida*, New York: Hill & Wang.
Langley, E. (1997) *The Lusty Ladies*, Zurich: Scalo.
Sontag, S. (1980) *On Photography*, Harmondsworth, Mx: Penguin.

First We Take Manhattan: Four American Women and the New York School of Dance Criticism

Diana Theodores
Amsterdam: Harwood Academic Press, 1996.
180 pp. ISBN: 3-7186-5886-0 (hb)

First We Take Manhattan is a kind of testament to the relationship between what the author identifies as a golden age of American dance and a golden age of dance criticism in the years 1965–85. Dance and dance criticism as a 'new literature' (2) are seen to be interlocked in their extraordinary development. As the book's title suggests, Theodores presents us with a narrative of how a new frontier of dance writing was forged and, through it, how an American dance ideal was defined.

The book celebrates the work of four North American dance critics: Arlene Croce, Nancy Goldner, Deborah Jowitt and Marcia Siegel, who are identified as forming a 'New York School' of dance criticism (1). Three opening chapters introducing context, influences and stylistic elements are followed by four 'files' outlining each writer's specific contribution. Rather than taking a critical approach in the broader sense, Theodores writes something more like an extremely favourable review of this group of writers. They are, indeed, her models and mentors.

The dance criticism of Croce, Goldner, Jowitt and Siegel has often been dubbed 'descriptive' – sometimes pejoratively, to suggest that there is something 'beyond description' that these writers should really be doing. In Theodores' terms, however, this kind of writing constitutes 'a new literature' – one that is truly able to do justice to, and that helps to shape, the analytic and formal values of the various traditions of American concert dance.

Theodores invokes an earlier generation of 'pioneering' American choreographers as a kind of model for her four critics:

> I cannot help being fascinated with the parallel that exists between this group of contemporary American women writers who were the pioneers of a new dance criticism and the women choreographers who pioneered the American modern dance (7).

Theodores suggests here a kind of lineage of pioneering American women – some dancing, the others seeking to define the values of that dancing for a public. Deborah Jowitt is quoted, writing of Martha Graham's *Frontier*: 'The conquest of the land is analogous to the forging of her body' (2).

Here the Americanness of American dance is closely associated with women and their spatially powerful physical presences. Watching over their legacy are the four critics, 'always poised between heritage and vanguard' (4). They are a 'sacred sisterhood' who 'wrote into their critic's job description a self-appointed guardianship' (4) of America's dance.

However, *First We Take Manhattan* is even more, perhaps, the story of a *paternity* in American dance and its criticism, because the figures of Edwin Denby and George Balanchine are used to represent founding ideals in writing and choreography respectively. Denby even takes on a god-like aspect as the 'spiritual' exemplar (19). Chapter 2, 'Under the influence', is devoted to claiming a central role for these two men during the 1940s and 1950s, in establishing the values of formalism and classicism as definitional of American dance. According to Theodores' dates, the end of the golden age 'dance boom' came just two years after Balanchine's death.

The emphasis on an aesthetics of classicism, formalism and 'purity of means', of which both Denby's criticism and Balanchine's 're-invention' of classical ballet are seen to be the epitome, is the means by which Theodores comes to generalize both her New York School of critics and the dance about which they write. 'Purity of means' is the bridge between elite/virtuoso (uptown) and democratic/pedestrian (downtown) dance. But in supporting her argument by taking her examples from reviews that are almost exclusively about dances from the former category, Theodores avoids important, fundamental differences between and even within these two broad divisions. She observes that 'the New York School critics enjoyed, during the time span discussed, a more wide ranging, active dance environment than any other dance critics in the world' (15); and yet the works reviewed, pictured, discussed are selected very narrowly from this broad spectrum, and were mostly made before the 'golden age' in question. The influence or presence of seminal choreographers and dancers from the Judson Church group – such as Yvonne Rainer – who played a crucial role in making the 'golden age' what it was, are missing from the book. Theodores' construction of coherence, rather than of diversity and difference, is an ideological one: American dance is pure, morally exemplary and noble – America and its greatest dances and dancers are forged in mutual reflection. Furthermore, in this ideology she can be seen to take her cue from the critics themselves. She quotes Marcia Siegel writing in *The Shapes of Change*:

> Perhaps it is not too much to suggest a relationship between these confident unadorned bodies of Balanchine's and the sense Americans have of being at ease in space (38).

The sense we get in Theodores' book is that the best dance and dancing, whether it be Balanchine's, Graham's, or Tharp's, is the best because it is seen to embody certain universal truths, and moral and aesthetic values which in turn make this dance quintessentially 'American'. In her account, the New York School critics are enlightened by these dances within which such durable values are already given, awaiting identification through a descriptive style in which the subjectivity of the writer is passionate but never, itself, in question. Here also, the critics' guardianship of a national dance ideal is at the expense of the differentiation between different lineages that they elsewhere fervently insist upon.

Indeed, the great value of *First We Take Manhattan* is in the way it makes us aware of the role played by a committed, literate and intelligent dance criticism in the development of a rich dance culture. Within the time period discussed we can see how these critics met the challenge of an essentially ephemeral art form, developing a kind of writing that enabled the experience and resonance of dance to be extended beyond the immediacy of its performance. Concerned to meet the challenge of ever new forms of dance and to guard against 'undifferentiated' viewing, Croce, Goldner, Jowitt and Siegel worked untiringly in their reviews, books and teaching, to identify and document the heritages out of or against which these new manifestations were emerging. The four critics encompass an unparalleled dance literacy made possible both by an environment that afforded them 'access not only to an unprecedented volume of performance but also to changing casts, retrospectives of large bodies of choreographers' works, to revivals and reconstructions as much as to rebellions' (3), and by their own deep commitments and perceptions.

Sally Gardner

Archive Review

The archives of Viennese Actionism

The historical period of *Wiener Aktionismus* (Viennese Actionism) comprises the years from 1962 to approximately 1971.[1] During this period of time, Günter Brus, Otto Muehl, Hermann Nitsch and Rudolf Schwarzkogler, the protagonists of this Austrian contribution to modern performance art, were active in Vienna, exchanging experiences and occasionally completing projects together. In the 1960s, these artist friends were also called, although less frequently, *Wiener Aktionsgruppe* (Viennese Action Group) and *Institut für Direkte Kunst Wien* (Institute for Direct Art Vienna).[2]

Especially in the early phase of Viennese actionism – the classic period of this movement – the artists met with enormous difficulties. Actual or threatened imprisonments came close to imposing a work ban on the actionists and caused them either to emigrate, to retreat into the isolation of the studio, or to express their ideas exclusively in the form of theoretical concepts. Because of these difficulties, up to now no archive dedicated to this historic chapter in the development of modern Austrian art and culture has been established as a public institution. But at least two steps in this direction have been undertaken over the last years.

RUDOLF SCHWARZKOGLER AT THE MUSEUM MODERNER KUNST (STIFTUNG LUDWIG) IN VIENNA

More than two years ago, Lorant Hegyi established a permanent showroom on Viennese Actionism at the Palais Liechtenstein. It assembles the most important works that the Viennese Museum of Modern Art owns from these artists. Moreover, since 1982 nearly the complete œuvre of Rudolf Schwarzkogler (1940–69), especially his drafts and photographic work, as well as all his theoretical concepts created in the context of Viennese actionism, have come into the possession of the Museum Moderner Kunst (Stiftung Ludwig) in Vienna. In the rooms of the so-called *Zwanziger Haus* ('Twenties House'), the Schwarzkogler Archive is run by Dr Eva Badura-Triska. Visits to the archive can be arranged by telephone. Since Schwarzkogler sold hardly any of his works during his lifetime and, moreover, his output was exceptionally limited in quantity, most of them are in the archive of the Wiener Museum. In addition, all of Schwarzkogler's important actions were carried out in front of the photographic camera, which means that photographic images are the sole artistic form designed for viewing. In 1992, a detailed catalogue of Schwarzkogler's complete photographic œuvre was published on the occasion of a comprehensive retrospective exhibition,

curated by Eva Badura-Triska and Hubert Klocker on behalf of the Museum Moderner Kunst (Stiftung Ludwig) in Vienna.[3]

As regards the remaining protagonists of Viennese actionism, those interested in their work have to visit private archives dedicated to individual artists. There are also two collections of material which deal comprehensively with the phenomenon of performance art.

OTTO MUEHL

Until recently, there existed under the highly confusing title *Archiv des Wiener Aktionismus* (Archive of Viennese Actionism), a collection of material documenting the work of Otto Muehl. It was located on the premises of the Friedrichshof, a former farming estate in Burgenland, approximately one hour's drive from Vienna. The buildings, which used to house a commune originally led by Muehl and now dissolved, were taken over by a housing association and have consequently been subject to several extensions and conversions. The farm can be reached only via a cart track from the neighbouring villages of Parndorf or Zurndorf, and this position reflects the seclusion that Otto Muehl's commune sought in its day. The archive includes some original works of all four Viennese actionists, but the bulk of material relates to the actionist and later commune leader Otto Muehl. Only a

Performance Research 3(3), pp.130-133 © Routledge 1998

few editions, books and catalogues of the other actionists can be found in the Muehl archive, with the exception of documentary material on work jointly undertaken and actions carried out together with other members of the group.

The Friedrichshof archive offers a wide range of information on Muehl's early *Materialaktionen* (material actions): notebooks with draft sketches of the main sections of the actions; artistic and pseudo-political manifestos; information sheets on individual performances; an abundance of photographs taken during the actions, partly ordered and systematized by Muehl himself in photograph albums. Although the material at the Friedrichshof is representative of Muehl's work, it is by no means exhaustive (see below the report on the Sohm Archive and the Conz Archive). All photographic editions, originally published by Muehl himself and later by various institutions, are included in the archive and will be made available to visitors by appointment only. Although these photographs are essential sources for the study of Muehl's œuvre, they are usefully complemented in the Friedrichshof archive by personal notes made by the actionist and related to his early actions, his increasingly sociopolitical ideas in the late 1960s, and the concept of the commune he founded. Some major publications are missing (e.g. *mama & papa* [Frankfurt: Kohlkunst Verlag, 1970), and Muehl's film work is hardly represented at all. However, the former can be found in the Sohm Archive, the latter at Karlheinz and Renate Hein's P.A.P. Filmagentur in Munich (which will arrange screenings by written appointment).

HERMANN NITSCH

Obtaining information on Hermann Nitsch is, comparatively, much easier. All important materials, action paintings, videos, photographs and publications, as well as manuscripts, are collected at the Prinzendorf Castle in lower Austria (also approximately one hour's drive away from Vienna). Schloss Prinzendorf, built in 1750, has been the artist's residence since 1971. It lies at the centre of the Austrian wine-growing region with its inviting taverns and simple country folk. The artist spent some parts of his youth here; and knowing the landscape and inhabitants is helpful to our understanding of Nitsch's artistic approach and its realization in the *OrgienMysterienTheater*, which takes place in the vicinity of the castle. In order to gain a comprehensive understanding of the artist's work, one should visit the castle, the ideal venue for performances of Nitsch's *OrgienMysterienTheater*, which found its ultimate realization in the form of a six-day performance on 3–9 August 1998. It is also advisable to visit Heinz Cibulka in nearby Ladendorf. Heinz Cibulka, also a close friend of the late Schwarzkogler and his favourite model, has been, for almost twenty years, the only photographer authorized by Nitsch to document his actions. Previously, he was also a main actor in Nitsch's performances and can be regarded as one of the most knowledgeable experts on the *OrgienMysterienTheater*.

Photography is an essential source for assessing the work of those artists who are no longer working with the medium of actionism. However, in order to evaluate this specific form of reception and documentation it is important to attain a clear idea of the photographer's own perspective and to be aware of how multifaceted the medium can be. In comparison to Rudolf Schwarzkogler, much more published material is available on Nitsch's work, and written requests to see the archive at Castle Prinzendorf are always answered. It should be noted, though, that it is advisable to get in touch with any institution mentioned in this review well in advance of an intended visit, because exhibitions and, in the case of Nitsch, new actions can make access to the collections impossible and cause delay in responding to letters.

GÜNTER BRUS

Regarding the work of Günter Brus, Hubert Klocker's publications on Viennese Actionism cited below[4] can be recommended, or volumes 8a, b and c of the journal *Die Schastrommel*,[5] published by Brus himself and offering a very lucid survey of his actionist œuvre. The most complete documentation of all actions from the earliest period to 1996 can be found in the Brus Archive, which has been run since 1972 in Hohengebraching near Regensburg by Arnulf and Franziska Meifert. For the past two years now, Günter Brus himself, assisted by his daughter Diana, has been working on a detailed chronology of his actions. As in the case of Schwarzkogler, photography represents an adequate medium to give an impression of the artist's concepts, particularly because from 1964 to 1970 they developed cogently from action to action. This fact is beneficial to later studies, since this material suffices for gaining an impression of the artist's highly ordered œuvre and allows an understanding of the principal artistic approach behind the actions, which were exclusively intended to be experienced as live events.

Following this summary report on the archives dedicated to individual artists, mention should be made of two collections documenting in more general terms the phenomena of performative and intermedia art. They provide a link between the Viennese and the international scenes and offer a useful reservoir of material gathered by two experts eminently knowledgeable in these matters.

THE SOHM ARCHIVE IN STUTTGART

The first is the Sohm Archive in the Staatsgalerie Stuttgart, founded by Hanns Sohm at the beginning of the 1960s to collect material on Happening, Fluxus, *Wiener Aktionismus*, concrete poetry, underground literature and artists' books. Viennese Actionism takes a prominent place in this comprehensive documentation. Sohm has been personally acquainted with the protagonists of this art form since 1966 ('Destruction in Art' symposium), and he has often taken photographs of their performances. Some rare items (e.g. photo collages by Brus and Muehl, sketches and drawings, manifestos, etc.) can be found only there. Besides the films made by Kurt Kren of various actionist works by Brus and Muehl, Hanns Sohm also acquired in 1975 a set of photographs of Viennese actionism by Ludwig Hoffenreich. The Sohm Archive also contains material about the literary association Wiener Gruppe, founded in the late 1950s, which had strong links with Viennese Actionism. In addition, it documents other progressive artists active in Vienna in the 1950s and 1960s, such as Friedensreich

Hundertwasser or Arnulf Rainer. At the Staatsgalerie Stuttgart, the Sohm Archive is looked after by Ina Conzen, together with Ilona Lütken, and can be visited by appointment.

THE CONZ ARCHIVE IN VERONA

Since 1973, the Italian city of Verona has housed an archive established by Francesco Conz, which, among other tendencies of intermedia art, also deals with Viennese actionism. The inventory lists about 8,000 photographs of works by all four Viennese actionists. Conz was friendly with Nitsch, Brus and Muehl from the early 1970s and not only acquired whole blocks of works – documentary material as well as originals – but also invited the artists repeatedly to his home in Asolo and inspired them to create works for him. Important examples are Hermann Nitsch's installation *Asolo-Raum* (now on permanent loan at Castle Prinzendorf), or Günter Brus' cycle of drawings, *La Croce del Veneto* (now in the Museum Moderner Kunst, Stiftung Ludwig, in Vienna).

Visiting the archives of Hanns Sohm and Francesco Conz is indispensable for putting into perspective the impressions one can gain in the archives dedicated to the individual artists mentioned above. In both cases, the archive owners' personal assessment is highly informative, since they were witnesses of many actions and, having been personal acquaintances of the artists, they were able to compare their work with that of artists from other movements.

Hanno Millesi
[trans. Daniel Meyer-Dinkgräfe]

NOTES

1 For an explanation of these dates see, among others, Hanno Millesi, Zur Fotographie im Wiener Aktionismus (Wolkersdorf: Foto Fluss, 1998).
2 Wiener Aktionsgruppe on the occasion of a special edition of the journal Le Marais, edited by Günter Brus in 1965; Institut für Direkte Kunst Wien on the occasion of the 'Destruction in Art' symposium, 1966 in London.
3 Klocker and Badura-Triska (1992).
4 Klocker (1989).
5 Brus (1972).

REFERENCES

Amanshauser, Hildegund and Ronte, Dieter (eds) (1986) *Günter Brus: Der Überblick, hg. im Auftrag des Museums Moderner Kunst Stiftung Ludwig*, Salzburg/Wien: Residenzverlag.
Brus, Günter (ed.) (1970) *Die Schastrommel 3*, Berlin.
Brus, Günter (ed.) (1972) *Die Schastrommel 8a*, Berlin; 8b–c, Stuttgart/ London: Verlag Hansjörg Mayer.
Brus, Günter (1993) *Limite de visible*, Paris: Editions du Centre Pompidou.
Klocker, Hubert (1989) *Wiener Aktionismus 1960–1971: Der zertrümmerte Spiegel. Hg. in Zusammenarbeit mit der Graphischen Sammlung Albertina, Wien und dem Museum Moderner Kunst, Stiftung Ludwig, Köln*, Klagenfurt: Ritter Verlag.
Klocker, Hubert and Badura-Triska, Eva (eds) (1992) *Rudolf Schwarzkogler: Leben und Werk. Hg. im Auftrag des Museums Moderner Kunst, Stiftung Ludwig, Wien*, Klagenfurt: Ritter Verlag.
Muehl, Otto (1969) *mama & papa, materialaktionen 63–69*, Frankfurt: Kohlkunst-verlag.
Muehl, Otto (1992) *Arbeiten auf Papier aus den 60er Jahren*, Frankfurt: Edition Portikus.
Nitsch, Hermann (1969) *Das Orgien Mysterien Theater*, Darmstadt: März-Verlag.
Nitsch, Hermann (1983) *Das O.M. Theater Lesebuch*, Wien: Freibord Verlag.
Nitsch, Hermann (1985–6) *Die Partituren aller aufgeführten Aktionen*, Vol. 1: 1–32, Aktion, 1979, Vol. 2: 33–65, Aktion, Vol.

4: Partitur der 80, Aktion. All volumes
published Naples: Studio Morra, Vols 2
and 4 in collaboration with Edition
Freibord, Vienna.
Nitsch, Hermann (1990) *Das O. M.
Theater: Manifeste, Aufsätze, Vorträge*,
Wien/Salzburg: Residenzverlag.
Nitsch, Hermann (1995) *Zur Theorie des
O.M. Theaters: Zweiter Versuch*,
Salzburg/Wien: Residenzverlag.
Noever, Peter, Schwarz, Dieter and
Loers, Veit (eds) (1988)
*Aktionsmalerei–Aktionismus, Wien
1960–65*, Museum für Angewandte
Kunst in Wien, Museum Fridericianum,
Kassel, Kunstmuseum Winterthur,
Scottish National Gallery of Modern Art,
Edinburgh, Klagenfurt: Ritterverlag.
Weibel, Peter (in collaboration with Valie
Export) (1970) *bildkompendium wiener
aktionismus und film*, Frankfurt:
Kohlkunst-verlag.

IMPORTANT ADDRESSES
Almost all the institutions listed
below prefer initial contact via mail
or fax, followed by a telephone
appointment. It is not advisable for a
would-be visitor to seek an appointment only on arrival.

Museum Moderner Kunst
Stiftung Ludwig Wien (20er Haus)
Contact: Dr Eva Badura-Triska
Arsenalstr. 1
A-1030 Vienna
Tel. + 43 1 799 6900
Fax + 43 1 799 6901

Museum Moderner Kunst
Stiftung Ludwig Wien
Palais Liechtenstein
Fürstengasse 1
A-1090 Vienna
Tel. + 43 1 317 6900–0
Fax + 43 1 317 6901

Sammlung Friedrichshof
Contact: Amelia Rausch

Römerstr. 1
A-2424 Zurndorf
(approx. one hour from Vienna)
Tel. + 43 2147 239 3171
Fax + 43 2147 239 3116

P.A.P. Kunstagentur
Galerie Film Video Musik
Renate und Karl-Heinz Hein
Friedenstr. 22
D-81671 Munich
Tel. + 49 89 408 828
Fax + 49 89 498 356

Atelier Hermann Nitsch
Contact: Hanno Millesi
Schloss 1
A-2185 Prinzendorf/Zaya
(approx. one hour by car from
Vienna)
Tel. + 43 2533 89380
Fax + 43 2533 89693

Heinz Cibulka
Contact through Atelier Hermann
Nitsch

Brus-Archiv
Arnulf und Franziska Meifert
Kirchplatz. 6
D-93080 Hohengegebraching (bei
Regensburg)
(Written requests only)

Archiv Sohm
Staatsgalerie Stuttgart
Konservatorin Dr Ina Conzen
Dokumentation Ilona Lütken
Urbanstr. 35
Postfach 104342
D-70038 Stuttgart
Tel. + 49 711 212 4054
Fax + 49 711 212 4068

Francesco Conz
Vicolo Quadrelli 7
I-37129 Verona
Fax + 39 45 800 1128

Performance Research: On Ritual

Notes on Contributors

THE EDITORS

Ric Allsopp is a joint editor of *Performance Research*. He is co-founder of Writing Research Associates, an international partnership organizing, promoting and publishing performance. He is currently a research fellow at Dartington College of Arts. He has been a research associate with the Centre for Performance Research since 1986, and has been associated with the School for New Dance Development, Amsterdam since 1990.

Richard Gough is general editor of *Performance Research*. He is senior research fellow in the Department of Theatre, Film and Television Studies at the University of Wales, Aberystwyth and Artistic Director of the Centre of Performance Research (CPR), the successor of Cardiff Laboratory Theatre, of which he was a founder member. He edited *The Secret Art of the Performer* (London: Routledge, 1990) and has curated and organized numerous conference and workshop events over the last twenty years as well as directing and lecturing internationally.

Claire MacDonald is a joint editor of *Performance Research*. She is a writer and critic and a founder member of *Impact and Insomniac* Theatre Companies. Formerly Head of Theatre at Dartington College of Arts she was Senior Lecturer and Research Fellow in Theatre at De Montfort University, UK, from 1994 to 1998 and most recently a visiting lecturer at Mount Holyoak College in Massachusetts. She is currently living in Maryland, USA, where she is completing several writing projects.

GUEST EDITOR – ON RITUAL

Günter Berghaus is a Reader in Theatre History and Performance Studies at the Drama Department, University of Bristol. He has published many articles on dance history, avant-garde performance, Renaissance and Baroque theatre. He has directed numerous plays from the classical and modern repertoire and devised many productions of an experimental nature. His books include *Nestroys Revolutionspossen* (1978), *A. Gryphius' 'Carolus Stuardus'* (1984), *The Reception of the English Revolution, 1640–1669* (1989), *Theatre and Film in Exile* (1989), *The Genesis of Futurism* (1995), *Fascism and Theatre* (1996), *Futurism and Politics* (1996), *Italian Futurist Theatre* (1998).

THE CONTRIBUTORS

Rev. Dr. Martin Boord trained extensively in tantric Buddhist ritual systems and their underlying philosophy with Tibetan lamas in India, prior to reading Religious Studies at the University of London. Currently working in Oxford on a translation of the *Phur 'grel 'bum nag*, his published works include *The Cult of the Deity Varjrakila*, Tring, 1993, and *Overview of Buddhist Tantra*, Dharamsala, 1996.

Sally Gardner is a dancer and writer living in Melbourne, Australia. She is co-editor of the journal *Writings on Dance*.

David George was based at Murdoch University in Australia for twenty one years and has spent the last twenty five years researching into Asian performing arts. He is the author of *India: Three Ritual Dance-Dramas* and *Balinese Ritual Theatre*, published by Chadwick-Healey. He is currently completing a new book on Buddhism as/in Performance, and has recently taken a new position as Chair of the Drama and Dance Department at Queens College, City University of New York.

Graham Harvey is Senior Lecturer in Religious Studies at King Alfred's College, Winchester, UK. His main publications include *The True Israel* (E.J. Brill, 1996) and *Listening People, Speaking Earth: Contemporary Paganism* (C. Hurst, 1997). He is now combining interests in Judaism, Paganism and Indigenous religions in research concerning 'returning to tradition'.

Mutsumi Izeki specializes in Aztec archaeology. She studied at the National University of Mexico from 1993–5 and gained an MA in History at Keio University, Tokyo, Japan in 1997. She is now a PhD candidate at the Institute of Archaeology, University College, London.

Linda S. Kauffman is Professor of English at the University of Maryland, USA. She is the author of *Discourses Of Desire: Gender, Genre, And Epistolary Fictions* (Cornell UP 1986); *Special Delivery: Epistolary Modes in Modern Fiction* (U. Chicago Press, 1992), and editor of 3 volumes of feminist essays for Blackwell, most recently *American Feminist Thought At Century's End*. Her essay in this issue is a revised version of a chapter in *Bad Girls And Sick Boys: Fantasies In Contemporary Art & Culture* (U. California Press, 1998).

Grace Lau has a degree in Documentary Photography from Newport College of Art, UK and an MA in Photography: History and Culture from the London Institute. She is a practicing photographer working mainly from a documentary approach and lectures part time at the London Institute. She has tutored at Pentonville and Holloway prisons in London and led workshops for women to photograph the male nude and for men to 'Re-view women' as well as other educational workshops to explore social issues. A retrospective of her work entitled *Adults in Wonderland* was published in July 1997 by Serpents Tail.

Josephine Leask is a dance writer, lecturer and performer based in London. She is the editor of *Dance UK News* and freelance writer for a number of specialist dance and art magazines, including *Dance Theatre Journal* and *Make – Women's Art Magazine*. She currently lectures in dance and cultural studies at the London Studio Centre. Her most recent performance work includes a commissioned show which investigated women who work as strippers.

Graham Ley has taught at the Universities of London and Auckland, and is currently Lecturer in Drama at the University of Exeter. He writes on theory for *New Theatre Quarterly*, and will be publishing a study of theatrical and performance theory with the University of Exeter Press in 1999.

Roland Littlewood is currently Professor of Social Anthropology at University College London, and a consultant psychiatrist. He holds degrees in biochemistry, medicine, psychiatry and anthropology and is the author of *Aliens and Alienists*, *Pathology and Identity*, *Reason and Necessity* and *Intercultural Therapy*.

Gordon MacLellan is the main worker of Creeping Toad, an environmental education and celebration company, working across the country on projects that encourage people to discover their 'sense of wonder'. Gordon is the author of *Talking to the Earth: Environmental Art Activities for Children* and *Sacred Animals*, both published by Capall Bann, and is the administrator of the Sacred Earth Drama Trust. More information on Creeping Toad work can be obtained from Gordon MacLellan, Creeping Toad, 3 Vernon Street, Old Trafford, Manchester, M16 9JP. Tel: 0161 226 8127.

Peter Malekin, now retired, was formerly Senior Lecturer at the University of Durham. He is currently working with others on a project to develop the potential of pashyanti, a pre-verbal holistic stage of the speech process, in drama and performance. He is Co-author, with Ralph Yarrow, of *Consciousness, Literature and Theatre: Theory and Beyond*.

Daniel Meyer-Dinkgräfe studied English, Philosophy and German Literature at the University of Düsseldorf, Germany and obtained his PhD from the University of London in 1994. Since then he has been a lecturer in the Department of Theatre, Film and Television Studies at the University of Wales, Aberystwyth. The relation of consciousness and performance represents his major research interest, documented by *Consciousness and the Actor* (Peter Lang, 1996), as well as several articles and conference presentations.

Maria de Marias is a performer and video artist. She trained at the Universitat Autònoma de Barcelona and

The London Institute. In 1989, she won the National Award for Creativity, Oviedo, Spain.

Hanno Millesi is an art historian and author based in Vienna. He studied at the University of Vienna and since 1993 has been assistant to Herman Nitsch working on the archive of the Orgies Mysteries Theatre. He has completed a PhD about the possibilities of photography in relation to performance art.

Cláudia Neiva de Matos is a professor of literary theory, Brazilian literature and comparative literature at the Federal University Fluminense. For a long time she has researched the manifestations of oral, colloquial and marginal literatures. Her publications include: *Antologia da floresta: Literatura selecionada e ilustrada pelos professores indígenas do Acre* (Rio de Janeiro: Multiletras, 1997); *A poesia popular na república das lettras: Silvio Romero folclorista* (Rio de Janeiro: Funarte/Ed.UFRJ, 1994); *Gentis guerreiros: O indianismo de Gonçalves Dias* (São Paulo: Atual, 1988); and *Acertei no milhar: Samba e malandragem no tempo de Getúlio* (Rio de Janeiro: Paz e Terra, 1982)

Daniel C. Noel is Visiting Professor of Liberal Studies in Religion and Culture in the Adult Degree Program at Vermont College of Norwich University in Montpelier, Vermont. He also serves as Adjunct Faculty in Mythological Studies at Pacifica Graduate Institute in Carpinteria, California. Noel is the author or editor of six books, including, most recently, *The Soul of Shamanism: Western Fantasies, Imaginal Realities* (New York: Continuum, 1997; available in the UK through Cassell), as well as numerous articles and reviews. He presents papers and lectures widely, often in the UK. He also leads study tours of the British Isles and is co-organizing a symposium, 'black sun, deep end–re-imagining millennium,' to be held in the Penzance area at the time of the solar eclipse in August of 1999.

Ted Polhemus is an author, journalist, photographer and curator based in London. He holds an MPhil in anthropology (body image and adornment) from University College, London. He is author and co-editor of several books including *Diesel: World Wide Wear* (Thames & Hudson); *The Customised Body* (Serpents Tail); *Streetstyle* (Thames & Hudson); *Rituals of Love: sexual experiments, erotic possibilities* (Picador). His current projects include a computer game, Mirror Mirror, and a book on fashion for children. He acts as an advisor to advertising agencies on youth marketing and style trends.

Inés María Martiatu Terry is a theatre anthropologist, writer and researcher, who lives in Santiago de Cuba. She has published numerous essays and articles on performance, ritual and culture, and is currently preparing an anthology of Cuban plays.

Lisa Wolford is Assistant Professor of Theatre at Bowling Green State University, USA. She has worked recurrently with Grotowski since 1989 and is the author of *Grotowski's Objective Drama Research* (University of Mississippi Press; 1996). Her writings have appeared in various journals including *The Drama Review, New Theatre Quarterly, Slavic & East European Performance, Contemporary Theatre Review* and *Canadian Theatre Review*. She is resident dramaturg for Theatre Labyrinth, an experimental performance company based in Cleveland, Ohio.

Ralph Yarrow teaches drama at the University of East Anglia, where he has been Chair both of Drama and French. He writes, directs and performs in a variety of languages and locations, and recently published *Consciousness, Literature and Theatre: Theory and Beyond* (MacMillan, 1997) with Peter Malekin.